Where do I go for answers to my travel questions?

What's the best and easiest way to plan and book my trip?

frommers.travelocity.com

Frommer's, the travel guide leader, has teamed up with **Travelocity.com**, the leader in online travel, to bring you an in-depth, easy-to-use resource designed to help you plan and book your trip online.

At **frommers.travelocity.com**, you'll find free online updates about your destination from the experts at Frommer's plus the outstanding travel planning and purchasing features of Travelocity.com. Travelocity.com provides reservations capabilities for 95 percent of all airline seats sold, more than 47,000 hotels, and over 50 car rental companies. In addition, Travelocity.com offers more than 2,000 exciting vacation and cruise packages. Travelocity.com puts you in complete control of your travel planning with these and other great features:

> **Expert travel guidance from Frommer's** - over 150 writers reporting from around the world!
>
> **Best Fare Finder** - an interactive calendar tells you when to travel to get the best airfare
>
> **Fare Watcher** - we'll track airfare changes to your favorite destinations
>
> **Dream Maps** - a mapping feature that suggests travel opportunities based on your budget
>
> **Shop Safe Guarantee** - 24 hours a day / 7 days a week live customer service, and more!

Whether traveling on a tight budget, looking for a quick weekend getaway, or planning the trip of a lifetime, Frommer's guides and Travelocity.com will make your travel dreams a reality. You've bought the book, now book the trip!

Travelocity.com
A Sabre Company

Frommer's®

A New Star-Rating System & Other Exciting News from Frommer's!

In our continuing effort to publish the savviest, most up-to-date, and most appealing travel guides available, we've added some great new features.

Frommer's guides now include a new star-rating system. Every hotel, restaurant, and attraction is rated from 0 to 3 stars to help you set priorities and organize your time.

We've also added seven brand-new features that point you to the great deals, in-the-know advice, and unique experiences that separate travelers from tourists. Throughout the guide look for:

Finds	Special finds—those places only insiders know about
Fun Fact	Fun facts—details that make travelers more informed and their trips more fun
Kids	Best bets for kids—advice for the whole family
Moments	Special moments—those experiences that memories are made of
Overrated	Places or experiences not worth your time or money
Tips	Insider tips—some great ways to save time and money
Value	Great values—where to get the best deals

PORTABLE

Florence

1st Edition

Reid Bramblett

Hungry Minds

Best-Selling Books • Digital Downloads • e-Books
Answer Networks • e-Newsletters • Branded Web Sites • e-Learning
New York, NY • Cleveland, OH • Indianapolis, IN

About the Author

Reid Bramblett learned Italian on the playground of a Roman parochial school when he was 12, explored Italy with his parents for 2 years in a hippie-orange VW camper, and spent a year studying there during a break from the anthropology department at Cornell. After a stint in Frommer's editorial offices, Reid vaulted over the desk to write Frommer's first guide to Tuscany and Umbria and hasn't stopped exploring, learning, interviewing, taking notes, and reporting it all in guidebooks since. He has also written *Frommer's Memorable Walks in New York,* is a coauthor of *Frommer's Italy from $70 a Day,* and contributes to *Frommer's Europe* and *Frommer's Europe from $70 a Day.* When not on the road, he lives in Plymouth Meeting, Pennsylvania, outside Philadelphia.

Published by:

Hungry Minds, Inc.

909 Third Ave.
New York, NY 10022

ISBN 0-7645-6594-X
ISSN 1536-9625

Editor: Suzanne Jannetta
Production Editors: Bethany André and Christina Van Camp
Photo Editor: Richard Fox
Cartographer: Roberta Stockwell
Production by Hungry Minds Indianapolis Production Services

Special Sales

For general information on Hungry Minds' products and services, please contact our Customer Care department; within the U.S. at 800-762-2974, outside the U.S. at 317-572-3993 or fax 317-572-4002. For sales inquiries and reseller information, including discounts, bulk sales, customized editions, and premium sales, please contact our Customer Care department at 800-434-3422.

Manufactured in the United States of America

5 4 3 2 1

Contents

List of Maps

An Invitation to the Reader

In researching this book, we discovered many wonderful places—hotels, restaurants, shops, and more. We're sure you'll find others. Please tell us about them, so we can share the information with your fellow travelers in upcoming editions. If you were disappointed with a recommendation, we'd love to know that, too. Please write to:

Frommer's Portable Florence, 1st Edition
Hungry Minds, Inc. • 909 Third Avenue • New York, NY 10022

An Additional Note

Please be advised that travel information is subject to change at any time—and this is especially true of prices. We therefore suggest that you write or call ahead for confirmation when making your travel plans. The authors, editors, and publisher cannot be held responsible for the experiences of readers while traveling. Your safety is important to us, however, so we encourage you to stay alert and be aware of your surroundings. Keep a close eye on cameras, purses, and wallets, all favorite targets of thieves and pickpockets.

What the Symbols Mean

The following abbreviations are used for credit cards:

AE American Express	DISC Discover	V Visa
DC Diners Club	MC MasterCard	

FROMMERS.COM

Now that you have the guidebook to a great trip, visit our website at www.frommers.com for travel information on nearly 2,000 destinations. With features updated regularly, we give you instant access to the most current trip-planning information available. At Frommers.com, you'll also find the best prices on airfares, accommodations, and car rentals—and you can even book travel online through our travel booking partners. At Frommers.com, you'll also find the following:

- Daily Newsletter highlighting the best travel deals
- Hot Spot of the Month/Vacation Sweepstakes & Travel Photo Contest
- More than 200 Travel Message Boards
- Outspoken Newsletters and Feature Articles on travel bargains, vacation ideas, tips & resources, and more!

Planning Your Trip to Florence

Florence, the capital of Tuscany, is one of Italy's most famous cities. It was once the home of the colorful Medici dynasty, which actively encouraged the development of the Renaissance by sponsoring masters such as Donatello, Leonardo, and Michelangelo. Art treasures like those found at the Accademia (Michelangelo's *David*), the Uffizi Galleries (Botticelli's *Birth of Venus*), and the Pitti Palace (Raphael's *La Velata*) draw millions of visitors every year. Throw into the mix fabulous architecture (the Duomo with Brunelleschi's dome, Giotto's campanile, Santa Croce), fine restaurants and earthy trattorie, and leading designer boutiques and bustling outdoor markets, and the city of the Renaissance becomes quite simply one of the world's must-see sights.

This chapter addresses everything you'll need to know to plan a trip to Florence—from when to go to how to get there.

1 Visitor Information

TOURIST OFFICES

For general information in your home country, try your local branch of the **Italian State Tourist Board (ENIT)** or the ENIT-sponsored website **www.enit.it**. Unfortunately, Frommer's readers have reported that the office isn't really that helpful.

In the United States: 630 Fifth Ave., Suite 1565, New York, NY 10111 (© **212/245-4822;** fax 212/586-9249); 500 N. Michigan Ave., Suite 2240 Chicago, IL 60611 (© **312/644-0996;** fax 312/644-3019); and 12400 Wilshire Blvd., Suite 550, Los Angeles, CA 90025 (© **310/820-1898** or 310/820-1898; fax 310/820-6357).

In Canada: 1 place Ville Marie, Suite 1914, Montréal, Québec H3B 2C3 (© **514/866-7667** or 514/866-0975; fax 514/392-1429).

In the United Kingdom: 1 Princes St., London W1R 9AY England (© **020/7355-1557;** fax 020/7493-6695-1429).

USEFUL WEBSITES

Websites and e-mail addresses are included throughout this guide for everything from tourist offices, hotels, and restaurants to museums and festivals.

The official Florence information site, **www.firenze.turismo. toscana.it**, is currently available only in Italian (English is coming) but contains a wealth of up-to-date information (events, museums, practical details) on Florence and its province. Included is a searchable "hotels" form allowing you to specify amenities, categories, and the like; it responds by spitting out a list of where you can get contact info and see current room rates.

Firenze By Net (www.mega.it/florence), **Firenze.Net** (english. firenze.net), and **FlorenceOnLine** (www.fol.it) are all Italy-based websites with English translations and good general information on Florence. **Informacittà** (www.informacitta.net) is an excellent little guide to this month's events, exhibits, concerts, and theater; the English version is pending, however. And of course there's **Arthur Frommer's Budget Travel Online** (www.frommers.com), where Arthur Frommer himself, the man who helped reinvent the travel guide, chimes in with his own take on Tuscany's capital.

2 Entry Requirements & Customs

ENTRY REQUIREMENTS

U.S., Canadian, U.K., Irish, Australian, and New Zealand citizens with a **valid passport** don't need a visa to enter Italy if they don't expect to stay more than 90 days and don't expect to work there. If after entering Italy you find you want to stay more than 90 days, you can apply for a permit for an extra 90 days, which as a rule is granted immediately. Go to the nearest *questura* (police headquarters) or your home country's consulate. If your passport is lost or stolen, head to your consulate as soon as possible for a replacement.

Passport applications are downloadable from the Internet at the following sites: **www.travel.state.gov** (U.S.), **www.dfait-maeci. gc.ca/passport** (Canada), **www.open.gov.uk/ukpass/ukpass.htm** (U.K.), and **www.dfat.gov.au/passports** (Australia).

CUSTOMS

WHAT YOU CAN BRING INTO ITALY   Foreign visitors can bring along most items for personal use duty-free, including fishing tackle, a sporting gun and 200 cartridges, a pair of skis, two tennis racquets, a baby carriage, two hand cameras with 10 rolls of film,

and 400 cigarettes (two cartons) or a quantity of cigars or pipe tobacco not exceeding 500 grams (1.1 lb.). There are strict limits on importing alcoholic beverages. However, limits are much more liberal for alcohol bought tax-paid in other countries of the European Union.

WHAT YOU CAN TAKE HOME   For U.S. Citizens   You can bring back into the States $400 worth of goods (per person) without paying a duty. On the first $1,000 worth of goods over $400 you pay a flat 10% duty. Beyond that, it works on an item-by-item basis. There are a few restrictions on amount: 1 liter of alcohol (you must be over 21), 200 cigarettes, and 100 cigars. Antiques over 100 years old and works of art are exempt from the $400 limit, as is anything you mail home. Once per day, you can mail yourself $200 worth of goods duty-free; mark the package "For Personal Use." You can also mail to other people up to $100 worth of goods per person, per day; label each package "Unsolicited Gift." Any package must state on the exterior a description of the contents and their values. You can't mail alcohol, perfume (it contains alcohol), or tobacco products.

For more information on regulations, check out the **U.S. Customs Service website** (www.customs.ustreas.gov) or write to them at P.O. Box 7407, Washington, DC, 20044 to request the free *Know Before You Go* pamphlet.

To prevent the spread of diseases, **you cannot bring into the States** any plants, fruits, vegetables, meats, or most other foodstuffs. This includes even cured meats like salami (no matter what the shopkeeper in Europe says). You may bring in the following: bakery goods, all but the softest cheeses (the rule is vague, but if the cheese is at all spreadable, don't risk confiscation), candies, roasted coffee beans and dried tea, fish, seeds for veggies and flowers (but not for trees), and mushrooms. Check out the **USDA's website** (www.aphis.usda.gov/oa/travel.html) for more info.

For British Citizens   You can bring home almost as much as you like of any goods from any EU country (theoretical limits run along the lines of 90 liters of wine). If you're returning home from a non-EU country or if you buy your goods in a duty-free shop, you're allowed to bring home 200 cigarettes, 2 liters of table wine, plus 1 liter of spirits or 2 liters of fortified wine. Get in touch with **Her Majesty's Customs and Excise Office,** New King's Beam House, 22 Upper Ground, London SE1 9PJ (© **020/7620-1313**), for more information.

For Canadian Citizens For a clear summary of Canadian rules, write for the booklet *I Declare,* issued by **Revenue Canada,** 2265 St. Laurent Blvd., Ottawa K1G 4KE (℡ **613/993-0534** or 800/461-9999; www.ccra-adrc.gc.ca). Canada allows its citizens a $500 exemption, and you're allowed to bring back duty-free 200 cigarettes, 2.2 pounds of tobacco, 40 imperial ounces of liquor, and 50 cigars. In addition, you're allowed to mail gifts to Canada from abroad at the rate of Can$60 a day, provided they're unsolicited and aren't alcohol or tobacco (write on the package "Unsolicited Gift, Under $60 Value"). All valuables should be declared on the Y-38 form before departure from Canada, including serial numbers of, for example, expensive foreign cameras that you already own. *Note:* The $500 exemption can be used only once a year and only after an absence of 7 days.

For Australian Citizens The duty-free allowance in Australia is A$400 or, for those under 18, A$200. Personal property mailed back from Italy should be marked "Australian Goods Returned" to avoid payment of duty. On returning to Australia, citizens can bring in 250 cigarettes or 250 grams of loose tobacco, and 1125ml of alcohol. If you're returning with valuable goods you already own, such as foreign-made cameras, you should file form B263. A helpful brochure, available from Australian consulates or Customs offices, is *Know Before You Go.* For more information, contact **Australian Customs Services,** GPO Box 8, Sydney NSW 2001 (℡ **1300/363-263** within Australia; 02/6275-6666 from overseas).

For New Zealand Citizens The duty-free allowance for New Zealand is NZ$700. Citizens over 17 years can bring in 200 cigarettes, or 50 cigars, or 250 grams of tobacco (or a mixture of all three if their combined weight doesn't exceed 250 grams); plus 4.5 liters of wine and beer, or 1.125 liters of liquor. New Zealand currency doesn't carry import or export restrictions. Fill out a certificate of export, listing the valuables you are taking out of the country; that way, you can bring them back without paying duty. Most questions are answered in a free pamphlet available at New Zealand consulates and Customs offices: *New Zealand Customs Guide for Travellers, Notice no. 4.* For more information, contact **New Zealand Customshouse,** 50 Anzac Ave., Box 29, Auckland, NZ (℡ **09/ 359-6655;** www.customs.govt.nz).

3 Money

In January 2002, Italy retired the lira and joined most of Western Europe in switching to the euro. Coins are issued in denominations of .01€, .02€, .05€, .10€, .20€, and .50€ as well as 1€ and 2€; bills come in denominations of 5€, 10€, 20€, 50€, 100€, 200€, and 500€.

Exchange rates are established daily and listed in most international newspapers. To get a transaction as close to this rate as possible, pay for as much as possible with credit cards and get cash out of ATM machines.

At this writing, US$1 = approximately 2,000L, and this was the rate of exchange used to calculate the dollar values throughout this book. The rate fluctuates from day to day, depending on a complicated series of economic and political factors, and might not be the same when you travel to Italy. The rate for lira to euro is fixed at 1,936L = 1€.

Likewise, the ratio of the British pound to the lira fluctuates constantly. At press time, £1 = approximately 3,230L, an exchange rate reflected in the following table.

Traveler's checks, while still the safest way to carry money, are going the way of the dinosaur. The aggressive evolution of international computerized banking and consolidated ATM networks has led to the triumph of plastic throughout the Italian peninsula—even if cold cash is still the most trusted currency. Never rely on credit cards alone, however. Although you should be safe in most hotels and many restaurants, smaller towns and cheaper places are still wary; always carry some cash.

You'll get the best rate if you **exchange money** at a bank or one of its ATMs. The rates at "Cambio/change/wechsel" exchange booths are invariably less favorable but still a good deal better than what you'd get exchanging money at a hotel or shop (a last-resort tactic only). The bill-to-bill changers you'll see in some touristy places exist solely to rip you off.

CREDIT CARDS

Visa and **MasterCard** are now almost universally accepted at most hotels, restaurants, and shops; the majority also accept **American Express. Diners Club** is gaining some ground, especially in Florence and in more expensive establishments throughout the region. The only places you'll sometimes find all your credit cards useless are the smaller, cheaper mom-and-pop joints, be they

Tips **A Pricing Dilemma**

Note that we're in an unusual situation for this edition. The research was done in 2001, when all prices were still set in lire with the euro amount merely calculated (the fixed rate was 1,936 lire to the euro) and mentioned parenthetically. But this book hits the shelves in 2002, when the lira will only be a fond memory and prices will all be in euros. The problem is that lira prices were usually nice round numbers, while the strict conversion to euros led to awkward amounts. Though there were laws in place to prevent initial inflation when the euro switch happened, you can bet they are going to start rounding the euro amounts somehow—there's no way the museum that charged 10,000 lira admission is going to start demanding precisely 5.16€. They'll probably drop the price, but to 5.15€, or to 5€ flat? Or will it go up to 5.20€? There's no way to know. I beg your forgiveness if the actual rates in this edition are slightly off and the hotel room I was told cost 150,000 lire now runs 78€ rather than the 77.50€ it says in the book. Trust me, this problem is slight compared with all the Italian businesses that had to maintain two register tills, accepting payment for a candy bar in lire and making change in euros, during the 2-month switch-over!

one-star hotels, budget dining spots, or neighborhood shops. If you arrange with your card issuer to enable the card's cash advance option (and get a PIN as well), you can also use them at ATMs (see "ATMs" below).

If you **lose your card,** call toll-free *in Italy*: **Visa** (© 800/ 819-014), **MasterCard** (© 800/870-866), or **American Express** (collect © 336/393-1111 from anywhere, or toll-free in Italy © 800/872-000).

ATMs

The ability to access your personal checking account through the **Cirrus** (© 800/424-7787; www.mastercard.com) or **Plus** (© 800/ 843-7587; www.visa.com) network of ATMs—or get a cash advance on an enabled Visa or MasterCard—has been growing by leaps and bounds in Italy in the last few years. It works just like at home. All you need do is search out a machine that has your network's symbol displayed (which these days is practically all of them), pop in your card, and punch in your PIN (see "A PIN Alert" below). It'll spit out local currency drawn directly from your home checking account (and at a more favorable rate than converting traveler's checks or cash).

An ATM in Italian is a ***Bancomat*** (though Bancomat is a private company, its name has become the generic word for ATMs). Increased internationalism has been slowly doing away with the old worry that your card's PIN, be it on a bank card or credit card, need be specially enabled to work abroad, but it always pays to check with the issuing bank to be sure. If at the ATM you get a message saying your card isn't valid for international transactions, it's likely the bank just can't make the phone connection to check it (occasionally this can be a citywide epidemic); try another ATM or another town.

When you withdraw money with your **bank card,** you technically get the interbank exchange rate—about 4% better than the "street rate" you'd get exchanging cash or traveler's checks. Note, however, that some U.S. banks are now charging a 1% to 3% "exchange fee" to convert the currency. (Ask your bank before you leave.) Similarly, **Visa** has begun charging a standard 1% conversion fee for cash advances, and many credit card–issuing banks have begun tacking on an additional 1% to 3%. And, unlike with purchases, interest on a credit card cash advance starts accruing immediately, not when your statement cycles. Both methods are still a slightly better deal than converting traveler's checks or cash and considerably more convenient (no waiting in bank lines and pulling out your passport as ID).

ATM withdrawals are often limited to 300,000L (155€, $150) or 500,000L (258€, $250) per transaction regardless of your cash advance allowance. **American Express** card cash advances are

A PIN Alert

Make sure the PINs on your bank cards and credit cards will work in Italy. You'll need a **four-digit code** (six digits often won't work), so if you have a six-digit code, play it safe by getting a new four-digit PIN for your trip. If you're unsure about this, contact Cirrus or Plus (see "ATMs," above). Be sure to check the daily withdrawal limit at the same time.

usually available only from the American Express offices in Florence (see "Fast Facts: Florence" in chapter 2, "Getting to Know Florence," for more information).

TRAVELER'S CHECKS

Most banks issue checks under the names of **American Express** (© **800/721-9768** in the United States and Canada; www. americanexpress.com) and **Thomas Cook** (© **800/223-7373** in the U.S. and Canada, or 44/1733-318-950 collect from anywhere in the world; www.thomascook.com)—both offer versions that can be countersigned by you or your companion—**Visa** (© **800/ 227-6811** in the U.S. and Canada, or 44/171-937-8091 collect from anywhere in the world; www.visa.com), or **Citicorp** (© **800/ 645-6556** in the U.S. and Canada, or 813/623-1709 collect from anywhere in the world). AAA will sell Amex checks to their members without a commission. Note that you'll get the worst possible exchange rate if you pay for a purchase or hotel room directly with a traveler's check; it's better to trade in the traveler's checks for lire at a bank or the American Express office.

To report **lost or stolen traveler's checks,** call toll-free *in Italy:* **American Express** (© **800/872-000**), **Thomas Cook** (© **800/ 872-050**), **Visa** (© **800/874-155**), or **Citicorp** (© **813/623-1709** collect from anywhere).

4 When to Go

The best times to visit Florence are in the **spring** and **fall.** Starting in late May, the **summer** tourist rush really picks up, and from July to mid-September the country is teeming with visitors. August is the worst month to visit. Not only does it get uncomfortably hot, muggy, and crowded (the lines for the Uffizi and the Accademia can stretch for blocks), but the entire country goes on vacation at least from August 15 until the end of the month, and many Italians take off the entire month. Many hotels, restaurants, and shops are closed—except at the spas, beaches, and islands, which are where 70% of the Italians are headed. In **winter** (late October to Easter), most sights go on shorter winter hours or are closed for restoration and rearrangement, many hotels and restaurants take a month or two off between November and February, spa and beach destinations become padlocked ghost towns, and it can get much colder than most people expect—it may even snow on occasion.

WEATHER

It can get uncomfortably hot at the height of August in Florence. The long spring is temperate and very comfortable, with occasional showers. Fall is also fairly mild, with lots of rainfall being the only drawback. Winter, though mild for most months, can get quite cold in late December or January, it can drizzle a great deal, and snowfall isn't impossible.

HOLIDAYS

Official state holidays include January 1, January 6 (Epiphany), Easter Sunday and Monday, April 25 (Liberation Day), May 1 (Labor Day), August 15 (Ferragosto and Assumption Day), November 1 (All Saints Day), December 8 (Day of the Immaculate Conception), December 25, and December 26 (Santo Stefano). Florence also shuts down to honor its patron, St. John the Baptist, on June 24.

5 Health & Insurance

STAYING HEALTHY

There are no special health risks you'll encounter in Italy. The tap water is safe, and medical resources are of a high quality. If you need to take any **prescription medicine** with you, have the bottle's label printed with the generic (chemical) name of the drug for customs purposes; and, if you need to take a prescription, have your doctor make it out with the chemical name instead of a brand name so that Italian pharmacists can fill it with the local equivalent.

For advice on travel and health in general, and a list of English-speaking doctors in your area of travel, contact the **International Association for Medical Assistance to Travelers (IAMAT),** 417 Center St., Lewiston, NY 14092 (© **716/754-4883;** www.sentex.net/~iamat); in **Canada** at Regal Road, Guelph, Ont., N1K 1B5 (© **519/836-0102;** fax 519/836-3412); and in **New Zealand** at P.O. Box 5049, Christchurch 5 (fax 03/352-4630).

INSURANCE

Before you look into additional trip and medical insurance, check your existing insurance policies—homeowner's, medical, credit card, and the like—to see if and what they may cover. Often, purchases made with a credit card, including airline tickets, are covered in some way. Several large national and multinational companies provide a variety of policies to cover your vacation, including full-fledged packages that cover trip cancellation, lost luggage, accident, illness, emergency assistance, and death, among others. Packages often cost no more than $40 to $60 per person for a vacation valued at $1,000.

Try **Access America,** 6600 W. Broad St., Richmond, VA 23286-4991 (© **800/284-8300**); **Travelex Insurance Services,** 1717 Burt St., Suite 202, Omaha, NE 68154 (© **888/457-4602**); **Travel Guard International,** 1145 Clark St., Stevens Point, WI 54481 (© **800/826-1300;** www.travel-guard.com); and **Travel Insured International,** P.O. Box 280568, East Hartford, CT 06128-0568 (© **800/243-3174;** www.travelinsured.com). British travelers can try **Columbus Travel Insurance,** 17 Devonshire Square, London EC2M 4SQ (© **020/7375-0011** in London; www.columbusdirect.com).

Most health insurance plans covering out-of-country illnesses and hospital stays require you to pay your local bills up front—your coverage takes the form of a refund after you've returned and filed the paperwork. However, **Blue Cross/Blue Shield members** (© **800/ 810-BLUE** or www.bluecares.com for a list of participating hospitals) can now use their plans and cards at select hospitals abroad as they would at home, which means much lower out-of-pocket costs. In Florence, the card is honored at the **Villa Donatello,** Piazza Donatello 14 (© **055-323-3373**).

6 Tips for Travelers with Special Needs

FOR PEOPLE WITH DISABILITIES

Italy certainly doesn't win any medals for being overly accessible, though a few of the top museums and churches are beginning to at least install ramps at the entrances, and a few hotels are converting first-floor rooms into accessible units by widening the doors and baths. Buses and trains can cause problems as well, with high, narrow doors and steep steps at entrances. There are, however, seats reserved for travelers with disabilities on public transportation.

Luckily, there's an endless list of organizations to help you plan your trip and offer specific advice before you go. The **Moss Rehab Hospital** in Philadelphia has been providing phone advice and referrals to travelers with disabilities for years; call the **Travel Information Service** at © **215/456-9603;** 215/456-9602 TTY. The **American Foundation for the Blind,** 11 Penn Plaza, Suite 300, New York, NY 10001 (© **800/232-5463** or 212/502-7600; www.afb.org), can fill you in on travel in general and how to get your Seeing-Eye dog into Europe. Travelers with a hearing impairment should contact the **American Academy of Otolaryngology,** 1 Prince St., Alexandria, VA 22314 (© **703/ 836-4444** or 703/519-1585 TTY; www.entnet.org).

FOR GAYS & LESBIANS

Italy isn't the most tolerant country regarding same-sex couples, but it has grown to accept homosexuality, especially over the past few decades. Florence has the largest and most visible homosexual population (not that that's saying much). Homosexuality is legal, and the age of consent is 16. Condoms are *profilatici* (pro-feel-*aht*-tee-chee). Luckily, Italians are already more affectionate and physical than Americans in their general friendships, and even straight men regularly walk down the street with their arms around each other—however, kissing anywhere other than on the cheeks at greetings and goodbyes will certainly draw attention.

Italy's national association and support network for gays and lesbians is **ARCI-Gay/ARCI-Lesbica,** in Florence at Via San Zanobi 54r (© and fax **055/476-557** or 055/488-288; www.azionegaye lesbica.it). They also publish a **gay guide** (in Italian and English) to Florence and Tuscany called *Il Giglio Fuscia,* listing everything from gay bars and beaches to useful addresses and resources. It's free and available at the ARCI-Gay offices, local gay nightspots, and other places that cater to gay interests, as well as some Florentine bookstores. A *Gay Map of Florence* pointing out nightspots and the like is available from c/o Omo Edizioni, Via Casilina 1712, 00133 Roma, Italia (© and fax **06/205-7878**).

Frommer's Gay & Lesbian Europe has a fabulous chapter on Florence (as well as ones on Rome, Venice, Milan, and many other cities).

The **International Gay & Lesbian Travel Association** (IGLTA), 52 W. Oakland Park Blvd. #237, Wilton Manors, FL 33311 (© **800/448-8550;** fax 954/776-3303; www.iglta.org), is your best all-around resource. Members ($100 to join plus $150 a year) get a newsletter and membership directory, but even nonmembers can get advice on specialist travel agencies (or search for local ones on their website).

FOR SENIORS

Italy is a multigenerational culture that doesn't tend to marginalize its seniors, and older people are treated with a great deal of respect and deference throughout Italy. But there are few specific programs, associations, or concessions made for them. The one exception is on admission prices for museums and sights, where those over 60 or 65

A Note for Families & Seniors

At most state-run museums, children under 18 and seniors get in free *but only if* they hail from one of the countries that has signed a reciprocal international cultural agreement to allow children and seniors this privilege. These countries include England, Canada, Ireland, Australia, New Zealand, and indeed much of the world—but *not* the United States. (However, many museum guards either don't ask for citizenship ID or wave kids and seniors on through anyway.) Children and seniors, no matter what their nationality, also get discounts on trains.

will often get in at a reduced rate or even free. As a senior in Italy, you're *un anciano* (*una anciana* if you're a woman) or "ancient one"—look at it as a term of respect and let people know you're one if you think a discount may be in the works.

Your best resource before leaving home is the **AARP** (formerly known as the **American Association of Retired Persons**), 601 E St. NW, Washington, DC, 20049 (© **800/424-3410;** www.aarp.org), which can get you discounts on some car rentals and chain hotels. Most major **airlines offer discount programs** for senior travelers; be sure to ask whenever you book a flight. Of the big car-rental agencies, only National currently gives an AARP discount (10%), but the many rental dealers that specialize in Europe—Auto Europe, Kemwel, Europe-by-Car—offer seniors 5% off their already low rates. In most European cities, people over 60 or 65 get reduced admission at theaters, museums, and other attractions, and they can often get discount fares or cards on public transportation and national rail systems. Carrying ID with proof of age can pay off in all these situations.

FOR STUDENTS & YOUTHS

The best resource for students is the **Council on International Educational Exchange,** or CIEE (© **800/2COUNCIL;** www.ciee.org). They can set you up with an ID card (see below), and their travel branch, **Council Travel Service (CTS),** is the biggest student travel agency in the world. For discounts on plane tickets, railpasses, and the like, you can call them at © **800/2-COUNCIL;** (www.counciltravel.com), or contact the New York office at 205 E. 42nd St., New York, NY 10017 (✆ **212/ 822-2600**). Also ask them for a list of CTS offices in major European cities so you can keep the discounts flowing and aid lines open as you travel. In Canada, **Travel CUTS,** with offices in every major city (✆ **888/838-CUTS** or 800/667-2887 or 416/979-2406; www.travelcuts.com), offers similar services. They also have a London office, 295A Regent St., London W1R 7YA (✆ **020/ 7255-1944**), or try **Campus Travel,** 52 Grosvenor Gardens, London SW1W 0AG (✆ **020/7730-3402;** www.campustravel. co.uk), Britain's leading specialist in student and youth travel.

From CIEE (or its Canadian or British counterparts) you can obtain for $20 the student traveler's best European friend, the **International Student Identity Card (ISIC).** It's the only officially acceptable form of student ID, good for cut rates on railpasses, plane tickets, and other discounts. It also provides you with basic health and life insurance and a 24-hour help line. If you're no longer a student but are still under 26 you can get a **GO 25** card from the same people—it will get you the insurance and some of the discounts (but not student admission prices in museums).

The University of Florence is on the north edge of the center around Piazza San Marco. Two travel agencies cater specifically to students, getting you great deals and discounts on transportation from airline tickets to car rentals and selling discount passes and the like. **S.T.S.—Student Travel Services,** Via Zanetti 18r, off Via de' Cerretani (✆ **055/284-183**), sells plane, train, and bus tickets and passes and accepts credit cards. **CTS,** Via Ginori 25r (✆ **055/ 289-570;** www.cts.it), offers similar but even wider services, including car rental and hotel reservations (but no train reservations or Eurail; only B.I.J. youth tickets). It doesn't accept credit cards and has longer lines. There's also an info office specifically for youths and students called **Informagiovani,** Vicolo Santa Maria Maggiore 1 (✆ **055/218-310**), an alley a few steps down Via de' Vecchietti from Via de' Cerretani.

7 Getting There

BY PLANE

Airline fares rates are divided into three seasons: **High season** is June to early September, the Christmas season (December 15 to 31), and Easter week. **Shoulder season,** with good-value prices, is April to May and early September to October. **Low season** runs November to March, excluding Christmas and Easter, and is the cheapest time to travel. Fares to Italy are constantly changing, but you can expect to pay somewhere from $400 to $800 for a direct, round-trip ticket from New York to Rome in coach class.

FROM NORTH AMERICA   No carrier flies directly from the United States or Canada to Florence; however, with most airlines (and their affiliates) you can connect through a handful of European cities to the small international airports at Pisa or Florence. You may find it most convenient simply to fly to Rome and connect to Florence by plane (a bit over 1 hour) or by train (close to 3 hours; see below).

The Major Airlines   Italy's national airline, **Alitalia** (© 800/ 223-5730; www.alitalia.it), offers more flights daily to Italy than any other airline. It flies direct to both Rome and Milan from New York, Newark, Boston, Chicago, Los Angeles, and Miami. You can connect in Rome or Milan to any other Italian destination, including Pisa or Florence. If you're flying from the New York City area and planning to connect directly to Florence, fly out of Newark instead of JFK and you'll shave 4 hours off the layover in Rome's airport.

   British Airways (© 800/247-9297; www.british-airways.com) flies direct from dozens of U.S. and Canadian cities to London, where you can get connecting flights to Pisa, Rome, or Milan. **Air Canada/Canadian Airlines** (© 888/247-2262; www.aircanada.ca) flies daily from Toronto and Vancouver to Rome. **Continental** (© 800/231-0856; www.continental.com) doesn't fly to Italy itself, but it's partnered with Alitalia for the Newark-to-Rome and New York JFK-to-Milan flights, so if you're a Continental Frequent Flyer you can reserve through Continental and rack up the miles.

   Delta (© 800/241-4141; www.delta.com) flies daily out of New York JFK (you can connect from most major U.S. cities) to Rome and Milan, where it's possible to change to one of Delta's local

---

Tips **The Milan Connection**

Note that if you find yourself flying into Milan, the domestic airport is separate from the international one, and transferring planes to a connecting flight to Florence or Pisa requires switching airports, sometimes changing airlines, and an innate trust in the gods of luggage transfer. If you fly into Milan, a train to Tuscany is probably your best bet.

partner airlines (Lufthansa, Iberia, and so on) for the last leg to Tuscany. **TWA** (© **800/892-4141;** www.twa.com) flies direct from New York JFK to Rome and Milan. From either city you can take a train to Tuscany, or from Rome you can connect to an Alitalia flight to Florence or Pisa.

Possibly less convenient alternatives are **American Airlines** (© **800/433-7300;** www.im.aa.com), whose flights from the United States to Milan all go through Chicago; **United** (© **800/ 241-6522;** www.ual.com), which flies once daily to Milan out of Washington, D.C. Dulles; or **US Airways** (© **800/622-1015;** www.usairways.com), which offers one flight daily to Rome out of Philadelphia. (You can connect through Philly from most major U.S. cities.)

FROM GREAT BRITAIN & IRELAND **British Airways** (© **0845/7799-977;** www.british-airways.com) flies twice daily from London's Gatwick to Pisa. **Alitalia** (**020/8745-8200;** www. alitalia.it) has six daily flights from London to both Rome and Milan and one daily from London Gatwick into Pisa. **KLM UK** (formerly Air UK; © **08705/074-074;** www.klmuk.com) flies several times per week from London Stansted to Milan (both airports) and Rome. No-frills upstart **Ryanair** (© **0906/766-1000** in the U.K.; www.ryanair.ie) will fly you from London to Pisa starting at around £84.

The best and cheapest way to get to Italy from Ireland is to make your way first to London and fly from there to Rome or direct to Pisa (see above; to book through **British Airways** in Ireland, dial © **01/610-666**). **Aer Lingus** (© **01/844-4711;** www.aerlingus.ie) flies direct from Dublin to both Rome and Milan about 5 days a week. **Alitalia** (© **01/677-5171**) puts you on a British Midland to get you to London, where you change to an Alitalia plane for the trip to Rome.

BY TRAIN

Every day up to 14 **Eurostar** trains (reservations in London © **0990/186-186;** www.eurostar.com) zip from London to Paris's Gare du Nord via the **Chunnel** (Eurotunnel) in a bit over 4 hours. In Paris, you can transfer to the Paris Gare de Lyon station for one of three daily trains to **Milan** (from which you can transfer to Florence), two to **Pisa,** or one to **Florence.** Some of the Milan runs are high-speed TGV trains, a 6½-hour ride requiring a seat reservation. At least one will be an overnight Euronight (EN) train, with reservable sleeping couchettes; the Euronight leaves Paris around

10pm and gets into Milan around 8:45am. The two Euronight trains going directly from Paris to Pisa take about 10 hours; to Florence, it takes 12½ hours.

The definitive 500-page book listing all official European train routes and schedules is the ***Thomas Cook European Timetable of Railroads,*** available in the United States for $27.95 (plus $4.50 shipping and handling) from Forsyth Travel Library, P.O. Box 2975, Shawnee Mission, KS 66201 (✆ **800/367-7984**) or at travel specialty stores.

8 Arriving in Italy

BY PLANE

GETTING TO FLORENCE FROM ROME'S AIRPORTS
Most international flights to Rome will arrive at **Fiumicino Airport** (officially named **Leonardo da Vinci International Airport,** but few, including the airlines themselves, call it that). Some inter-European and transatlantic charter flights may land at the less convenient **Ciampino Airport.** You can connect to a plane at either to take you to Pisa's or Florence's airport, but it's often simpler, almost as fast in the long run, and cheaper to take the train.

Fiumicino (✆ **06/659-51** for switchboard; 06/659-52640 for flight information; 06/65-643 for Alitalia desk) is 19 miles (30km) from Rome's center. You can take the **express train** (15,000L, 8€, $8) from Fiumicino to Rome's central train station, Termini. A taxi to the station costs about 70,000L (36€, $35). From Termini, you can grab one of many daily trains to Florence, Pisa, and most other destinations. If you happen to fly into **Ciampino Airport** (✆ **06/7934-0297**), 9¼ miles (15km) south of the city, a none-too-frequent COTRAL bus (2,000L, 1.05€, $1) will take you to the Anagnina metro station, where you can take the metro to Termini (1,500L, .80€, 75¢). A taxi to Rome's center from Ciampino should run about 40,000L to 50,000L (21€ to 26€, $20 to $25).

GETTING TO FLORENCE FROM MILAN'S AIRPORT
Your flight may land at either **Linate Airport,** about 5 miles (8km) southeast of the city, or **Malpensa Airport,** 28 miles (45km) from downtown. For general information on either, call ✆ **02-74-851.** From **Linate,** buses (4,000L, 2.05€, $2; 5,000L, 2.60€, $2.50 if you buy your ticket on board) make the 15-minute trip to Milan's central train terminal, Stazione Centrale, every 20 to 30 minutes daily 7am to 11pm. From **Malpensa,** buses (12,000L, 6€, $6) leave for the station hourly, daily 6:30am to 11pm for the hour-long trip.

(You can buy tickets on board when the ticket office at the airport is closed.) There are also buses connecting the two airports, in case you have to transfer for a final leg to Florence. From Stazione Centrale, you can get trains to Florence.

FLORENCE-AREA AIRPORTS   Florence's tiny **Aeroporto Amerigo Vespucci** (© 055/373-498; www.safnet.it) is 3 miles (5km) northwest of the town center in Peretola. Alitalia's desk at the airport is at © **055/27-888,** but for general flight info call © **055/373-498.** Alitalia's office in Florence is at Lungarno degli Acciaiuoli 10–12 (© **055/27-881**). City bus no. 62 runs between the airport and Florence's Santa Maria Novella train station every 20 minutes. The 15-minute taxi ride should cost about 30,000L (16€, $15.00).

More flights land at Tuscany's main international airport, **Pisa's Galileo Galilei Airport** (© 050/500-707; www.pisa-airport.com), about 50 miles (80km) from Florence. Every hour or two daily 7am to 7pm, a shuttle train makes the trip (slightly over an hour, costing 8,000L, 4.15€, $4) between the airport and Florence's Santa Maria Novella train station. At track 5 in the station is an **Alitalia desk** (© **055/216-073**), so you can check in for your plane before boarding the train.

BY TRAIN

Florence is Tuscany's rail hub, with connections to all the region's major cities. To get here from Rome, you can take the Pendolino (4 daily, 1¾ hours; make sure it's going to Santa Maria Novella station, not Rifredi; you must reserve tickets ahead), an EC or IC train (24 daily, just under 2 hr.), or an interregionale (7 daily, around 3 hr.). There are also about 16 trains daily from Milan (3 hours) through Bologna (1 hr.).

The **main station** in Florence is **Santa Maria Novella** (© 055/ **288-785,** or 055/23-521 for train information). The **tourist office** (© **055/212-245**) across from track 16 is open daily 8:30am to 9pm and gives out free maps and general information and will reserve a hotel room for you for a small fee. You'll find train information across from track 5. The yellow posters on the wall inside the anteroom list all train times and routes for this and other major Italian stations. Another copy of the Florence poster is just inside the sliding glass doors of the second, main room. For personalized help, you have to take a number from the color-coded machine (pink is for train information) and wait your turn—often for more than an hour.

The **ticketing room** (Salone Biglietti) is located through the central doors; at *sportelli* (windows) 9 to 18 you can buy ordinary unreserved train tickets. The automatic ticket machines were installed mainly to taunt us and rarely work. Around the corner from this bank of ticket windows is a smaller room where you can buy **international tickets** (window 7), make **reservations** for high-speed and overnight trains (windows 1 to 4), or pay for a spot on the **Pendolino/ETR express** to Milan, Bologna, or Rome (window 5).

Exit out to the left coming off the tracks and you'll find many bus lines as well as stairs down to the underground **pedestrian underpass** which leads directly to Piazza dell'Unità Italiana and saves you from the crazy traffic of the station's piazza.

TRAIN TRAVEL TIPS   Italian trains tend to be very clean and comfortable, and most of the longer-haul ones are made up of *couchette* compartments that seat only six or occasionally eight. (Try to find one full of nuns for a fighting chance at a smoke-free trip.) First class (*prima classe*) is usually only a shade better than second class (*seconda classe*), with four to six seats per couchette instead of six to eight. The only real benefit of first class comes if you're traveling overnight, in which case four berths per compartment are a lot more comfortable than six. Few visitors are prepared for how **crowded** Italian trains can sometimes get, though with the increase in automobile travel, they're not as crowded as they were in decades past. An Italian train is only full when the corridors are packed solid and there are more than eight people sitting on their luggage in the little vestibules by the doors. Overcrowding is usually only a problem on Friday evenings and weekends, especially in and out of big cities, and just after a strike.

The **ETR/Pendolino** (P) is the "pendulum" train that zips back and forth between Rome and Milan, stopping at Florence and Bologna along the way. It's the fastest but most expensive option (first class only, a meal included); it has its own ticket window at the stations and *requires* a seat reservation. **Eurocity** (EC, EN if it runs overnight) trains connect Italian cities with cities outside the country; these are the speediest of the standard trains, offering both first and second class and always requiring a supplement (except for Eurailpass holders, though the conductors won't always believe you on this one); **Intercity** (IC) trains are similar to Eurocity trains in that they offer both first and second class and require a supplement, but they never cross an international border.

When buying a **regular ticket,** ask for either *andata* (one-way) or *andata e ritorno* (round-trip). If the train you plan to take is an EC or IC, ask for the ticket *con supplemento rapido* (with speed supplement) to avoid on-train penalty charges.

BY CAR

The **A1 autostrada** runs north from Rome past Arezzo to Florence and continues to Bologna. The **A11** connects Florence with Lucca, and **unnumbered superhighways** run to Siena and Pisa. There are many private parking lots in town, but it's difficult to find spots, and they often keep weird hours, so your best bet is one of the city-run garages. Although the finally finished parking lot under Santa Maria Novella (3,000L, 1.55€, $1.50 per hour) is closer to the city center, the best deal if you're staying the night (better than most hotels' garage rates) is at the **Parterre parking lot** under Piazza Libertà, north of Fortezza del Basso. If you're staying at least 1 night in Florence at a hotel, you can park here, are welcome to a free bike, and (on presentation of your hotel receipt as you leave or the hotel's stamp on your parking receipt) pay only 15,000L (8€, $8) per night.

If you're **renting a car** in Italy, you'll get the best rental rate if you book your car from home instead of renting direct in Italy—in fact, if you decide to rent once you're over there, it's worth it to call home to have someone arrange it all from there. You must be over 25 to rent from most agencies (some accept 21).

Though it once was smart shopping to see what rates Italian companies were offering, they're all now allied with the big agents in the States: **Avis** (© 800/331-2112; www.avis.com), **Budget** (© 800/527-0700; www.budgetrentacar.com), **Hertz** (© 800/654-3131; www.hertz.com), and **National** (© 800/227-7368; www.nationalcar.com). You can usually get a better rate by going through one of the rental companies specializing in Europe: **Auto Europe** (© 800/223-5555; www.autoeurope.com), **Europe by Car** (© 800/223-1516, 212/581-3040 in New York City, 800/252-9401 in California; www.europebycar.com), and **Kemwell** (© 800/678-0678; www.kemwell.com). With constant price wars and special packages, it always pays to shop around among all the above.

DRIVING TIPS   Italian drivers aren't maniacs; they only appear to be. Actually, they tend to be very safe and alert drivers, if much more aggressive than Americans are used to. If someone races up behind you and flashes her lights, that's the signal for you to slow down so she can pass you quickly and safely. Stay in the right lane on highways; the left is only for passing and for cars with large engines and the pedal to the metal. If you see someone in your rearview mirror speeding up with his hazard lights blinking, get out of the way because it means his Mercedes is opened up full throttle. On a two-lane road, the idiot passing someone in the opposing traffic who has swerved into your lane expects you to veer obligingly over into the shoulder so three lanes of traffic can fit—he would do the same for you.

Autostrade are superhighways, denoted by green signs and a number prefaced with an A, like the A1 from Rome to Florence. A few aren't numbered and are simply called *raccordo,* a connecting road between two cities (such as Florence-Siena and Florence-Pisa). On longer stretches, autostrade often become toll roads. **Strade Statale** are state roads, usually two lanes wide, indicated by blue signs. Their route numbers are prefaced with an SS or an S, as in the SS222 from Florence to Siena. On signs, however, these official route numbers are used infrequently. Usually, you'll just see blue signs listing destinations by name with arrows pointing off in the appropriate directions.

The **speed limit** on roads in built-up areas around towns and cities is 31 mph (50 kmph). On rural roads and the highway it's 68 mph (110 kmph), except on weekends when it's upped to 81 mph (130 kmph).

2

Getting to Know Florence

Mary McCarthy famously described Florence (*Firenze*) as a "City of Stone." This assessment digs deeper than merely the fact that the buildings, streets, doorjambs, sidewalks, windowsills, towers, and bridges are all cobbled together in shades of gray, stern rock hewn by generations of the stonecutters Michelangelo grew up with. Florence's stoniness is evident in both its countenance and its character. Florentines often seem more serious and slower to warm to strangers than the stereotypical Italians. The city's fundamental rhythms are medieval, and it's fiendishly difficult to get beyond the touristy surface and see what really makes Florence tick. Although the historic center is compact, it takes time and effort to get to know it personally, get the hang of its alleys, and understand the deep history of its palace-lined streets.

This chapter will equip you with the basic tools (the hammer and chisel, so to speak) you'll need to get under the stony skin of Florence. It breaks down the city layout and neighborhoods and explains the sorts of facts and services you'll need.

1 Essentials

VISITOR INFORMATION

The city's largest tourist office is at **Via Cavour 1r** (✆ 055/233-20; www.firenze.turismo.toscana.it), about 3 blocks north of the Duomo. This office offers lots of literature, including details on current (sometimes extended) museum hours and concert schedules. March to October, it's open Monday to Saturday 8:15am to 7:15pm and Sunday 8:30am to 6:30pm; November to February, hours are Monday to Saturday 8:15am to 1:45pm (though lately they've been experimenting with keeping it open to 7:15pm in winter).

At the head of the tracks in Stazione Santa Maria Novella is a tiny info office with some maps and a hotel-booking service (see chapter 3, "Where to Stay") open Monday to Saturday 9am to 9pm (to 8pm November to March), but the **station's main tourist office** (✆ 055/212-245) is outside at Piazza della Stazione 4. With

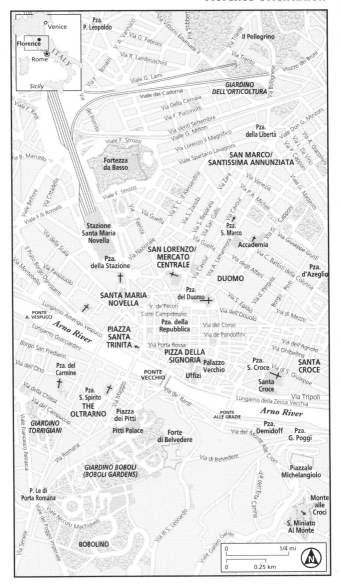

your back to the tracks, take the left exit, cross onto the concrete median, and turn right; it's about 100 feet (30m) ahead. The office is usually open Monday to Saturday 8:30am to 7pm (often to 1:30pm in winter) and Sunday 8:30am to 1:30pm.

Ignore publications carrying the address of the information office just off Piazza della Signoria at Chiasso Baroncelli 17r; it relocated in 1998 to an obscure side street south of Piazza Santa Croce, Borgo Santa Croce 29r (© **055/234-0444**), open Monday to Saturday 9am to 7pm and Sunday 9am to 2pm.

For upcoming events, shows, theater, exhibitions, and other entertainment, look for one of the events magazines, like *Events in Florence and Tuscany* (bimonthly and very good, sometimes at news-stands for 4,000L, 2.05€, $2) and *Vista* (better in-depth articles, not as good a calendar, harder to find), often found in hotel lobbies. Another free magazine is *Concierge Information,* full of good bilin-gual hints and tips. At the Via Cavour tourist office you can also pick up the free *Firenze Avventimenti* events brochure, giving you but the barest facts about each major event for the year but includ-ing contact phone numbers. Also be on the lookout at tourist offices and hotels for the free *Informacittà* monthly pamphlet. Otherwise, you'll have to be able to decipher the Italian of the monthly *Firenze Spettacolo* (2,700L, 1.40€, $1.35), available at most newsstands.

CITY LAYOUT

Florence is a smallish city, sitting on the Arno River and petering out to olive-planted hills rather quickly to the north and south but extending farther west and to a lesser extent east along the Arno val-ley with suburbs and light industry. The *centro storico* (historic cen-ter), where visitors spend most of their time, is a compact tangle of medieval streets and *piazze* (squares). The bulk of Florence, and most of the tourist sights, lies north of the river, with an old artisans' working-class neighborhood hemmed in between the Arno and the hills on the south side.

MAIN STREETS & PIAZZE   The center is encircled by a traffic ring of wide boulevards, the Viale, that were created in the late 1800s by tearing down the city's medieval defensive walls. The descriptions below all refer to the *centro storico* as the visitor's city. From Piazza Santa Maria Novella, south of the train station, Via de' Panzani angles into Via de' Cerretani to Piazza del Duomo and the connected Piazza San Giovanni, the city's religious heart around the cathedral. From Piazza del Duomo, Via dei Calzaiuoli, the wide

The Red & the Black

Florence's address system has a split personality. Private homes, some offices, and hotels are numbered in black (or blue), while businesses, shops, and restaurants are numbered independently in red. This means that 1, 2, 3 (black) addresses march up the block numerically oblivious to their 1r, 2r, 3r (red) neighbors. You might find the doorways on one side of a street numbered: 1r, 2r, 3r, 1, 4r, 2, 3, 5r . . .

Florence keeps proclaiming that it's busily renumbering the whole city without the color system—plain 1, 3, 5 on one side, 2, 4, 6 on the other—and will release the new standard soon, but no one is quite sure when. Conservative Florentines who don't want their addresses to change have been helping to hold up the process. This is all compounded by the fact that the color codes occur only in the centro storico and other older sections of town; outlying districts didn't bother with the codes and use the international standard system common in the United States.

road popular during the *passeggiata* (evening stroll), leads south to Piazza della Signoria, Florence's civic heart near the river, home to the Palazzo Vecchio and the Uffizi galleries. Traffic winds its way from the back of the Duomo to behind the Uffizi along Via del Proconsolo.

Another route south from the Duomo takes you down Via Roma, through cafe-lined Piazza della Repubblica, and continues down Via Calimala and Via Por Santa Maria to the Ponte Vecchio, the most popular and oldest bridge over the Arno, lined with overhanging jewelry shops. Via degli Strozzi leads east of Piazza della Repubblica to intersect Florence's main shopping drag, Via de' Tornabuoni, running north toward Piazza Santa Maria Novella and south to Piazza Santa Trínita on the river. Borgo de' Greci connects Piazza della Signoria with Piazza Santa Croce on the city center's western edge.

North from the Duomo, Via dei Servi leads to Florence's prettiest square, Piazza Santissima Annunziata. Via Riscasoli leads from the Duomo past the Accademia Gallery (with Michelangelo's

David) to Piazza San Marco, where many city buses stop. Via de'
Martelli/Via Cavour is a wide traffic-laden road also connecting the
Duomo and Piazza San Marco. From the Duomo, Borgo San
Lorenzo leads to Piazza San Lorenzo, the old neighborhood of the
Medici that's these days filled with the stalls of the outdoor leather
market. This area is also just east of the train station.

On the Oltrarno side of the river, shop-lined Via Guicciardini
runs toward Piazza dei Pitti and its museum-filled Pitti Palace. From
here, Via Mazzetta/Via Sant'Agostino takes you past Piazza Santo
Spirito to Piazza della Carmine; these two squares are the Oltrarno's
main centers.

STREET MAPS   The tourist offices hand out two versions of a
Florence *pianta* (city plan) free: Ask for the one *con un stradario*
(with a street index), which shows all the roads and is better for nav-
igation. The white pamphlet-size version they offer you first is okay
for basic orientation and Uffizi-finding, but it leaves out many
streets and has giant icons of major sights that cover up Florence's
complicated back-alley systems.

If you want to buy a more complete city plan, the best selections
are at the newsstand in the ticketing area of the train station and at
Feltrinelli International and **Libreria Il Viaggio** bookstores
(see chapter 6, "Shopping," for more information). Falk puts out a
good pocket-sized version, but my favorite is the palm-sized 1:9,000
Litografica Artistica Cartografia map with the yellow and blue
cover. It covers the city in three overlapping indexed sections that
fold out like a pop-up book. If you need to find a tiny street not on
your map, ask your hotel concierge to glance at his or her
TuttoCittà, a very complete magazine of fully indexed streets that
you can't buy but residents (and hotels and bars) get along with their
phone books.

NEIGHBORHOODS IN BRIEF

I've used the designations below to group hotels, restaurants, and sights in
Florence. Although the city does contain six "neighborhoods" centered around
the major churches (Santa Maria Novella, Il Duomo, Santa Croce, San Lorenzo,
and Santo Spirito and San Frediano in the Oltrarno), these are a bit too broad
to be useful here. I've divided the city up into more visitor-oriented sections
(none much more than a dozen square blocks) focused around major sights
and points of reference. The designations and descriptions are drawn to give
you a flavor of each area and help you choose a zone in which to base
yourself.

The Duomo   The area surrounding Florence's gargantuan cathedral is about as central as you can get. The Duomo is halfway between the two great churches of Santa Maria Novella and Santa Croce as well as at the midpoint between the Uffizi Galleries and the Ponte Vecchio to the south and San Marco and the Accademia Gallery with Michelangelo's *David* to the north. The streets north of the Duomo are long and often traffic-ridden, but those to the south make up a wonderful medieval tangle of alleys and tiny squares heading toward Piazza della Signoria.

This is one of the most historic parts of town, and the streets still vaguely follow the grid laid down when the city began as a Roman colony. Via degli Strozzi/Via dei Speziali/Via del Corso was the *decumanus maximus,* the main east-west axis; Via Roma/Via Calimala was the key north-south *cardo maximus.* The sight of the Roman city's forum is today's Piazza della Repubblica. The current incarnation of this square, lined with glitzy cafes, was laid out by demolishing the Jewish Ghetto in a rash of nationalism during Italian unification in the late 19th century, and (until the majority of neon signs were removed) it was by and large the ugliest piazza in town. The area surrounding it, though, is one of Florence's main shopping zones. The Duomo neighborhood is, understandably, one of the most hotel-heavy parts of town, offering a range from five-star luxury inns to one-star student dives and everything in between.

Piazza Della Signoria   This is the city's civic heart and perhaps the best base for museum hounds, because the Uffizi Galleries, Bargello sculpture collection, and Ponte Vecchio leading toward the Pitti Palace are all nearby. It's a well-polished part of the tourist zone but still retains the narrow medieval streets where Dante grew up—back alleys where tour-bus crowds running from the Uffizi to the Accademia rarely set foot. The few blocks just north of the Ponte Vecchio have good shopping, but unappealing modern buildings were planted here to replace the district destroyed during World War II. The whole neighborhood can be stiflingly crowded in summer, but in those moments when you catch it off-guard and empty of tour groups, it remains the most romantic heart of pre-Renaissance Florence.

San Lorenzo and the Mercato Centrale   This small wedge of streets between the train station and the Duomo, centered around the Medici's old church of San Lorenzo with its Michelangelo-designed tombs, is market territory. The vast indoor food market is here, and most of the streets are filled daily with hundreds of stalls hawking leather jackets and other wares. It's a colorful neighborhood, though perhaps not the quietest.

Piazza Santa Trinita   This piazza sits just off the river at the end of Florence's shopping mecca, Via de' Tornabuoni, home to Gucci, Armani, Ferragamo, Versace, and more. Even the ancient narrow streets running out either side of the square are lined with the biggest names in high fashion. It's a very pleasant, well-to-do, but still medieval neighborhood to stay in even if you don't care about haute couture. But if you're a shopping fiend, there's no better place to be.

Santa Maria Novella   This neighborhood, bounding the western edge of the *centro storico,* really has two characters: the run-down unpleasant zone around Santa Maria Novella train station and the much nicer area south of it between the church of Santa Maria Novella and the river. In general, the train station area is the least attractive part of town in which to base yourself. The streets are mostly outside the pedestrian zone and hence heavily trafficked, noisy, and dirty, and you're removed from the major sights and the action. This area does, however, have more budget options than any other quarter. Some streets, like Via Faenza and its tributaries, contain a glut of one- and two-star joints, with dozens of choices every block and often two, three, or even six bottom-scraping dives crammed into a single building. It's the best place to go if you can't seem to find a room anywhere else; just walk up the street and try each place you pass. And while many hotels simply pander uninspiredly to tourists, a few (those recommended later) seem to try twice as hard as central inns to cater to their guests and are among the friendliest hotels in town.

The situation improves dramatically as you move into the San Lorenzo area and pass Santa Maria Novella church and head toward the river. Piazza Santa Maria Novella and its tributary streets are attracting something of a bohemian nightlife scene (but parts of it can be seedy). Two of Florence's premier inns, the Excelsior and the Grand, are on the Arno at Piazza Ognissanti— just a bit south of the station but miles away in atmosphere.

San Marco and Santissima Annunziata   These two churches are fronted by piazze—Piazza San Marco, now a busy traffic center, and Piazza Santissima Annunziata, the most beautiful in the city—that together define the northern limits of the *centro storico.* The neighborhood is home to the University, Michelangelo's *David* at the Accademia, the San Marco monastery, and long, quiet streets with some real hotel gems. The daily walk back from the heart of town up here may tire some, but others welcome its removal from the worst of the high-season tourist crush.

Santa Croce   This eastern edge of the *centro storico* runs along the Arno. The bulky Santa Croce church is full of famous Florentine art and famous dead Florentines. The church is also the focal point of one of the most genuine neighborhoods left in the old center. While the area's western edge abuts the medieval district around Piazza della Signoria—Via Bentacordi/Via Torta actually trace the outline of the old Roman amphitheater—much of the district was rebuilt after World War II in long blocks of creamy yellow plaster buildings with residential shops and homes. Few tourists roam off Piazza Santa Croce, so if you want to feel like a city resident, stay here. This neighborhood also boasts some of the best restaurants in the city.

The Oltrarno   "Across the Arno" is the artisans' neighborhood, still packed with workshops where craftspeople hand-carve furniture and hand-stitch leather gloves. It began as a working-class neighborhood to catch the overflow from the expanding medieval city on the Arno's opposite bank, but it also became a rather chic area for aristocrats to build palaces on the edge of the countryside. The largest of these, the Pitti Palace, later became the home of the grand dukes and today houses a set of museums second only to the Uffizi. Behind it spreads the landscaped baroque fantasies of the Boboli Gardens, Florence's best park. Masaccio's frescoes in Santa Maria della Carmine here were some of the most influential of the early Renaissance.

Florence tacitly accepted the Oltrarno when the 14th-century circuit of walls was built to include it, but the alleys and squares across the river continued to retain that edge of distinctness. It has always attracted a slightly Bohemian crowd—the Brownings lived here from just after their secret marriage in 1847 until Elizabeth died in 1861. The Oltrarno's lively tree-shaded center, Piazza Santo Spirito, is a world unto itself, lined with bars and trendy salad-oriented restaurants (good nightlife, though young druggies have recently been encroaching on it); and, its Brunelleschi-designed church faces pointedly away from the river and the rest of Florence.

In the Hills   From just about any vantage point in the center of Florence, you can see the city ends abruptly to the north and south, replaced by green hills spotted with villas, small farms, and the expensive modern homes of the upper-middle class. To the north rises Monte Ceceri, mined for the soft gray *pietra serena* that accented so much of Renaissance architecture and home to the hamlet of Settignango, where Michelangelo was wet-nursed by a stonecutter's wife. The high reaches harbor the Etruscan village of Fiesole, which was here long before the Romans built Florence in the valley below. Across the Arno, the hills hemming in the Oltrarno—with names like Bellosguardo (Beautiful View) and Monte Uliveto (Olive Grove Hill)—are blanketed in farmland. With panoramic lookouts like Piazzale Michelangiolo and the Romanesque church of San Miniato al Monte, these hills offer some of the best walks around the city, as Elizabeth Browning, Henry James, and Florence Nightingale could tell you. They're crisscrossed by snaking country roads and bordered by high walls over which wave the silvery-green leaves of olive trees.

Because of the lack of public transportation, first-time visitors who plan a strenuous sightseeing agenda probably will not want to choose accommodations in the hills. But for those who don't need to be in town every day and want a cooler, calmer, and altogether more relaxing vacation, they can be heaven.

2 Getting Around

Florence is a walking city. You can leisurely stroll between the two top sights, the Duomo and the Uffizi, in less than 5 minutes. The hike from the most northerly sights, San Marco with its Fra' Angelico frescoes and the Accademia with Michelangelo's *David,* to the most southerly, the Pitti Palace across the Arno, should take no more than 30 minutes. From Santa Maria Novella across town to Santa Croce is an easy 20- to 30-minute walk.

Most of the streets, however, were designed to handle the moderate pedestrian traffic and occasional horse-drawn cart of a medieval city. Sidewalks, where they exist, are narrow—often less than 2 feet wide. Though much of the *centro storico* is closed to traffic, this doesn't include taxis, residents with parking permits, people without permits who drive there anyway, and the endless swarm of noisy Vespas and *motorini* (scooters). In high season, especially July and August, the cars and their pollution (catalytic converters aren't yet standard), massive pedestrian and tourist traffic, maniac moped drivers, and stifling heat can wear you down. On some days Florence can feel like a minor circle of Dante's Inferno. However, on calmer, less-crowded Sunday mornings and in the off-season, wandering the City of Stone can be quite pleasant indeed. Evenings tend to be cool year-round, bringing residents and visitors alike out for

---

(Kids) **A Walking Warning**

Florentine streets are mainly cobbled or flagstone, as are the sidewalks, and thus can be rough on soles, feet, and joints after awhile. Florence may be one of the world's greatest shoe-shopping cities, but a sensible pair of quality walking shoes or sneakers is highly recommended over loafers or pumps. In dress shoes or heels, forget it.

---

the traditional before-dinner *passeggiata* stroll up and down Via Calzaiuoli and down Via Roma and its continuations across the Ponte Vecchio.

BY BUS   Buses (*autobus*) are useful only to reach outlying destinations or to get to your hotel with luggage. Florence is a walkable city, and many first-timers coming from Rome or Milan misjudge distance and hop on a bus only to find themselves in the suburbs or hills within minutes. The train station is the city's bus hub, and many buses pass through Piazza San Marco as well, but the pedestrian zone historic center isn't well serviced, though the new electric minibuses A, B, C, and D do dip into it.

A **single ticket** costs 1,500L (.80€, 75¢) and is good for 60 minutes. There are also a 2,500L (1.30€, $1.25) 3-hour ticket, a 6,000L (3.10€, $3) 24-hour ticket, and a 11,000L (6€, $6) 3-day pass. You can ride unlimited buses within the time limits—just stamp one end in the orange box on the first bus you board. Tickets are available at newsstands and *tabacchi* (tobacconists shops, marked by a white "T" against brown). I've provided buses that stop nearest the hotels and restaurants below, but this usually doesn't mean doorstep service. Ask the tourist office for a bus map. Regular buses run daily between 5:30 and 8am to between 7 and 9pm. **Night buses** include nos. 67, 68, and 71 (running 9pm to 1am) and no. 70 (running 12:30 to 6am) from the main train station through the center to the suburban Campo Marte station (where some express and night trains stop). For more information, contact the **ATAF** at Piazza della Stazione and Piazza del Duomo 57 (© **055/565-0222;** www.ataf.net).

BY TAXI   Taxis aren't cheap, and with the city so small and the one-way system forcing drivers to take convoluted routes, they aren't an economical way to get about town. Taxis are most useful to get you and your bags between the train station and your hotel in the virtually busless *centro storico*. The standard rate is 1,500L (.80€, 75¢) per kilometer, with a 6,500L (3.35€, $3.25) minimum (9,500L, 4.90€, $4.75 minimum 10pm to 6am; 7,500L, 3.90€, $3.75 on Sundays), plus 1,000L (.50€, 50¢) per bag. There's a taxi stand outside the train station; otherwise you have to call for one (a Radio Taxi) at ℭ **4242,** 4798, or 4390.

BY BICYCLE & SCOOTER Though traffic can be heavy on the narrow streets, the city is mainly flat and not bad for biking (on uncrowded Sunday mornings it can actually be pleasant). *Motorini* (**mopeds**) are the quintessential Italian way to get around and can be especially useful for exploring the hills. **Alinari,** Via Guelfa 85r (ℭ **055/280-500**), is one of the biggest outfits renting scooters (9,000L to 10,000L, 4.65€ to 5.15€, $4.50 to $5 per hour; 40,000L to 50,00L, 21€ to 26€, $20 to $25 per day) and bikes (4,000L to 5,000L, 2.05€ to 2.60€, $2 to $2.50 per hour; 12,000L to 20,000L, 6€ to 10€, $6 to $10 per day). To rent a moped, you'll need to bring a credit card (for deposit) and passport, be over 18, and pay for your own gas. A helmet (*casco*) is included, but you have to ask for it; closed Sunday.

In the last year or so, the city has set up temporary sites about town in summer (look for stands at the train station, Piazza Mercato Centrale, Piazza Strozzi, and Via della Nina along the south side of the Palazzo Vecchio to name a few) where **bikes** are furnished free of charge 8am to 8pm; you must return the bike to any of the other sites. If this is no longer being done or there are no bikes left, you can rent one from **Florence by Bike,** Via San Zanobi, 120–122 R (ℭ **055/488-992**).

BY CAR Trying to drive in the *centro storico* is a frustrating, useless exercise. Florence is a maze of one-way streets and pedestrian zones, and it takes an old hand to know which laws to break in order to get where you need to go—plus you need a permit to do anything beyond dropping off and picking up bags at your hotel. Again, Florence is a walking town, so park your vehicle in one of the huge underground lots on the center's periphery and pound the pavement. For car rental firms in town, see "By Car" under "Arriving in Italy" in chapter 1.

As far as *parcheggio* (**parking**) is concerned, on **streets** white lines indicate free public spaces and blue lines pay public spaces. Meters don't line the sidewalk; rather, there's one machine on the block where you punch in how long you want to spend, it spits out a ticket, and you leave this on your dashboard; sometimes streets will have an attendant who'll come around and give you your time ticket (pay him or her when you get ready to leave). If you park in an area marked PARCHEGGIO DISCO ORARIO, root around in your rental car's glove compartment for a cardboard parking disc (or buy one at a gas station). With this device, you dial up the hour of your arrival (it's the honor system) and display it on your dashboard. You're allowed *un ora* (1 hr.) or *due ore* (2 hr.), according to the sign. **Parking lots** have ticket dispensers but usually *not* manned booths as you exit. Take your ticket with you when you park; when you return to the lot to get your car and leave, first visit the office or automated payment machine to exchange your ticket for a paid receipt you then use at the automated exit.

BY GUIDED TOUR **American Express** (see "Fast Facts: Florence," below) teams with **CAF Tours,** Via Roma 4 (© 055/283-200), to offer two, half-day bus tours (57,000L, 29€, $29), including visits to the Uffizi, the Medici Chapels, and Piazzale Michelangiolo. They also offer several walking tours (35,000L to 45,000L, 18€ to 23€, $18 to $23); day trips to Pisa, Siena/San Gimignano, and the Chianti region (57,000L to 83,000L, 29€ to 43€, $29 to $42); and farther afield to Venice and Perugia/Assisi (140,000L to 180,000L, 72€ to 93€, $70 to $90). You can book the same tours through most other travel agencies around town.

Recently introduced is a daily walking tour called **Enjoy Florence** (© 800/274-819 toll-free from anywhere in Italy; www.florencewalkingtour.com). It departs Monday to Saturday at 10am (sometimes with a second tour on Monday, Wednesday, and Friday at 5pm) from the Thomas Cook exchange office just off the Ponte Vecchio on the Duomo side of the river; it lasts 3 hours and costs 30,000L (16€, $15) for those over 26 and 25,000L (13€, $13) for those under 26. **Walking Tours of Florence** (© 055/234-6225;** www.artviva.com) offers 3-hour tours Monday to Saturday at 10am for 35,000L (18€, $18) adults or 10,000L (5€, $5) children. Meet at the doors of Caffè Giubbe Rosse on Piazza della Repubblica. They also provide private guides and custom requests.

Call **I Bike Italy** (© 055/234-2371; www.ibikeitaly.com) to sign up for 1-day rides in the surrounding countryside (Fiesole, Chianti, or a 2-day trip to Siena) March to November, or you can book Country Walks in Tuscany year-round at the same number. Guided walks are 75,000L (39€, $38) and guided bike rides (21-speed bikes supplied) 95,000L (49€, $48). A shuttle bus picks you up at 9am at the Ponte delle Grazie and drives you to the outskirts of town, and an enjoyable lunch in a local trattoria is included. You're back in town by 5pm. It may stretch your budget, but you should get out of this tourist-trodden stone city for a glimpse of the incomparable Tuscan countryside. **The Accidental Tourist** (© 055/699-376 or 0348/659-0040; fax 055-699-048) offers slightly more genteel 1-day jaunts, either a bike ride through the hills around Florence with a countryside meal or a cooking course and lunch in the Chianti. (You needn't pedal; you're shuttled back and forth to this one.)

 ***FAST FACTS:* Florence**

American Express Amex, Piazza Cimatori/Via Dante Alghieri 22r, 50122 Firenze (© **055/50-981**), will act as a travel agent (for a commission), accept mail on your behalf, and cash traveler's checks at no commission. (They don't have to be Amex checks.) The office is open Monday to Friday 9am to 5:30pm and Saturday 9am to 12:30pm (no travel services Saturday).

Business Hours General open hours for **stores, offices,** and **churches** are 9:30am to noon or 1pm and again 3 or 3:30pm to 7:30pm. That early afternoon shutdown is the *riposo,* the Italian *siesta.* Most stores close all day Sunday and many also on Monday (morning only or all day). Some shops, especially grocery stores, also close Thursday afternoons. Some services and business offices are open to the public only in the morning. In Florence, however, many of the larger and more central shops stay open through the midday *riposo* (*orario no-stop*). The traditional closed day for **museums** is Monday, and though some of the biggest stay open all day long, many close for *riposo* or are only open in the morning (9am to 2pm is popular). Some churches open earlier in the morning, but the largest often stay open all day. **Banks** tend to be open Monday to Friday 8:30am to 1:30pm and 2:30 to 3:30pm or 3 to 4pm.

Use the *riposo* as the Italians do—take a long lunch, stroll through a city park, cool off in the Duomo, travel to the next town, or simply go back to your hotel to rest and regroup your energies. The *riposo* is an especially welcome custom during the oppressive afternoon heat of August when a few hours respite from sightseeing is the only thing that can keep you going.

Doctors/Dentists A **Walk-in Clinic** (℅ 055/483-363 or 0330/774-731) is run by Dott. Giorgio Scappini. Monday, Tuesday, and Thursday office hours are 5:30pm to 6:30pm or by appointment at Via Bonifacio Lupi 32 (just south of the Tourist Medical Service, see "Hospitals" below); Monday, Wednesday, and Friday go to Via Guasti 2 from 3 to 4pm (north of Fortezza del Basso). Dr. Stephen Kerr keeps an office at Piazza dei Giuochi 5–6r, near American Express (℅ 0335/ 836-1682, or 055/436-8775 at home), with home visits or clinic appointment 24 hours a day.

For general **dentistry,** try Dr. Camis de Fonseca, Via Nino Bixio 9, northeast of the city center off Viale dei Mille (℅ 055/587-632), Monday to Friday 3 to 7pm; he's also available for emergency weekend calls. The U.S. consulate can provide a list of other English-speaking doctors, dentists, and specialists. Also see "Hospitals," below, for medical translator service.

Electricity Italy operates on a 220 volts AC (50 cycles) system, as opposed to the United States' 110 volts AC (60 cycle) system. You'll need a simple adapter plug (to make our flat pegs fit their round holes) and, unless your appliance is dual-voltage (as some hair dryers and travel irons are), a currency converter.

E-mail To check or send e-mail head to the **Internet Train** (www.fionline.it), with locations at Via dell'Oriuolo 25r, 3 blocks from the Duomo (℅ 055/263-8968); Via Guelfa 24a near the train station (℅ 055/214-794); and Borgo San Jacopo 30r in the Oltrarno (℅ 055/265-7935). Access is 10,000L (5€, $5) per hour or 8,000L (4.15€, $4) for students. You get a free membership and e-mail address with your first hour, and they also provide printing, scanning, Webcam, and fax services. So does **www village**, Via Alfani 11–13r (℅ 055/247-9398), where online charges are 3,000L (1.55€, $1.50) for 15 minutes, 10,000L (5€, $5) per hour (9,000L, 4.65€, $4.50 for students), or 60,000L (31€, $30) for 8 hours. **Netgate**, Via Sant'Egidio 10–20r (℅ 055/234-7967), has similar rates, but also offers a Saturday "happy hour" of free access 10:30 to 11am and 2 to 2:30pm. All are open daily from around 10am to midnight or later (on Sundays, www village opens 2 to 8pm; Netgate closes at 10:30pm, 8:30pm in winter).

Embassies/Consulates The **U.S. Embassy** is in Rome at Via Vittorio Veneto 121 (© **06/46-741;** fax 06/488-2672). The **U.S. consulate in Florence**—for passport and consular services—is at Lungarno Amerigo Vespucci 46 (© **055/239-8276;** fax 055/284-088), open to drop-ins Monday to Friday 8:30am to 12:30pm and 2 to 4:30pm. The **U.K. Embassy** is in Rome at Via XX Settembre 80a (© **06/482-5441** or 06/852-721; fax 06/487-3324), open in summer Monday to Friday 8am to 1:30pm and off-season Monday to Friday 9am to 12:30pm and 2 to 4:30pm. The **U.K. consulate in Florence** is at Lungarno Corsini 2 (© **055/284-133**).

Of English-speaking countries, only the United States and Great Britain have consulates in Florence. Citizens of other countries must go to their consulates in Rome for help: The **Canadian** consulate in Rome is at Via Zara 30, on the fifth floor (© **06/445-0981** or 06/440-3028), open Monday to Friday 10am to noon and 2 to 4pm. **Australia's** Rome consulate is at Via Alessandria 215 (© **06/852-721;** fax 06/8527-2300), open Monday to Thursday 9am to noon and 1:30 to 5:30pm and Friday 9am to 1:30pm. **New Zealand's** Rome consulate is at Via Zara 28 (© **06/440-2028;** fax 06/440-2984), open Monday to Friday 8:30am to 12:45pm and 1:45 to 5pm.

Emergencies Dial © **113** for an emergency of any kind. You can also call the **Carabinieri** (the national police force; more useful than local branches) at © **112,** dial an **ambulance** at © **118,** and report a **fire** at © **115.** All these calls are free from any phone. For **car breakdowns,** call ACI at © **116.**

Hospitals The **emergency ambulance number** is © **118.** A **Tourist Medical Service,** Via Lorenzo il Magnifico 59, north of the city center between the Fortezza del Basso and Piazza della Libertà (© **055/475-411**), is open 24 hours; take bus no. 8 or 80 to Viale Lavagnini or bus no. 12 or night bus no. 91 to Via Poliziano.

Thanks to socialized medicine, you can walk into most any Italian hospital when ill (but not an emergency) and get taken care of speedily with no insurance questions asked, no forms to fill out, and no fee charged. They'll give you a prescription and send you on your way. The most central are the **Arcispedale di Santa Maria Nuova** (© **055/27-581**), a block northeast of the Duomo on Piazza Santa Maria Nuova, and the **Misericordia Ambulance Service** (© **055/212-222** for ambulance) on Piazza del Duomo across from Giotto's bell tower.

For a free translator to help you describe your symptoms, explain the doctor's instructions, and aid in medical issues in general, call the **Associazione Volontari Ospedalieri (AVO)** at C **055/425-0126** or 055/234-4567 Monday, Wednesday, and Friday 4 to 6pm and Tuesday and Thursday 10am to noon.

Liquor Laws Driving drunk is illegal and not a smart idea anyway on Italy's twisty, narrow roads. Legal drinking age in Italy is 14, but that's just on paper. Public drunkenness (aside from people getting noisily tipsy and flush at big dinners) is unusual except among some street people—usually among foreign vagabonds, not the Italian homeless.

Luggage Storage/Lockers Leave your bags at Santa Maria Novella train station (5,000L, 2.60€, $2.50 per bag for each 12-hour period; first 5,000L payable up front). It's open daily 4:30am to 1:30am.

Mail The Italian mail system is notoriously slow, and friends back home may not receive your postcards or aerograms for anywhere from 1 to 8 weeks (sometimes longer). Postcards, aerograms, and letters, weighing up to 20 grams (0.7 oz.), to North America cost 1,300L (.70€, 65¢), to the United Kingdom and Ireland 800L (.40€, 40¢), and to Australia and New Zealand 1,400L (.70€, A$1.05).

You can buy *francobolli* (stamps) from any *tabacchi* (tobacconists) or from the central post office. The most central **post office** is at Via Pellicceria 3 (C **160** for general info or 055/211-147), under the arcade at Piazza della Repubblica, to the left of the Banco Nazionale del Lavoro. September to July, it's open Monday to Saturday 8:15am to 7pm and Sunday 8:30am to 7pm (on Sunday and holidays, you can enter only from Piazza Davazanti 4, around the back). August, it's open daily 8:30am to 1:30pm. It's closed January 1, May 1, Easter, August 15, and December 25.

Drop postcards and letters into the boxes outside. To mail larger packages, drop them at sportello (window) 9/10, but first head across the room to window 21/22 for stamps. If that window is closed, as it often is, you buy your stamps at the next window, 23/24, which is also the pickup for Fermo Posta (poste restante, or held-mail).

Pharmacies You'll find **green neon crosses** above the entrances to most *farmacie* (pharmacies). You'll also find many *erborista* (herbalist) shops, which usually offer more traditional herbal remedies (some of which are marvelously effective) along with the standard pharmaceuticals. Most *farmacie* of any stripe keep everything behind the counter, so be prepared to point or pantomime. *Some help:* Most minor ailments start with the phrase *mal di* in Italian, so you can just say "Mahl dee" and point to your head, stomach, throat, or whatever. Some male toilette items, such as razor blades, are sold at *tabacchi*. Pharmacies rotate which will stay open all night and on Sundays, and each store has a poster outside showing the month's rotation.

For pharmacy **information,** dial ℂ **110.** There are 24-hour pharmacies (also open Sundays and state holidays) in **Santa Maria Novella train station** (ℂ **055/216-761;** ring the bell between 1 and 4am); at **Piazza San Giovanni 20r,** just behind the Baptistery at the corner of Borgo San Lorenzo (ℂ **055/211-343**); and at **Via Cazzaiuoli 7r,** just off Piazza della Signoria (ℂ **055/289-490**).

Police For emergencies, dial ℂ **112** for the **Carabinieri police.** To report lost property or passport problems, call the *questura* (urban police headquarters) at ℂ **055/49-771.** Also see "Emergencies," above.

Post Offices See "Mail," above.

Restrooms Public toilets are going out of fashion in northern Italy, but most *bars* will let you use their bathrooms without a scowl or forcing you to buy anything. Ask "*Posso usare il bagno?*" (*poh*-soh oo-*zar*-eh eel *ban*-yo). *Donne/signore* are women and *uomini/signori* men. Train stations usually have a bathroom, for a fee, often of the two-bricks-to-stand-on-and-a-hole-in-the-floor Turkish toilet variety. In many of the public toilets that remain, the little old lady with a basket has been replaced by a coin-op turnstile.

Safety Central Italy is an exceedingly safe area with practically no random violent crime. There are, as in any city, plenty of **pickpockets** out to ruin your vacation, and Florence has the added joy of light-fingered gypsy children (especially around the train station), but otherwise you're safe. Do steer clear of the Cascine Park after dark, when it becomes somewhat seedy and you may run the risk of being mugged, and you probably won't want to hang out with the late-night heroin addicts shooting up on the Arno mudflats below the Lungarno embankments on the edges of town.

Taxes There's no sales tax added onto the price tag of your purchases, but there is a **value-added tax** (in Italy: IVA) automatically included in just about everything. For major purchases, you can get this refunded (see "Getting Your VAT Refund" in chapter 6, "Shopping"). Some five-star and four-star hotels don't include the 13% luxury tax in their quoted prices. Ask when making your reservation.

Telephones/Fax The **country code** for Italy is **39**. In 1988, Italy incorporated what were once separate **city codes** (for example, Florence's was 055) into the numbers themselves. Therefore, you must dial the entire number, *including the initial zero,* when calling from *anywhere* outside or inside Italy.

In other words, to call Florence from the States, dial **011/39-055-xxx-xxxx** (soon, newly issued Florence numbers may begin with something other than 055). Phone numbers in Italy can range from 6 to 12 digits in length (including those former "city codes").

Local calls in Italy cost 200L (.10€, 10¢). There are three types of public pay phones: those that take coins only, those that take both coins and phonecards, and those that take only **phonecards** (*carta* or *scheda telefonica*). You can buy these prepaid phonecards at any *tabacchi* (tobacconists), most newsstands, and some bars in denominations of 5,000L (2.60€, $2.50), 10,000L (5€, $5), and 15,000L (8€, $8). Break off the corner before inserting it; a digital display counts down how much money is left on the card as you talk. Don't forget to take the card with you when you leave!

For **operator-assisted international calls** (in English), dial toll-free ✆ **170**. Note, however, that you'll get better rates by calling a home operator for collect calls, as detailed here: To make **calling card calls,** insert a phonecard or 200L (.10€, 10¢)—it'll be refunded at the end of your call—and dial the local number for your service. For **Americans:** AT&T at ✆ **172/1011,** MCI at ✆ **172/1022,** or Sprint at ✆ **172/1877.** These numbers will raise an American operator for you, and you can use any one of them to place a **collect call** even if you don't carry that phone company's card. **Canadians** can reach Teleglobe at ✆ **172/1001. Brits** can call BT at ✆ **172/0044** or

Mercury at ✆ **172/0544.** The **Irish** can get a home operator at ✆ **172/0353. Australians** can use Optus by calling ✆ **172/1161** or Telstra at ✆ **172/1061.** And **New Zealanders** can phone home at ✆ **172/1064.**

To **dial direct internationally from Italy,** dial ✆ **00,** then the country code, the area code, and the number. Country codes are as follows: the United States and Canada 1; the United Kingdom 44; Ireland 353; Australia 61; New Zealand 64. Make international calls from a public phone if possible because hotels charge ridiculously inflated rates for direct dial, but take along plenty of *schede* to feed the phone. Italy has also introduced a *scheda telefonica internazionale* for calling overseas. You buy these at the same outlets as a regular phonecard (most often found at *tabacchi* and newsstands in train stations). They come in increments of 50 (12,500L, 6€, $6), 100 (25,000L, 13€, $13), 200 (50,000L, 26€, $25), and 400 (100,000L, 52€, $50) *unita* (units). Each *unita* is worth 250L (.15€, 15¢) of phone time; it costs 5 *unita* (1,250L, .65€, 65¢) per minute to call within Europe or to the States or Canada and 12 *unita* (3,000L, 1.55€, A$2.95) per minute to call Australia or New Zealand. You don't insert this card into the phone; merely dial ✆ **1740,** then "*2" for instructions in English when prompted.

To call free national **telephone information** (in Italian) in Italy, dial ✆ **12.** International information for Europe is available at ✆ **176** but costs 1,200L (.60€, 60¢) a shot. For international information beyond Europe, dial ✆ **1790** for 1,000L (.50€, 50¢).

Your hotel will most likely be able to send or receive **faxes** for you, sometimes at inflated prices, sometimes at cost. Otherwise, most *cartoleria* (stationery stores), *copista* or *foto-copie* (photocopy shops), and some *tabacchi* (tobacconists) offer fax services.

Time   Italy is 6 hours ahead of Eastern Standard Time in the United States. When it's noon in New York, it's 6pm in Florence.

Tipping   In **hotels,** a service charge is usually included in your bill. In family-run operations, additional tips are unnecessary and sometimes considered rude. In fancier places with a hired staff, however, you may want to leave a 1,000L (.50€, 50¢) daily tip for the maid, pay the bellhop or porter 2,000L (1.05€,

$1) per bag, and a helpful concierge 5,000L (2.60€, $2.50) for his or her troubles. In **restaurants,** 10% to 15% is almost always included in the bill—to be sure, ask *"è incluso il servizio?"*—but you can leave up to an additional 10%, especially for good service. At **bars and cafes,** leave at least 100L (.05€, 5¢) per espresso on the counter for the barman, 200L (.10€, 10¢) for a cappuccino, and 1,000L (.50€, 50¢) for a cocktail; if you sit at a table, leave 15%. **Taxi** drivers expect 10% to 15%.

Water Although most Italians take mineral water with their meals, tap water is safe everywhere, as are any public drinking fountains you run across. Unsafe sources will be marked *"acqua non potabile."* If tap water comes out cloudy, it's only the calcium or other minerals inherent in a water supply that often comes untreated from fresh springs.

3

Where to Stay

Throughout the 1990s, inflation ran rampant in Italy, and hotel prices more than tripled in cities like Florence. It's now fairly difficult to find a double you'd want to stay in for less than 100,000L (52€, $50). Because hotel prices actually outpaced inflation, the hoteliers stockpiled some surplus, and in the last few years they've been reinvesting in their properties. In many hotels, the amenity levels are now at or above what Americans expect to find at home, and the days of the bathroom-down-the-hall cheap pensione are fading—or at least those properties are now mostly student dives. Almost everyone seems to have put in new bathrooms. Extras like heated towel racks, whirlpool tubs, satellite TVs receiving CNN and the BBC, and direct-dial phones that once only the top few inns boasted are now in three-quarters of the properties below. I've tried to balance the selections to suit all tastes and budgets and assigned stars to the properties that really offer excellent value for your money.

For **help finding a room,** visit the Santa Maria Novella train station for the **Consorzio Informazioni Turistiche Alberghiere (ITA)** office, near track 9 (© **055/282-893**), and the tiny tourist office, near track 16, both of which will find you a room in your price range (for a small commission).

To help you decide in which area you'd like to base yourself for exploring the city, consult the "Neighborhoods in Brief" section in chapter 2.

1 Near the Duomo

VERY EXPENSIVE

Hotel Brunelleschi ⊛ The mishmash of historical structures making up this hotel—including a Roman *calidarium* in the foundations—was so confusing they installed a small museum in the basement to explain it all. The property rambles through the remains of various medieval houses, a deconsecrated church, and a 6th-century Byzantine tower (the Brunelleschi's pride and joy, today serving as meeting rooms and a hotel bar). Most of the interiors mix curving modern lines with the salvaged vestiges of the medieval buildings. The rooms are spacious and very comfortable, with large bathrooms, but are disappointingly modern. A few, especially on the upper floors, share with the panoramic roof terrace a view of the Duomo. The location is prime but the price a bit steep for those who don't get a thrill from sleeping near the fossilized remnants of the Middle Ages.

Piazza Sant'Elisabetta 3 (off Via de' Calzioli), 50122 Firenze. ℂ **800/860-076** toll-free in Italy or 055/27-370. Fax 055/219-653. www.hotelbrunelleschi.it. 96 units. 570,000L (294€, $285) double; 900,000L (465€, $450) suite. Rates include breakfast. AE, DC, MC, V. Valet parking in garage 60,000L (31€, $30). Bus: B, 14, 23, 71. **Amenities:** Intimate Tuscan nouvelle restaurant, American bar (in the tower); concierge; tour desk; car-rental desk; courtesy car (pay); business center and secretarial services; room service; massages (in-room); baby-sitting; laundry service; dry cleaning (same day); nonsmoking rooms. *In room:* A/C, TV, minibar, hair dryer, safe.

Hotel Savoy ⋞⋞ The Savoy was built in 1893 and closed in 1999 to 2000 for a complete transformation by Sir Rocco Forte and his sister, who designed the warm, stylishly minimalist modern interiors. Rooms are standardized in off-white and wheat shades accented with slips of color and dark-stained wood furnishings under soft sconce lighting, with walk-in closets, dark brown marble bathrooms, and mosaics over the tubs. The different room "styles"—classic, executive, and deluxe—really just refer to size. "Studios" are code for junior suites consisting of a single very large room. Four suites (two rooms, two TVs, leather easy chairs, white marble bathrooms) are on the back, four on the piazza. Rooms on the fifth floor, added in 1958, just peep over the surrounding buildings for spectacular views, especially those on the Duomo (back) side. As with the Hotel Pensione Pendini (below), you're just a few steps in any direction from all the sights and the best shopping. The building actually belongs to Ferragamo (their decor tip o' the hat is to include shoe images in most public area art).

Piazza della Repubblica 7, 50123 Firenze. ℂ **800/223-6800** in the U.S.; 055/27-351 in Italy. Fax 055/273-5888. www.rfhotels.com. 107 units. 825,000L–968,000L (426€–500€, $413–$484) double; 1,210,000L (625€, $605) studio; 1,650,000L–2,090,000L (852€–1,080€, $825–$1045) suite; 2,750,000L (1,420€, $1,375) Repubblica suite. Breakfast 44,000L (23€, $22). AE, DC, MC, V. Bus: A, 22, 6, 11, 36, 37. **Amenities:** Tuscan restaurant, bar; concierge; tour desk; car-rental desk; courtesy car (from airport; pay); secretarial services; room service (24-hour); massages (in-room); baby-sitting; laundry service; dry cleaning (same day); nonsmoking rooms. *In room:* A/C, TV w/ pay movies, VCR (on request), fax (on request), dataport, minibar, hair dryer, safe.

Florence Accommodations

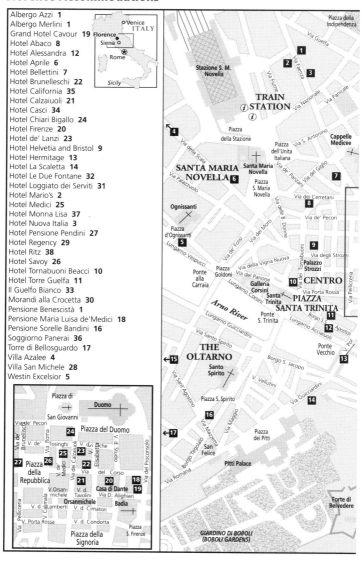

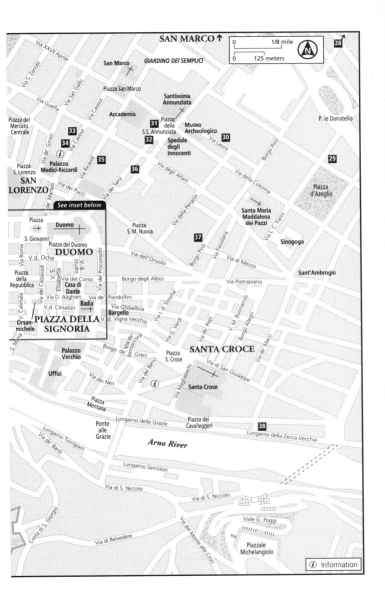

EXPENSIVE

Grand Hotel Cavour ✿ The Cavour is an address of some refinement in Dante's old neighborhood, and about as central as you can get. The plush chairs in the large vaulted lobby focus around an antique stone pillar, and the roof terrace has a positively spectacular view of the Duomo, the Palazzo Vecchio, and other Florentine landmarks. The rooms, carpeted and furnished with contemporary good taste, tend to be on the small side, though a few enjoy brick arches and other 10th-century holdovers. The bathrooms are new, and the firm beds are spread with patterned quilts. Accommodations along the front and side get a view of the towers sprouting from the Bargello and the Badia, but be warned: The double-glazed windows are no match for the clamorous buses that grumble down the busy street in front.

Via del Proconsolo 3 (next to the Badia), 50122 Firenze. ✆ 055/282-461. Fax 055/218-955. www.hotelcavour.com. 108 units. 360,000L (186€, $180) double. Rates include breakfast. AE, DC, MC, V. Valet parking in garage 50,000L (26€, $25). Bus: 14, 23, 71. **Amenities:** Elegant and famous Beatrice restaurant (refined traditional Tuscan); bike rental; concierge; tour desk; car-rental desk; salon; room service; baby-sitting; laundry service; dry cleaning (same day); nonsmoking rooms. *In room:* A/C, TV, dataport, minibar, hair dryer, safe.

Hotel Calzaiuoli ✿ As central as you can get, the Calzaiuoli offers comfortable, well-appointed rooms on the main strolling drag halfway between the Uffizi and the Duomo. The halls' rich runners lead up a *pietra serena* staircase to the midsize and largish rooms decorated with painted friezes and framed etchings. Refurbishment of all rooms was underway in 2001, with the addition of stylish wood furnishings and mirrored armoires. The firm beds rest on patterned carpets, in the older rooms surrounded by functional furniture beginning to show some wear. The bathrooms range from huge to cramped, but all have hair dryers and fluffy towels (and a few enjoy Jacuzzis). The rooms look over the street, with its pedestrian carnival and some of the associated noise, or out the back—either over the rooftops to the Bargello and Badia towers or up to the Duomo's cupola.

Via Calzaiuoli 6 (near Orsanmichele), 50122 Firenze. ✆ 055/212-456. Fax 055/268-310. www.calzaiuoli.it. 45 units. 420,000L (217€, $210) double. Discounts of 20%–25% in slow periods. Rates include breakfast. AE, DC, MC, V. Valet parking 45,000L–50,000L (23€–26€, $23–$25) in garage. Bus: 22, 36, 37. **Amenities:** Concierge; tour desk; car-rental desk; room service; baby-sitting; laundry service; dry cleaning. *In room:* A/C, TV, minibar, hair dryer, safe.

Hotel de' Lanzi 🏵🏵   A much quieter alternative to the Hotel Chiari Bigallo, its sister hotel around the corner (see below), the Lanzi is just as centrally located and more comfortable. A 1997 refurbishment left all the beds with firm mattresses and spreads embroidered in an antique Florentine pattern. The accommodations, in fact, are all done very tastefully for a hotel of this price. (Ask for a Frommer's discount and it may drop into the "Moderate" category.) The rooms are carpeted, have a unified decor, and come with shiny new bathrooms sporting heated towel racks (in most). Many rooms on the front get that magnificent window-filling side view of the Duomo to which hotels in this area are prone, but even if you don't get the vista, you can be assured of cozy, relaxing accommodations just a few steps from the city's major sights and shopping. Breakfast is a full buffet with fruit and ham.

Via delle Oche 11 (off Via Calzaiuoli around the corner from the Duomo), 50122 Firenze. ✆ and fax **055/288-043**. www.florence.ala.it/lanzi. 44 units. 330,000L (170€, $165) double. Ask for Frommer's discounts. Rates include breakfast. AE, DC, MC, V. Valet parking 35,000L (18€, $18). Bus: 22, 36, 37. **Amenities:** Concierge; tour desk; car-rental desk; room service; laundry service; dry cleaning; nonsmoking rooms. *In room:* A/C, TV, hair dryer, safe.

MODERATE

Hotel Medici 🏵 *Value*   In the heart of town with killer views, this place is more than worth it for budgeteers who can secure a room on the fifth or (better yet) sixth floor. All rooms are good-size but plain, with functional furniture, tile floors, tiny bathrooms, and firm beds. But who looks at the room when your window is filled with a vista of Florence's Duomo—facade, campanile, dome, and all? Only the top two levels of rooms get the full effect, but the sixth floor has a wraparound terrace everyone can enjoy. If you're lucky, you might happen in at a moment when one of the many regulars haven't booked one of the sixth-floor rooms with French windows opening directly onto the terrace. Fifth- and sixth-floor rooms have TVs, and by 2001 they expect to have them in all. The price is excellent for this kind of location and panorama.

Via de' Medici 6 (between Piazza della Repubblica and Via de' Calzaiuoli), 50123 Firenze. ✆ **055/284-818**. Fax 055/216-202. http://medici@dada.it. 39 units, 26 with bathroom (shower only). 90,000L–180,000L (46€–93€, $45–$90) double without bathroom; 120,000L–250,000L (62€–129€, $60–$125) double with bathroom. MC, V. Rates include breakfast. Valet parking 35,000L (18€, $17.50) in nearby garage. Bus: A, 22, 36, 37. **Amenities:** Concierge; tour desk; car-rental desk; room service (breakfast only). *In room:* TV (in some), minibar (in 6), hair dryer.

Hotel Pensione Pendini ⍟ Built during the heyday of the 1880s when Florence was briefly the capital of the newly unified Italy, the Pendini rises above the storefronts of Piazza della Repubblica. The Abolaffio brothers, Emmanuele and David, took over this former pensione in 1994 and have since installed double glazing on all windows so that street noise has virtually disappeared, and they're finishing up renovating the rooms on the lower story. All bathrooms are also being redone in green tile with large tubs. Many rooms boast an airy country style, with original and reproduction antiques and brass-framed beds. The rather large accommodations on the piazza are best, with views over the bustle of the cafe-lined square. Family suites have two small bedrooms with a common bathroom. The lounge, offering 24-hour bar service, will remain a comfortable mélange of 19th-century furnishings with scattered rugs, plus a computer with free Internet access. The location and price make this hotel a good choice for shoppers who'd rather give their money to Armani and Ferragamo.

Via Strozzi 1 (Piazza d. Repubblica), 50123 Firenze. ⓒ 055/211-170. Fax 055/281-807. www.florenceitaly.net. 42 units, all with bathroom. 213,000L–290,000L (110€–150€, $107–$145) double; 280,000L–416,000L (145€–215€, $140–$208) triple; 320,000L–494,000L (165€–255€, $160–$247) quad; 320,000L–648,000L (165€–335€, $160–$324) family suite. Rates include continental breakfast. AE, DC, MC, V. Valet garage parking 40,000L–60,000L (21€–31€, $20–$30). Bus: A, 6, 11, 22, 36, 37. **Amenities:** Concierge; tour desk; car-rental desk; room service (breakfast & bar; 24-hour). *In room:* A/C, TV, dataport, hair dryer (ask at desk).

INEXPENSIVE

Hotel Chiari Bigallo ⍟ *Finds* This place may be a bit noisy in the evenings, but if you get a room along the front you can lean out your window and practically poke Giotto's campanile with a stick. In fact, the view from these rooms (about four rooms get the view) is a living postcard—a foreshortened shot with the Duomo facade and campanile 50 feet away and Brunelleschi's dome rising above them. I was quite cross last year to find that they'd decided to renovate into three-star status—and double the prices—this old super-cheap standby (to bring it in line with their other two hotels, including the de' Lanzi; see above). It was closed in 2001 to completely revamp the largish rooms, each in a unique antique style, and to create four suites.

Vicolo degli Adimari 2 (off the Via Calzaiuoli near the Piazza Duomo), 50122 Firenze. ⓒ 055/216-086. Fax 055/214-496. 17 units. 300,000L–350,000L

(155€–181€, $150–$175) double. Rates include continental breakfast. AE, DC, MC, V. Valet parking in garage 40,000L (21€, $20). Bus: A, 1, 6, 11, 14, 17, 22, 23, 36, 37. **Amenities:** Concierge; tour desk; car-rental desk; room service; laundry service; dry cleaning; nonsmoking rooms. *In room:* A/C, TV, hair dryer, safe.

Hotel Firenze   A recent renovation has transformed this former student hangout (still partly used as a study-abroad dorm) into a two-star hotel. It's location is divine, tucked away on its own little piazza at the heart of the *centro storico*'s pedestrian zone, but it's a bit too institutional to justify the midrange rates. The rooms are simple, brightly tiled but bland. This is a large operation without any of the warmth or ambience of a small, family-run hotel, and the concierge and management are efficient but generally uninvolved.

Piazza Donati 4 (on Via del Corso, off Via dei Calzaiuoli), 50122 Firenze. ① 055/268-301 or 055/214-203. Fax 055/212-370. 60 units. 150,000L (77€, $75) double; 215,000L (111€, $108) triple; 260,000L (134€, $130) quad. Rates include continental breakfast. No credit cards. Bus: A, 14, 23. **Amenities:** Tour desk. *In room:* TV, hair dryer.

Pensione Maria Luisa de' Medici ★★★ *Kids Finds*   In the 1950s and '60s, Angido Sordi was into Italian design, and the rooms of his hotel—each frescoed with a different Medici portrait by his wife— have lamps, chairs, and tables you'd normally have to go to New York's Museum of Modern Art to see. In the 1970s and '80s, Sordi got into baroque art, so the halls are hung with canvases by the likes of Van Dyck, Vignale, and Sustermans. I can't wait to see what he gets into next. The 1645 palazzo setting goes well with the artistic theme, and Sordi's Welsh partner, Evelyn Morris, cooks hearty breakfasts served to you in your room. Most rooms are large enough to accommodate four to five people comfortably. The firm beds are set on carpeted or tiled floors scattered with thick rugs. There are four shared bathrooms, so you usually don't have to wait in the morning. One drawback: You have to walk up three flights. There is a curfew, which varies with the season.

Via del Corso 1 (2nd floor; between Via dei Calzaiuoli and Via del Proconsolo), 50122 Firenze. ① 055/280-048. 9 units, 2 with bathroom. 114,000L (59€, $57) double without bathroom, 144,000L (74€, $72) double with bathroom; 160,000L (83€, $80) triple without bathroom, 198,000L (102€, $99) triple with bathroom; 206,000L (106€, $103) quad without bathroom, 252,000L (130€, $126) quad with bathroom. Rates include breakfast. No credit cards. Nearby parking about 40,000L (21€, $20). Bus: A, 14, 23. **Amenities:** Concierge; tour desk. *In room:* Hair dryer, no phone.

2 Near Piazza Della Signoria

Hotel Hermitage ✦ This ever-popular hotel right at the foot of the Ponte Vecchio was renovated in 1998 to give each room wood floors or thick rugs, shiny new bathrooms (most with Jacuzzis), and fresh wallpaper. The rooms are of moderate size, occasionally a bit dark, but they're full of 17th- to 19th-century antiques and boast double-glazed windows to cut down on noise. Those that don't face the Ponte Vecchio are on side alleys and quieter but miss out on the view. Their famous roof terrace is covered in bright flowers that frame postcard views of the Arno, Duomo, and Palazzo Vecchio. The charming breakfast room full of picture windows gets the full effect of the morning sun. The owners and staff excel in doing the little things that help make your vacation go smoothly, like providing unerring restaurant recommendations—but prices are a bit inflated.

Vicolo Marzio 1/Piazza del Pesce (to the left of the Ponte Vecchio as you're facing it), 50122 Firenze ✆ **055/287-216.** Fax 055/212-208. www.hermitagehotel.com. 28 units. 410,000L (212€, $205) double; 530,000L (274€, $265) suite. Rates 20% lower in winter. Rates include breakfast. MC, V. Parking 40,000L–60,000L (21€–31€, $20–$30). Bus: 23, 71. **Amenities:** Concierge; tour desk; room service; baby-sitting; laundry service; dry cleaning. *In room:* A/C, TV, hair dryer, safe.

3 Near San Lorenzo & the Mercato Centrale
EXPENSIVE

Il Guelfo Bianco ✦✦ Once you enter this refined hotel (completely renovated in 1994 and enlarged in 2001), you'll forget it's on busy Via Cavour. Its windows are triple-paned, blocking out nearly all traffic noise, and many rooms overlook quiet courtyards and gardens out back. The room decor is very pretty, with marble-topped desks, modern art, painted tile work in the large new bathrooms, and tasteful futon chairs in the larger superior rooms. The ceilings faithfully reproduce the beam and terra-cotta look this 15th-century palazzo once had. Some rooms have retained such atmospheric 17th-century features as frescoed or painted wood ceilings, carved wooden doorways, antique furnishings, and the occasional parquet floor. The friendly staff is full of advice and strives to help make your stay memorable.

Via Cavour 29 (near the corner of Via Guelfa), 50129 Firenze. ✆ **055/288-330.** Fax 055/295-203. www.ilguelfobianco.it. 43 units. 330,000L (170€, $165) standard double; 395,000L (204€, $198) superior double. Rates include breakfast. AE, MC, V. Valet parking 35,000L–42,000L (18€–22€, $18–$21) in garage. Bus: 1, 6, 7, 11, 17, 33, 67, 68. **Amenities:** Bike rental (they have just a few they'll lend for free on

> (**Kids** **Family-Friendly Hotels**
>
> **Hotel Casci** (p. 52)   This inexpensive family favorite near the Palazzo Medici-Ricciardi has a series of extra-large rooms set aside especially for families. The hotel is housed in a 15th-century palazzo, and the family that runs it is very friendly and helpful. A great family value!
>
> **Hotel Nuova Italia** (p. 57)   The Italian-American couple that runs this hotel near the station are just about the most helpful hoteliers I've ever run across. The rooms aren't overly large but are immaculate. And here's an added perk: With this Frommer's guidebook in hand, you and your brood can get a discount off the already reasonable prices.
>
> **Pensione Maria Luisa de' Medici** (p. 49)   An amicable pair of proprietors runs this very central hotel just a few blocks from the Duomo. Most rooms are enormous, with multiple beds and dressers and tabletops on which to spread your family's stuff. The home-cooked Welsh breakfast served in your room is included in the low prices. Just be sure to admonish the more curious youngsters from touching the genuine—and valuable—baroque paintings in the hall.

first come, first serve); concierge; tour desk; car-rental desk; room service (24-hour); massages (in-room); baby-sitting; laundry service; dry cleaning (same day). *In room:* A/C, TV, VCR (in some), dataport, minibar, hair dryer, safe.

MODERATE

Hotel Bellettini ⭐ *Value*   A hotel has existed in this Renaissance palazzo since the 1600s. Gina and Marzia, sisters and third-generation hoteliers, run this gem of terra-cotta tiles, wrought-iron or carved wood beds, antiques, stained-glass windows, and hand-painted coffered ceilings. Room 44 offers a tiny balcony that, blooming with jasmine and geraniums by late spring, makes it second best only to room 45 with its view of the Medici chapels and the Duomo's dome. The two bedrooms of no. 20 make it perfect for families. In 2000, they added a lovely six-room annex with frescoes, marble bathrooms, minibars, and coffeemakers; rooms are about 20,000L (10€, $10) more than at the main hotel. The hotel shares management with the 26-room Le Vigne, Piazza Santa Maria Novella 24 (© **055/294-449;** fax 055/230-2263), which absorbs some of the overflow into large but simple renovated rooms. The rates are slightly lower than at the Bellettini, and duplex 119 is great for families. Breakfast is an impressive spread.

Via dei Conti 7 (off Via dei Cerretani), 50123 Firenze. © **055/213-561.** Fax 055/283-551. www.firenze.net/hotelbellettini. 28 units. 230,000L (119€, $115) double; 275,000L (142€, $138) triple; 345,000L (178€, $173) quad. Rates include buffet breakfast. AE, DC, MC, V. Nearby parking 35,000L (18€, $18). Bus: A, 1, 6, 14, 17, 22, 23, 36, 37. **Amenities:** Concierge; tour desk; room service; laundry service; dry cleaning. *In room:* A/C, TV, minibar (in annex rooms), coffeemaker (in annex rooms), hair dryer (ask at reception), safe.

INEXPENSIVE

Hotel California 🌴 *(Value* The California is a good budget option on a lightly trafficked street near the Duomo. Some of the painted tiled floors are very pretty, and rooms were completely overhauled in 2000/2001 with stylish modern furnishings, richly colored bedspreads, and spanking new bathrooms—a few with Jacuzzi tubs, and almost all with spacious marble sink counters. There are 18th-century fresco fragments and stuccoes on many of the ceilings, and breakfast is served on a flower-covered terrace in nice weather. A few of the rooms have balconies and views of the Duomo's cupola, and they offer good deals for families.

Via Ricasoli 30 (1½ blocks north of the Duomo), 50122 Firenze. © **055/282-753.** Fax 055/216-268. 30 units. 180,000L–280,000L (93€–145€, $90–$140) double. Rates include breakfast. AE, DC, MC, V. Valet parking 45,000L (23€, $23). Bus: 1, 6, 7, 10, 11, 17, 20, 25, 31, 32, 33, 67, 68, 91. **Amenities:** Concierge; tour desk; room service. *In room:* A/C, TV, dataport, minibar (in 10 rooms), hair dryer, safe.

Hotel Casci 🌴 *(Kids* This clean hotel in a 15th-century palazzo is run by the Lombardis, one of Florence's nicest families. It's patronized by a host of regulars who know a good value when they find it. The Lombardis bicker among themselves Italian style but are amazingly accommodating toward guests—their favorite phrase in English is "No problem!" The tiny frescoed bar room was part of composer Giacchino Rossini's apartment in the 1850s, as were the only two guest rooms on the street level, which sport a formidable double set of double-paned windows to block out the noise. All accommodations are plain, with unassuming modular furniture set on tile floors with a few rugs. The bathrooms were renovated in 1999 with fresh tile, heated towel racks, and hair dryers. The rooms ramble on toward the back forever, overlooking the gardens and Florentine rooftops, and are mouse-quiet except for the birdsong. A few large family suites in back sleep four to five. The breakfast room has 18th-century ceiling frescoes.

Via Cavour 13 (between Via dei Ginori and Via Guelfa), 50129 Firenze. ℭ **055/ 211-686**. Fax 055/239-6461. www.hotelcasci.com. 25 units. 220,000L (114€, $110) double; 300,000L (155€, $150) triple; 380,000L (196€, $190) quad. Off-season rates 20%–30% less; check website for special offers, especially Nov–Feb. Rates include buffet breakfast. AE, DC, MC, V. Valet parking 40,000L (21€, $20). Bus: 1, 6, 11, 17. **Amenities:** Concierge; tour desk; baby-sitting; laundry service; dry cleaning; nonsmoking rooms. *In room:* A/C, TV, minibar, hair dryer, safe.

4 Near Piazza Santa Trínita

VERY EXPENSIVE

Hotel Helvetia and Bristol ✶✶✶   This Belle Epoque hotel is the most central of the top five-star addresses in town, host in the past to the Tuscan Macchaioli painters as well as De Chirico, playwright Pirandello, and atom-splitting Enrico Fermi. The attentive staff oversees the rather cushy accommodations outfitted with marble bathrooms; large, firm beds; and heavy curtains. The suites have multiple phones and often multiple TVs. Rooms of deluxe category on up also have CD stereos, VCRs (free movies in English at the reception), and cordless phones. Most rooms have at least one antique work of art on the fabric-covered walls, and all are well insulated from the sounds of the outside world. The large 17th-century canvases add an air of dignity to the plush sofas of the lounge, while the Winter Garden bar/breakfast room is tricked out with trailing ivy and a splashing fountain.

Via dei Pescioni 2 (near the Palazzo Strozzi), 50123 Firenze. ℭ **888/770-0447** in the U.S., 800/505-050 toll-free in Italy or 055/287-814. Fax 055/288-353. 67 units. 635,000L–908,500L (328€–469€, $318–$454) double; 878,000L–1,995,000L (454€–1,030€, $439–$998) suite. Breakfast 46,000L (24€, $23). AE, DC, MC, V. Valet parking in garage 60,000L (31€, $30). Bus: 6, 11, 36, 37, 68. **Amenities:** Intimate restaurant (internationalized Italian); bike rental; concierge; tour desk; car-rental desk; Internet terminal; room service (24-hour); massages (in-room); baby-sitting; laundry service; dry cleaning (same day). *In room:* A/C, TV, VCR (in deluxe rooms), minibar.

EXPENSIVE

Hotel Tornabuoni Beacci ✶   The 80-year-old Beacci continues a 200-year hostelry tradition in this 16th-century Strozzi family palace. The staff greets return guests and new friends alike with genuine warmth. Everything is a bit worn, but there's a concerted effort to furnish the rooms with period pieces. The rooms on the upper floor are smaller, but their windows see over the rooftops. The bathrooms were recently redone in a modern style with tubs and heated towel racks. The dining room is sunny, and the lunches and dinners are well prepared. In summer, you can take breakfast on a terrace bursting with flowers and a view of the Bellosguardo hills. Off the terrace is a small bar, and there's an atmospheric reading room with a 17th-century tapestry and a large fireplace that roars to life in winter. They're currently expanding into the floor below with a small conference room and 12 more guest rooms, including a suite overlooking Piazza Santa Trínita and a honeymoon suite covered with beautiful 17th-century frescoes.

Via Tornabuoni 3 (off the north corner of Piazza Santa Trínita), 50123 Firenze. ✆ 055/212-645. Fax 055/283-594. www.BThotel.it. 28 units. 300,000L–400,000L (155€–207€, $150–$200) double; 700,000L (362€, $350) suite. Rates include buffet breakfast. AE, DC, MC, V. Parking 45,000L (23€, $23) in garage. Bus: 6, 11, 36, 37, 68. **Amenities:** Tuscan restaurant; concierge; tour desk; room service (24-hour); baby-sitting; laundry service; dry cleaning. *In room:* A/C, TV, minibar, hair dryer.

Hotel Torre Guelfa ★★★

Giancarlo and Sabina Avuri run one of the most atmospheric hotels in Florence. Here the tallest privately owned tower in the city offers a panorama of the city's monuments and stratospheric bar service during summer. The building dates back to 1280, and the new management successfully balances genuine antique charm with modern hotel comfort. The two large common rooms, separated by a few stairs and a pair of magnificent columns, are scattered with comfy sofas and filled with the soft strains of jazz or classical music every evening. In the guest rooms (most of which are air-conditioned), the walls are done in soft pastel washes, and many of the cast-iron bed frames support canopies.

The Avuri's newest hotel endeavor is the 18th-century **Palazzo Castiglione,** Via del Giglio 8 (✆ **055/214-886;** fax 055/ 274-0521), with four doubles (300,000L, 155€, $150) and two suites (380,000L, 196€, $190); breakfast is served in your room.

Borgo SS. Apostoli 8 (between Via dei Tornabuoni and Via Por Santa Maria), 50123 Firenze. ✆ **055/239-6338.** Fax 055/239-8577. www.hoteltorreguelfa.com. 16 units. 300,000L–350,000L (155€–181€, $150–$175) double; 390,000L (201€, $195) triple; 420,000L (217€, $210) quad. Ask about off-season discounts. Rates include continental breakfast. AE, MC, V. Bus: B, 6, 11, 36, 37. **Amenities:** Concierge; tour desk; car-rental desk; courtesy car (for airport); room service; baby-sitting; laundry service; dry cleaning. *In room:* A/C, minibar, TV, hair dryer.

Moderate

Hotel Alessandra ★ *Value*

This old-fashioned pensione in a 1507 palazzo just off the river charges little for its simple comfort and kind hospitality. The rooms differ greatly in size and style (none is overly small and some are very large), and while they won't win any awards from *Architectural Digest,* there are a few antique pieces and parquet floors to add to the charm. Air-conditioning was recently installed in 23 rooms. Most of the bathrooms have been overhauled and fitted with fluffy white towels, and the shared bathrooms are ample, clean, and numerous enough that you won't have to wait in line in the morning.

Borgo SS. Apostoli 17 (between Via dei Tornabuoni and Via Por Santa Maria), 50123 Firenze. ℂ 055/283-438. Fax 055/210-619. www.hotelalessandra.com. 25 units, 17 with bathroom (some with shower, most with tub and shower). 210,000L (108€, $105) double without bathroom, 270,000L (139€, $135) double with bathroom; 270,000L (139€, $135) triple without bathroom, 350,000L (181€, $175) triple with bathroom. Rates include breakfast. AE, MC, V. Parking in nearby garage 30,000L (16€, $15). Bus: B, 6, 11, 36, 37. **Amenities:** Concierge; tour desk; room service (breakfast only); massage; baby-sitting; laundry service; dry cleaning; non-smoking rooms. *In room:* A/C (in all but 2 singles), TV, hair dryer, safe (in some).

5 South of Santa Maria Novella

VERY EXPENSIVE

Westin Excelsior ℛ   This is Florence's prime luxury address; the sumptuousness will bowl you over, if the staggering price tags don't do it first. The old palazzi that make up the hotel, once partly owned by Napoléon's sister Caroline, were unified and decorated in 1927, the rooms decorated in three styles: Florentine 17th-century, Tuscan 18th-century, and Empire. All are done with a liberal use of colored marbles, walnut furniture, *pietra serena* accents, Oriental rugs, and neoclassical frescoes. Try to book a room overlooking the Arno (junior suites do not). The penthouses have terraces with drop-dead views over the city. Second-floor riverside doubles have balconies, and you can sometimes book half a luxurious suite at the price of a regular room. The staff is renowned for its genial attentiveness, offering a full array of amenities and services.

Piazza Ognissanti 3, 50123 Firenze. ℂ 800/WESTIN-1 in the U.S.; 055/264-201 or toll-free 800/837-024 in Italy. Fax 055/210-278. www.westin.com. 168 units. 990,000L–1,313,000L (511€–678€, $495–$657) double, add 155,000L (80€, $78) for Arno view; 2,310,000L (1,193€, $1,155) penthouse double; 2,200,000L–2,420,000L (1,136€–1,250€, $1,100–$1,210) junior suite; 3,200,000L–6,200,000L (1,653€–3202€, $1,600–$3,100) suite. Breakfast 48,400L–80,000L (25€–41€, $24–$40). AE, DC, MC, V. Valet parking 70,000L (36€, $35) in garage. Bus: B, C, 9. **Amenities:** Faux 18th-century restaurant (refined Italian and international), 3-story chic Donatello bar; bike rental; children's program; concierge; tour desk; car-rental desk; courtesy car (pay); business center; secretarial services; room service (24-hour); massages (in-room); baby-sitting; laundry service; dry cleaning (same day); no-smoking rooms; executive-level rooms (a few outfitted for business work). *In room:* A/C, TV, pay-TV, fax (on request), dataport, minibar, hair dryer, safe.

EXPENSIVE

Villa Azalee ⭐ *Finds*   The atmosphere of this 1870 villa on the city's edge, with its prizewinning flowers, soundproofed rooms, and comfortable beds, makes you forget the eight lanes of traffic a few dozen feet away. There's a sunroom in the main villa, tapestries on the walls, and a very friendly staff. The rooms are floral print–oriented—perfect for Laura Ashley buffs, but for others the pink taffeta and gauzy canopies can go over the top. The old *scuderia* (stables) out back were reconstructed in a hybrid Italian-English style, and many of the rooms in it echo of a cozy Cotswalds cottage. The best accommodations are on the *scuderia's* ground floor, with heavy beamed ceilings, and on the villa's first (upper) floor, with wood floors, sleigh beds, some walk-in closets and Empire bathrooms, and a few 19th-century frescoes.

Viale Fratelli Rosselli 44 (at the end of Via della Scala, between the station and Cascine Park), 50123 Firenze. © 055/214-242. Fax 055/268-264. www.villa-aza-lee.it. 25 units. 310,000L (160€, $155) double; 416,000L (215€, $208) triple. Rates include breakfast. AE, DC, MC, V. Parking 45,000L (23€, $23) in nearby garage. Bus: 1, 2, 9, 13, 16, 17, 26, 27, 29, 30, 35. **Amenities:** Bike rental (5,000L, 2.60€, $2.50 a day); concierge; tour desk; car-rental desk; room service (24-hour); laundry service; dry cleaning (same day). *In room:* A/C, TV, minibar, hair dryer.

MODERATE

Hotel Aprile   The Aprile fills a semi-restored 15th-century palace on this busy hotel-laden street near the station. The corridors are hung with (seriously deteriorated) detached fresco fragments from the palazzo's original facade. Portions of 16th- and 17th-century frescoes in much better shape grace many of the accommodations, and those on the ceiling of the breakfast room are beautifully intact (though in summer you can also breakfast in the garden out back). Aside from antique touches, the simple guest rooms are nothing to write home about, though they recently overhauled the bathrooms. The street noise gets through even the double glazing, so light sleepers will want to request a room off the road—besides, some of the back rooms have a breathtaking view of Santa Maria Novella. The frescoes and relative quiet of no. 16 make it an excellent choice. Historical footnote: Cavernous room no. 3 has had a tiny bathroom since the 15th century, one of the first "rooms with bathroom" ever.

Via della Scala 6 (1½ blocks from the train station), 50123 Firenze. © 055/216-237. Fax 055/280-947. 30 units, 27 with bathroom. 200,000L (103€, $100) double without bathroom; 320,000L (165€, $160) double with bathroom. Rates include breakfast. AE, DC, MC, V. Parking 35,000L–50,000L (18€–26€, $18–$25) in nearby garage. Bus: 1, 2, 12, 16, 17, 22, 29, 30. **Amenities:** Concierge; tour desk;

car-rental desk; baby-sitting; laundry service; dry cleaning (same day). *In room:* A/C (in all but 1), TV, minibar, hair dryer.

INEXPENSIVE

Hotel Abaco *Value*   Bruno runs a clean, efficient little hotel in a prime location, and is one of the more helpful, advice-filled hoteliers in town. It has inherited a few nice touches from its 15th-century palazzo, including high wood ceilings, stone floors (some are parquet), and in tiny no. 5 a carved *pietra serena* fireplace. They're slowly replacing the mismatched furnishings with quirky antique-style pieces like gilded frame mirrors. It's at a busy intersection, but the double-paned windows help, and there's a free Internet point.

Via dei Banchi 1 (halfway between the station and the Duomo, off Via de' Panzani), 50123 Firenze. ℭ 055/238-1919. Fax 055/282-2289. www.abaco-hotel.it. 7 units, 3 with shower and sink, 3 with full bathroom. 120,000L (62€, $60) double without bathroom; 130,000L (67€, $65) double with shower; 160,000L (83€, $80) double with bathroom. Rates include breakfast for Frommer's readers. AE, MC, V (they prefer cash). Valet parking 40,000L (21€, $20) in garage. Bus: 1, 6, 11, 14, 17, 22, 23, 36, 37. **Amenities:** Bike rental; concierge; tour desk; car-rental desk; coin-op washer/dryer. *In room:* TV, dataport, hair dryer.

6 Between Santa Maria Novella & Mercato Centrale

MODERATE

Hotel Mario's *★★*   Mario Noce runs a homey place, with 17th-century wood beams and floral-print sofas adding a hint of rural yesteryear to the public areas. There are Persian runners and modern art in the halls and tiled floors and reproduction Byzantine icons in the rooms, most of which are more cozy than spacious and contain vast old armoires. Mario's staff leaves a bowl of fresh fruit in your room each morning, and the general friendliness makes this one of the best choices near the station.

Via Faenza 89 (1st floor; near Via Cennini), 50123 Firenze. ℭ 055/216-801. Fax 055/212-039. www.webitaly.com/hotel.marios. 16 units. 160,000L–310,000L (83€–160€, $80–$155) double; 210,000L–380,000L (108€–196€, $105–$190) triple. Rates include continental breakfast. AE, DC, MC, V. Valet parking 35,000–45,000L (18€–23€, $18–$23). Bus: 7, 10, 11, 12, 25, 31, 32, 33. **Amenities:** Concierge; tour desk; room service (breakfast); baby-sitting; laundry service; dry cleaning; nonsmoking rooms. *In room:* A/C, TV, hair dryer, safe.

Hotel Nuova Italia *★★ Kids*   A Frommer's fairy tale: Once upon a time, the fair Eileen left the kingdom of Canada on a journey to faraway Florence, her trusty *Frommer's Europe on $5 a Day* in hand. At her hotel, Eileen met Luciano, her baggage boy in shining armor.

They fell in love, got married, bought a castle (er, hotel) of their own called the Nuova Italia, and their clients live happily ever after. The staff here really puts itself to task for guests, recommending restaurants, shops, day trips—they gave me tips the tourist office didn't know about. The rooms are two-star standard, medium to small, but the attention to detail makes the Nuova Italia stand out. Every room has a bathroom (with fuzzy towels), orthopedic mattress, and triple-paned windows (though some morning rumble from the San Lorenzo market street carts still gets through). It's also one of a handful of hotels in all Tuscany with mosquito screens in the windows. In 1999, everything was restructured and the furniture replaced. The large light-filled corner rooms have extra beds for families.

Via Faenza 26 (off Via Nazionale), 50123 Firenze. ✆ **055/268-430** or 055/287 508. Fax 055/210-941. http://hotel.nuova.italia@dada.it. 20 units. *For Frommer's readers:* 215,000L (111€, $108) double; 265,000L (137€, $133) triple. Rates include continental breakfast. AE, DC, MC, V (but 8% discount if you pay in cash or traveler's checks). Valet garage parking 35,000L (18€, $18). Bus: 7, 10, 11, 12, 25, 31, 32, 33. **Amenities:** Bike rental; concierge; tour desk; car-rental desk; massages (in-room); baby-sitting; laundry service; dry cleaning (same day). *In room:* A/C, TV, hair dryer (ask at desk).

INEXPENSIVE

Albergo Azzi   Musicians Sandro and Valentino, the new young owners of this ex-pensione (a.k.a. the Locanda degli Artisti/Artists' Inn), are creating here a haven for artists, artist manqués, and students. It exudes a relaxed Bohemian feel—not all the doors hang straight and not all the bedspreads match, though strides are being made (and they've even recently discovered some old frescoes in rooms 3 and 4). You'll love the open terrace with a view where breakfast is served in warm weather, as well as the small library of art books and guidebooks so you can enjoy a deeper understanding of Florence's treasures. Four of the rooms without a full bathroom have a shower and sink (but no toilet). In the same building, under the same management and with similar rates, are the **Anna** (8 units, 4 with bathroom; ✆ **055/239-8322**) and the **Paola** (7 units, 4 with bathroom and some with frescoes; ✆ **055/213-682**).

Via Faenza 56 (1st floor), 50123 Firenze. ✆ and fax **055/213-806** (fax in 2002 may be 055/264-8613). hotelazzi@hotmail.com. 12 units, 3 with bathroom (shower only). 100,000L (52€, $50) double with shower or without bathroom, 130,000L (67€, $65) double with bathroom; 120,000L (62€, $60) triple without bathroom, 150,000L (77€, $75) triple with bathroom; 160,000L (83€, $80) quad with or without bathroom. 40,000L (21€, $20) bed in shared room. Off-season rates about 20%

less. Rates include breakfast. AE, DC, MC, V. Parking in nearby private garage 30,000L (15€, $15). Bus: 7, 10, 11, 12, 25, 31, 32, 33. **Amenities:** Concierge; tour desk. *In room:* Hair dryer (ask at desk), no phone.

Albergo Merlini ⭐ *Value*   Family-run by a Sicilian, this cozy walkup boasts rooms appointed with carved wooden antique headboards and furnishings (and a few modular pieces to fill in the gaps). It's one of only a handful of hotels in all Florence with mosquito screens (which gets it the star rating). The optional breakfast is served on a sunny, glassed-in terrace decorated in the 1950s with frescoes by talented American art students. Enjoy your cappuccino with a view of the Medici Chapel's cupola, Florence's bell towers, and the city's terra-cotta roofscape. This is a notch above your average one-star place, the best in a building full of tiny pensioni. There's a 1am curfew.

Via Faenza 56 (3rd floor), 50123 Firenze. ℭ 055/212-848. Fax 055/283-939. 10 units, 2 with bathroom. 95,000L–105,000L (49€–54€, $48–$53) double without bathroom, 125,000L (65€, $63) double with bathroom; 135,000L–140,000L (70€–72€, $68–$70) triple without bathroom. Off-season rates about 15% less. Breakfast 9,000L (4.65€, $4.50). MC, V. Bus: 7, 10, 11, 12, 25, 31, 32, 33. **Amenities:** Concierge; tour desk. *In room:* Hair dryer (ask at desk), no phone.

7 Near San Marco & Santissima Annunziata

VERY EXPENSIVE

Hotel Regency ⭐⭐   The Regency, converted from two 19th-century mansions, is set on a wooded piazza at the edge of town that looks remarkably like a giant London residential square. The posh old England feel continues into the salon and bar lounge, furnished with worn antiques and darkly patterned carpets and wall fabrics. This decoration scheme dominates in the comfortable rooms as well, with a liberal use of mirrored wall panels in the smaller rooms (though none are tiny by any stretch). The marble-clad bathrooms feature heated towel racks, and the discreet service includes fresh fruit and candies left in your room and a complimentary *Herald Tribune* each morning.

Piazza Massimo d'Azeglio 3, 50121 Firenze. ℭ **055/245-247.** Fax 055/234-6735. www.regency-hotel.com. 35 units. 532,474L–894,577L (275€–462€, $266–$447) double; 873,258L–1,448,330L (451€–748€, $437–$724) suite. Rates include breakfast. AE, DC, MC, V. Valet parking 50,000L–55,000L (26€–28€, $25–$28). Bus: 6, 31, 32. **Amenities:** Justifiably famous Relais le Jardin restaurant (seasonal Tuscan), cozy bar; bike rental; concierge; tour desk; car-rental desk; conference room; 24-hour room service; in-room massage; baby-sitting; laundry service; dry cleaning; nonsmoking rooms. *In room:* A/C, TV, minibar, hair dryer, safe.

EXPENSIVE

Hotel Le Due Fontane   The only thing this place has over its neighbor the Hotel Loggiato dei Serviti (see below) is that the rooms get a view of all three loggia-blessed sides of the harmonious piazza (in the Loggiato, you look out from one of them). Although installed in a 15th-century palace, both the accommodations and the public areas are done along clean lines of a nondescript modern style, but the rooms are fairly large. The bathrooms were re-outfitted, some with Jacuzzis, in 1997. Unless you get a room with the view of the piazza (along with unfortunate traffic noise), it might not be the most memorable place to stay.

Piazza Santissima Annunziata 14, 50122 Firenze. (C) **055/210-185.** Fax 055/294-461. www.venere.it/firenze/leduefontane. 57 units. 387,000L (200€, $194) double. Lower rates off-season on request. Rates include breakfast. AE, DC, MC, V. Parking 35,000L (18€, $18) in nearby garage. Bus: 6, 31, 32. **Amenities:** Concierge; tour desk; car-rental desk; courtesy car; room service; baby-sitting; laundry service; dry cleaning; nonsmoking rooms. *In-room:* A/C, TV, minibar, hair dryer.

Hotel Loggiato dei Serviti ⭐⭐   The Loggiato is installed in the building designed by Antonio da Sangallo the Elder in 1527 to mirror the Ospedale degli Innocenti across the piazza, forming part of one of Italy's most beautiful squares. Twelve years ago, this was a student pensione, but the renovation that converted it into a three-star hotel has restored the Renaissance aura. High vaulted ceilings in soft creams abound throughout and are particularly lovely supported by the gray columns of the bar/lounge. The wood or brick-tiled floors in the rooms are scattered with rugs, and most of the beds have wood frames and fabric canopies for an antique feel. The rooms along the front can be a bit noisy in the evenings because traffic is routed through the edges of the piazza, but I usually reserve one anyway, just for the magical view.

Piazza Santissima Annunziata 3, 50122 Firenze. (C) **055/289-592.** Fax 055/289-595. http://loggiato_serviti@italyhotel.com. 29 units. 400,000L (207€, $200) double; 450,000L–700,000L (232€–387€, $225–$375) suite. Rates include breakfast. AE, DC, MC, V. Parking 42,000L (22€, $21). Bus: 6, 31, 32. **Amenities:** Concierge; tour desk; car-rental desk; room service; baby-sitting; laundry service; dry cleaning. *In room:* A/C, TV, minibar, hair dryer, safe.

Morandi alla Crocetta ⭐⭐ *(Finds)*   This subtly elegant pensione belongs to a different era, when travelers stayed in private homes filled with family heirlooms and well-kept antiques. Though the setting is indeed historic (it was a 1511 Dominican nuns' convent), many of the old-fashioned effects, like the wood beam ceilings, 1500s artwork, and antique furnishings, are the result of a recent redecoration. It has all been done in good taste, however, and there are still plenty of echoes of the original structure, from exposed brick arches to one room's 16th-century fresco fragments. A couple of rooms have viewless terraces, and all come with thick patterned rugs scattered over the wood floors, safes, and chenille bedspreads. An octogenarian Irishwoman, Katherine Doyle, still oversees the hotel business, but daily operations are mainly handled (with great care and hospitality) by her family and friends. By late 2002 they expect to finish work that will open up a few new rooms on the first floor and transfer the reception there alongside a bar and small library.

Via Laura 50 (a block east of Piazza Santissima Annunziata), 50121 Firenze. ℱ 055/234-4747. Fax 055/248-0954. www.hotelmorandi.it. 10 units. 290,000L–350,000L (150€–181€, $145–$175) double; 390,000L–420,000L (201€–217€, $195–$210) triple. Breakfast 20,000L (10€, $10). AE, DC, MC, V. Parking 30,000L (16€, $15) in garage. Bus: 6, 31, 32. **Amenities:** Concierge; tour desk; car-rental desk; room service; baby-sitting; laundry service; dry cleaning. *In room:* A/C, TV, minibar, hair dryer, safe.

INEXPENSIVE

Soggiorno Panerai *(Value)* This is a extremely bare-bones *affita-camere*, but still one of my favorites. A kind Russian woman who's lived here most of her life keeps an eye on the four rooms of this converted apartment, and she has bucked tradition by raising prices by only 10,000L in the past 10 years. The huge rooms (most sleep multiple persons) have the expected linoleum flooring and mismatched modern furnishings, but there are ancient throwbacks around to spice things up, like *pietra serena* doorjambs and marvelous old wood ceilings. The two rooms sharing a bathroom (they both open directly onto it from opposite sides) overlook an inner courtyard and are quiet, while the two on the road catch some traffic noise. There's a wide point in the hall with a fridge, coffee machine, and table for guests inclined to picnic.

Via dei Servi 36, 50122 Firenze (just down from Piazza Santissima Annunziata). ℱ 055/264-103. 4 units; 2 share a connecting bathroom, 2 share a hall bathroom. 65,000L (34€, $33) double; 80,000L (41€, $40) triple. No breakfast. No credit cards. Parking in public garage nearby. Bus: 6, 31, 32. *In room:* No phone.

8 Near Santa Croce

VERY EXPENSIVE

Hotel Monna Lisa *(★★)* There's a certain old-world elegance to the richly decorated sitting and breakfast rooms and the gravel-strewn garden of this 14th-century palazzo. Among the potted plants and framed oils, the hotel has Giambologna's original rough competition piece for the Rape of the Sabines, along with many pieces by neoclassical sculptor Giovanni Duprè, whose family's descendants own the hotel. The room decor varies widely, as they try their best to keep the whole place looking like a private home, but many rooms have the original coffered and painted wood ceilings, as well as antique furniture and richly textured wallpaper or fabrics. (Those in the new wing beyond the garden, however, are done in a slightly more modern style.) Most bathrooms were overhauled in the past few years, and if you're lucky you might land one with a Jacuzzi. By late 2002, they expect to have finished restructuring 15 rooms in another, recently acquired building bordering the courtyard.

Borgo Pinti 27, 50121 Firenze. (C) 055-247-9751. Fax 055-247-9755. www.monnalisa.it. 34 units. 400,000–640,000L (206€–331€, $200–$320) double. Rates include breakfast. AE, DC, MC, V. Parking 20,000L (10€, $10). Bus: B, 14, 23, 71. **Amenities:** American bar; concierge; tour desk; car-rental desk; room service; massage; baby-sitting; laundry service; dry cleaning (not on weekends). *In room:* A/C, TV, minibar, hair dryer, safe.

EXPENSIVE

Hotel Ritz 🐾 One of the more intimate hotels along the Arno, the Ritz was taken over in 1996 by the Abolaffio brothers—who also own the Hotel Pensione Pendini (see earlier in this chapter)— and renovations are underway. The walls are hung with reproductions of Italian art from the Renaissance to Modigliani, and the reading room and bar are cozy. The room decor varies—some floors have wood or marble, others are carpeted. The mix-and-match furniture is mostly modern yet tasteful, with iron-filigree bed frames. Two rooms on the front have balconies to better enjoy the Arno view, and two on the back (nos. 37 and 38) have small private terraces, and there's a roof terrace with its view of Fiesole. The rather roomy bathrooms are being completely redone with new tile and heated towel racks.

Lungarno della Zecca Vecchia 24, 50122 Firenze. (C) 055/234-0650. Fax 055/240-863. www.tiac.net/users/pendini/ritz. 30 units. 184,000L–348,000L (95€–180€, $92–$174) double; 280,000L–416,000L (145€–215€, $140–$208) triple; 320,000L–571,000L (165€–295€, $160–$286) quad; 320,000L–677,000L (165€–350€, $160–$339) family suite. Rates include breakfast. AE, DC, MC, V. Valet parking in garage 40,000L–60,000L (21€–31€, $20–$30). Bus: B, 13, 14, 23. **Amenities:** Concierge; tour desk; car-rental desk; room service (breakfast and bar; 24-hour). *In room:* A/C, TV, dataport, minibar, hair dryer, safe.

9 In the Oltrarno

Hotel La Scaletta *Kids* The Barbiere family runs this well-worn old shoe of a place in one of the only remaining palazzi on this block between the Pitti Palace and Ponte Vecchio. The inn's star is the flower-bedecked, sun-kissed terrace offering a 360° vista over the Boboli Gardens, the Oltrarno rooftops, and (beyond a sea of antennas) the monumental heart of Florence, plus a shoe-biting turtle they found here when they bought the place 25 years ago. Return visitors book months in advance for the homey rooms that have tiny bathrooms and old tiled floors. Some beds are lumpy to a fault, others fully firm, but street-side accommodations have double-paned windows that really do block the noise, and the worn, dark wood lacquer furniture is pleasantly unassuming. Six of the rooms on the back were recently overhauled with new everything and peek out at the Boboli Gardens. Rooms 30 to 32 (the last a quad) have exceedingly high ceilings. At breakfast, you can ask Manfredo to cook you a superb 25,000L (13€, $13) dinner that night.

Via Guicciardini 13 (2nd floor; near Piazza de Pitti), 50125 Firenze. © 055/283-028 or 055/214-255. Fax 055/289-562. www.lascaletta.com. 14 units, 11 with bathroom. 190,000L (98€, $95) double without bathroom, 220,000L–250,000L (114€–129€, $110–$125) double with bathroom; 210,000L (108€, $105) triple without bathroom, 270,000L (139€, $135) triple with bathroom; 300,000L (155€, $150) quad with bathroom. Ask about off-season discounts. Rates include continental breakfast. MC, V. Nearby parking 20,000L–40,000L (10€–21€, $10–$20). Bus: D, 11, 36, 37. **Amenities:** Concierge; tour desk; room service (breakfast); babysitting; laundry service; dry cleaning. *In room:* A/C (in 8), TV (on request, 10,000L, 5€, $5 per day), hair dryer.

Pensione Sorelle Bandini *Value* A 15th-century palazzo on Piazza Santo Spirito, the pulsing heart of the Oltrarno, is home to one of Florence's last great pensioni. This place is for romantics only, full of large, echoey rooms (a few two-room family suites) and halls stuffed with severely beat-up antiques on wonderfully worn wooden floors. The shared bathrooms are kept tolerably clean, and though some beds will have your back aching, others are firm. There are several sitting/reading rooms crawling with cats where dusty old professor-types in overstuffed easy chairs leaf through Byron. The proprietor, who was a 2-year pensione guest of the original Bandini sisters as a student, encourages you to "sit, read, paint, and write poetry!" Picnicking students hang around the outdoor loggia, a fixture that's stubbornly Oltrarno: It overlooks only the piazza below and the neighborhood churches on this side of the river. Zeffirelli used the pensione for some scenes in *Tea With Mussolini*.

Piazza Santo Spirito 9, 50125 Firenze. © **055/215-308.** Fax 055/282-761. 12 units, 5 with bathroom. 186,000L (96€, $93) double without bathroom; 224,000L (116€, $112) double with bathroom. Extra person 35% more. Rates include continental breakfast. No credit cards. Bus: D, 11, 36, 37. Parking in nearby garage 22,000L (11€, $11) **Amenities:** Tuscan restaurant; concierge; tour desk; car-rental desk; room service (breakfast only); baby-sitting; nonsmoking rooms. *In room:* No phone.

10 In the Hills

VERY EXPENSIVE

Villa San Michele 🕹🕹 The peaceful air this place exudes recalls its origins in the 15th century as a Franciscan monastery, but I doubt the good friars had a heated outdoor pool or Jacuzzis in their cells. The facade was reputedly designed by Michelangelo, and everything is in shades of creamy yellow with soft gray *pietra serena* accents. The antique furnishings are the epitome of simple elegance, and some rooms come with canopied beds and linen sheets; other are fitted with wrought-iron headboards and antiques. The new suites above the grassy terraces are done in a plush contemporary style. They've recently converted the tiny hillside chapel into a cozy honeymoon suite with sweeping views. The monks never had it this good.

Via Doccia 4, 50014 Fiesole (FI) (just below Fiesole off Via Fra Giovanni Angelico). © **800/237-1236** in the U.S. or 055/567-8200 in Italy. Fax 055/567-8250. http://villasanmichele.orient-express.com/. 41 units. 1,690,600L–2,129,300L (873€–1,100€, $845–$1,065) double; 2,782,000L–3,531,000L (1,437€–1,824€, $1,391–$1,766) suite. Rates include breakfast and half pension. AE, DC, MC, V. Free parking. Closed mid-Nov to mid-Mar. Bus: 7 (ask driver for stop, because you get off before Fiesole); free hourly shuttle bus from Piazza del Duomo. **Amenities:** Restaurant (Tuscan with a nouvelle twist), frescoed piano bar; heated outdoor pool; extensive park with nature trails and jogging track; bike rental; concierge; tour desk; car-rental desk; shuttle bus to/from town center; small business center and secretarial services; room service (24-hour); massage; baby-sitting; laundry service; dry cleaning (same day). *In room:* A/C, TV/VCR (front desk has free movies), dataport, minibar, hair dryer.

EXPENSIVE

Torre di Bellosguardo 🕹🕹🕹 *Finds* This castle was built around a 13th-century tower sprouting from a hillside on the southern edge of Florence. Spend a few days here above the city heat and noise, lazing by the pool, hiking the olive orchard roads, or sitting on a garden bench to enjoy the intimate close-range vista of the city. Don't come expecting another climate-controlled and carpeted bastion of

luxury. With its echoey halls, airy loggias, and imposing stone stair-
cases, the Bellosguardo feels just a few flickering torches shy of the
Middle Ages—exactly its attraction. It's packed with antiques, and
the beds from various eras are particularly gorgeous. Some rooms
have intricately carved wood ceilings, others sport fading frescoes,
and many have views, including a 360° panorama in the romantic
tower suite. There's no restaurant, but it's a 15-minute stroll down
the hill to Alla Vecchia Bettola (reviewed in chapter 4, "Where to
Dine").

Via Roti Michelozzi 2, 50124 Florence. (✆) **055/229-8145.** Fax 055/229-008.
http://members.aol.com/PuterBugzz/tbellos.html. 16 units. 500,000L (258€, $250)
double; 600,000L–700,000L (310€–362€, $300–$350) suite. Breakfast 37,000L
(19€, $19). AE, DC, MC, V. Free parking. Bus: 12, 13 to Piazza Tasso (then taxi up
hill). **Amenities:** Outdoor pool (June–Sept); small indoor pool; small exercise room;
Jacuzzi; sauna; concierge; tour desk; car-rental desk; room service (bar only, no
food; 24-hr.); massages; baby-sitting; laundry service; dry cleaning (same-day). *In
room:* A/C (in 3 suites), dataport, hair dryer.

MODERATE

Pensione Benescistà *Kids*   This comfortable and quiet family-run pensione in a rambling 14th-century villa gets you the same
view and escape from the city as the Villa San Michele above it at
one-fifth the price. The Benescistà seems to have changed little since
it opened in 1925. Antiques abound, and the elegantly cluttered
salons are straight out of an E.M. Forster novel. Many accommodations have big old chests-of-drawers, and some open onto the pretty
little garden. The dining room has a view of Florence, but in summer take in the vista by breakfasting on the terrace. Although service from the staff is occasionally off-handed, the owners are friendly
and truly consider you a guest in their home. They also expect to be
treated as hosts and require you to stay for most dinners. (I recom-
mend trading one dinner for a lunch to try the nearby Trattoria le
Cave di Maiano; see chapter 4, "Where to Dine.")

Via Benedetto da Maiano 4, 50014 Fiesole (FI) (just below Fiesole off the main
road). (✆)/fax **055/59-163.** 44 units, 34 with bathroom. 300,000L (155€, $150)
double without bathroom; 340,000L (176€, $170) double with bathroom. Rates
include required half pension (full pension available for small supplement).
Breakfast included. No credit cards. Free parking. Bus: 7 to Villa San Michele, then
backtrack onto side road following signs. **Amenities:** Restaurant (Tuscan and international); room service (breakfast only). *In room:* Hair dryer.

4

Where to Dine

Florence is thick with restaurants, though many in the most touristy areas (around the Duomo and Piazza della Signoria) are of low quality, charge high prices, or do both. I'll point out the few that aren't. The highest concentrations of excellent *ristoranti* and *trattorie* are around Santa Croce and across the river in the Oltrarno.

Florence's signature dish is the mighty **bistecca alla Fiorentina,** a massive steak carved from Chiana beef, brushed with olive oil, and sprinkled with cracked pepper before being grilled to perfection— though with the recent Mad Cow disease scare, T-bones are temporarily banned in Italy as we go to press.

1 Tips on Dining

For a quick bite, go to a **bar**—though it does serve alcohol, a *bar* in Italy functions mainly as a cafe. Prices at *bars* have a split personality: *al banco* is standing at the bar, while *à tavola* means sitting at a table where they'll wait on you and charge 2 to 4 times as much for the same cappuccino. In *bars* you can find *panini* sandwiches on various rolls and *tramezzini,* giant triangles of white-bread sandwiches with the crusts cut off. These run 2,000L to 6,000L (1.05€ to 3.10€, $1 to $3) and are traditionally stuck in a kind of tiny pants press to flatten and toast them so the crust is crispy and the filling hot and gooey; microwaves have unfortunately invaded and are everywhere turning *panini* into something that resembles a very hot, soggy tissue.

Pizza a taglio or *pizza rustica* indicates a place where you can order pizza by the slice, though Florence is infamous for serving some of Italy's worst pizza this way. Florentines fare somewhat better at *pizzerie,* casual sit-down restaurants that cook large, round pizzas with very thin crusts in wood-burning ovens. A *tavola calda* (literally "hot table") serves ready-made hot foods you can take away or eat at one of the few small tables often available. The food is usually very good, and you can get away with a full meal at a *tavola calda* for well under 25,000L (13€, $13). A ***rosticceria*** is the same type of place with some chickens roasting on a spit in the window.

Full-fledged restaurants go by the name *osteria, trattoria,* or *ristorante.* Once upon a time, these terms meant something—***osterie*** were basic places where you could get a plate of spaghetti and a glass of wine; ***trattorie*** were casual places serving simple full meals of filling peasant fare; and ***ristoranti*** were fancier places, with waiters in bow ties, printed menus, wine lists, and hefty prices. Nowadays, though, fancy restaurants often go by the name of *trattoria* to cash in on the associated charm factor, trendy spots use *osteria* to show they're hip, and simple inexpensive places sometimes tack on *ristorante* to ennoble their establishment.

The ***pane e coperto*** (bread and cover) is a 1,500L to 5,000L (.80€ to 2.60€, 75¢ to $2.50) cover charge you must pay at every Italian restaurant for the mere privilege of sitting at the table. Most Italians eat a full meal—appetizer and first and second courses—at lunch and dinner and will expect you to do the same, or at least a first and second course. To request the bill, ask *"Il conto, per favore"* (eel *con*-toh pore fah-*vohr*-ay). A tip of 15% is usually included in the bill these days, but if unsure ask *"è incluso il servizio?"* (ay een-*cloo*-soh eel sair-*vee*-tsoh?).

Many restaurants, especially larger ones and those in cities, serve a ***menù turistico*** (tourists' menu) costing from 10,000L to 40,000L (5€ to 21€, $5 to $20). This set-price menu usually covers all meal incidentals, including table wine, cover charge, and 15% service charge, along with a first and a second course. But it almost invariably offers an abbreviated selection of rather bland dishes: spaghetti in tomato sauce and slices of roast pork. Sometimes better is a ***menù a prezzo fisso*** (fixed-price menu), which usually doesn't include wine but sometimes covers the service and *coperto* and often has a wider selection of better dishes, occasionally including house specialties and local foods. Ordering a la carte, however, offers you the best chance for a memorable meal. Even better, forego the menu entirely and put yourself in the capable hands of your waiter.

Many eateries that really care about their food—from *osterie* to classy *ristoranti*—will also offer a ***menù degustazione*** (tasting menu), allowing you to sample small portions of the kitchen's bounty, usually several antipasti, a few primi, and a secondo or two (and sometimes several local wines to taste by the glass). They're almost always highly recommendable and usually turn out to be a huge feast.

Florence Dining

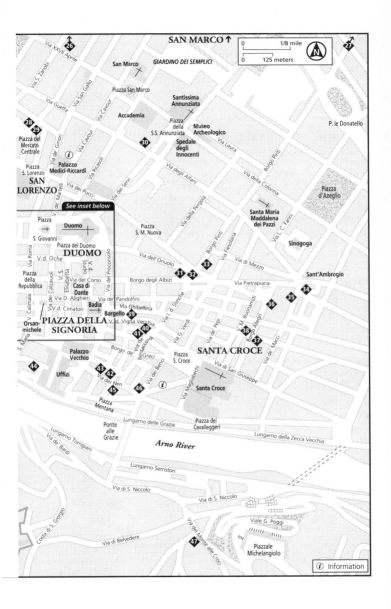

SAN MARCO ↑

0   1/8 mile

0   125 meters

San Marco

GIARDINO DEI SEMPLICI

Piazza San Marco

Santissima
Annunziata

Accademia

Piazza
della
S.S. Annunziata

Museo
Archeologico

P. le Donatello

Spedale
degli
Innocenti

Piazza del
Mercato
Centrale

Palazzo
Medici-Riccardi

Via degli Alfani

Via Laura

Piazza
S. Lorenzo

SAN
LORENZO

Via dei Pucci

Via della Pergola

Santa Maria
Maddalena
dei Pazzi

Piazza
d'Azeglio

See inset below

Piazza

Duomo

S. Giovanni

DUOMO

Piazza
S. M. Nuova

Sinogoga

Piazza del Duomo

Via dell'Oriuolo

Sant'Ambrogio

Piazza
della
Repubblica

Casa di
Dante

Borgo degli Albizi

Via Pietrapiana

Badia

Via Ghibellina

Orsan-
michele

Bargello

PIAZZA DELLA
SIGNORIA

Borgo de'

SANTA CROCE

Palazzo
Vecchio

Piazza
S. Croce

Uffizi

Via dei Neri

Via di San Giuseppe

Piazza
Mentana

Santa Croce

Lungarno delle Grazie

Piazza dei
Cavalleggeri

Ponte
alle
Grazie

Lungarno della Zecca Vecchia

Arno River

Lungarno Serristori

Via di S. Niccolo

Via di S. Niccolo

Viale G. Poggi

Via di Belvedere

Piazzale
Michelangiolo

ⓘ Information

69

The Courses of Italian Dining

The typical marathon Italian meal is drawn out by multiple courses, starting with the *antipasto* (appetizer; plural *antipasti*), then the *primo* (first course, usually pasta, risotto, or soup; plural *primi*), a *secondo* (second course, meat or fish; plural *secondi*), which doesn't automatically come with a *contorno* (side dish; plural *contorni*), rounded off by a *dolce* (dessert; plural *dolci*) before you get to your coffee and finish with a grappa or *vin santo*. At the very least, you'll be expected to order a *primo* and *secondo* (though at lunch, they might let you get away with an antipasto and a *primo*).

The *enoteca* (wine bar) is a growingly popular marriage of a wine bar and an osteria, where you can sit and order from a host of local and regional wines by the glass while snacking on finger foods and a number of simple primi. It's also possible to go into an *alimentari* (general food store) and have sandwiches prepared on the spot, or buy the makings for a picnic.

2 Near the Duomo

EXPENSIVE

Da Ganino FLORENTINE   The tiny family-run Ganino has long been a major destination for hungry tourists because it's across from the American Express office as well as halfway between the Duomo and the Uffizi. This has caused the place to jack its prices to eyebrow-raising levels but not sacrifice its friendly service and good food, from the big ol' chunk of mortadella that accompanies your bread basket through the tasty *ribollita* or *gnocchi al pomodoro* (ricotta-and-spinach gnocchi in tomato sauce) to the *filetto all'aceto basalmico* (veal filet cooked in basalmic vinegar) or *coniglio in umido* (rabbit with boiled potatoes on the side) that rounds out your meal. In summer, you can dine on tables out on the small piazza.

Piazza de' Cimatori 4r (near the Casa di Dante). ✆ **055/214-125.** Reservations recommended. Primi 12,000L–20,000L (6[eu–10€, $6–$10); secondi 16,000L–35,000L (8€–18€, $8–$18). AE, DC, MC, V. Mon–Sat noon–3pm and 7–11pm. Closed Aug. Bus: 14.

Paoli TUSCAN   Paoli has one of the most *suggestivo* (oft-used Italian word for "evocative") settings in town, with tables under a 14th-century vaulted ceiling whose ribs and lunettes are covered with fading 18th-century frescoes that variously mimic medieval, Renaissance, and Romantic art. It's in the heart of the sightseeing zone, meaning the prices are as high as they can reasonably push them; very few Italians drop by, but the food is actually quite good. The *ravioli verdi alla casalinga* (spinach ravioli in tomato sauce) may not be inspired, but it's freshly made and tasty. In mushroom season you can order *risotto ai funghi,* and year-round the scrumptious secondo *entrecôte di manzo arlecchino* (a thick steak in cognac-spiked cream sauce with peppercorns and sided with mashed potatoes). Also good is the cross-cultural *petti di pollo al curry* (curried chicken breasts with rice pilaf).

Via dei Tavolini 12r. ⓒ **055/216-215.** Reservations highly recommended. Primi 10,000L–22,000L (5[eu–11€, $5–$11); secondi 19,000L–30,000L (10€–16€, $10–$15); fixed-price menu with wine 36,000L (19€, $18). AE, MC, V. Wed–Mon noon–3pm and 7pm–midnight. Bus: A.

MODERATE

Ristorante Casa di Dante (Da Pennello) ITALIAN/TUSCAN The old name ("The Painter") and the original art on the walls serve as reminders that an *osteria* was opened here in the 16th century by a semiretired artist whose buddies Cellini, Pontormo, and Andrea del Sarto often dropped in for a meal. This incarnation opened in the late 1600s, and the restaurant's longevity is partly due to its buffet-style antipasto table full of vegetables, fish, and other delicacies. Make sure you leave room for a primo, perhaps *spaghetti alla carrettiera* (in piquant tomato sauce). Secondi include *spigola alla griglia* (grilled sea bass) and *scaloppine al limone* (veal scallop in light lemon sauce). To finish with a flourish, try *zucotto* (a liqueur-treated sponge cake stuffed with candy-studded frozen mousses).

Via Dante Alghieri 4r. ⓒ **055/294-848.** Reservations recommended. Primi 10,000L–14,000L (5€–7€, $5–$7); secondi 15,000L–22,000L (8€–11€, $8–$11); fixed-price menu without wine 30,000L (16€, $15). Tues–Sat noon–2:30pm and 7–10:15pm. Bus: 14.

INEXPENSIVE

I Fratellini 𝆑 SANDWICHES & WINE   Just off the busiest tourist thoroughfare lies one of the last of a dying breed: a *fiaschitteria* (derived from the word for a flask of wine). It's the proverbial hole in the wall, a doorway about 5 feet deep with rows of wine bottles against the back wall and Armando and Michele Perrino busy behind the counter, fixing sandwiches and pouring glasses of vino. You stand munching and sipping on the cobblestones of the narrow street surrounded by Florentines on their lunch break and a few bemused tourists. The *cinghiale piccante con caprino* (spicy raw wild boar sausage with creamy goat cheese) is excellent. Otherwise, choose your poison from among 30 stuffing combinations—the menu posted on the doorjamb has English translations—and accompany it with either a basic *rosso* (red) wine or point to any bottle to try *un bicchiere* (a glass).

Via dei Cimatori 38r (2 blocks from Piazza della Signoria, off Via Calzaiuoli). ✆ **055/239-6096.** Sandwiches 4,000L–5,000L (2.05€–2.60€, $2–$2.50); wine from 2,000L (1.05€, $1) a glass. No credit cards. Daily 8am–8:30pm (closed Sun in summer). Closed Aug 10–20. Bus: 14, 23, 71.

Le Mossacce FLORENTINE   Delicious, cheap, abundant, fast home cooking: This tiny *osteria*, filled with lunching businesspeople, farmers in from the hills, locals who've been coming since 1942, and a few knowledgeable tourists, is authentic to the bone. The waiters hate breaking out the printed menu, preferring to rattle off a list of Florentine faves like *ribollita, spaghetti alle vongole, crespelle,* and *lasagne al forno.* Unlike in many cheap joints catering to locals, the secondi are pretty good. You could try the *spezzatino* (goulashy beef stew) or a well-cooked, and for once cheap, *bistecca alla Fiorentina,* but I put my money on the excellent *involtini* (thin slices of beef wrapped tightly around a bread stuffing and artichoke hearts, then cooked to juiciness in tomato sauce).

Via del Proconsolo 55r (near the Bargello). ✆ **055/294-361.** Reservations recommended. Primi 7,500L–8,500L (3.85€–4.40€, $3.75–$4.25); secondi 9,000L–16,000L (4.65€–8€, $4.50–$8). AE, DC, MC, V. Mon–Fri noon–2:30pm and 7–9:30pm. Closed Aug. Bus: 14, 23, 71.

3 Near Piazza Della Signoria

EXPENSIVE

Antico Fattore FLORENTINE   The Antico Fattore was a literary watering hole early in the 20th century and remained a favorite trattoria just a few steps from the city's premier museum until the 1993 Uffizi bomb went off a few feet from its doors. The interior has been rebuilt and the restaurant reopened, but many claim it isn't what it used to be. Although it has indeed put on a few more airs, you can't deny they still make a tantalizing *lombatina all'aceto basalmico* (one of the thickest and most tender veal chops you'll ever find, cooked in basalmic vinegar). You can precede this with a

Quick Bites

For a light meal on the go, you can drop in on any bar for a *panino* (sandwich)—but avoid Florentine pizza-by-the-slice joints. One of the best quick lunches can be had at a *fiaschetteria*, an old-fashioned wine bar, such as **I Fratellini,** close by Piazza della Signoria, or **Antico Noè,** near Santa Croce (see listings in this chapter), where a glass of wine and a sandwich will run you no more than 7,000L (3.60€, $3.50).

Another good choice if you don't want to spend the time or money for lunch in a full-fledged restaurant is a *tavola calda* or *rosticceria,* where they sell very good pre-prepared Tuscan dishes by weight and often have tables in the back where you can sit and have a three-course meal for under 30,000L (16€, $15), wine and dessert included. **Giuliano** is a great one at Via dei Neri 74 (☏ 055/238-2723).

The classy bakery-cum-cafe **Cantinetta del Verrazzano,** at the very center of town at Via dei Tavolini 18–20r (☏ 055/268-590), is both an outlet for the wine and liqueurs of the historic Castello di Verrazzano vineyards in the Chianti and a perfect polished-wood sightseeing break where you can enjoy excellent pastries and stuffed *focacie sandwiches* (the salted flatbread is baked fresh in a wood oven at the back). It's open Monday to Saturday 8am to 9pm.

For a true Florentine experience, those who can stomach cows' stomach should try the **boiled tripe sandwich** called *lampredotto* sold on the street in front of the American Express office on Piazza de' Cimatori. It's 3,000L (1.55€, $1.50), and if you want it dipped in tripe juices, ask for it *bagnato.*

ribollita (more souplike than usual) or a traditional Tuscan *pappardelle sul cinghiale* (wide noodles in wild boar sauce). If veal's not your style, try their specialty *piccione* (grilled pigeon).

Via Lambertesca 1–3r (between the Uffizi and the Ponte Vecchio). ☏ 055/288-975. Reservations recommended. Primi 10,000L–15,000L (5€–8€, $5–$8); secondi 16,000L–25,000L (8€–13€, $8–$13). AE, DC, MC, V. Mon–Sat 12:15–3pm and 7:15–10:30pm. Bus: 23, 71.

> ### (Kids) Family-Friendly Restaurants
>
> It'd be a sin for any family to visit Florence and not drop by one of its premier gelato parlors to sample the rich Italian equivalent of ice cream. See "A Big Step Above Ice Cream: Florentine Gelato," later in this section. If the kids mutiny and absolutely insist on a hamburger, try the slightly American-style restaurant **Yellow Bar,** Via del Proconsolo 39r (© **055/211-766**). But be warned: The hamburger doesn't come with a bun (a form of blasphemy among certain preteens). They also serve pizzas.
>
> **Il Cantinone** (p. 91) This noisy old wine cellar is popular with students and has long tables where your family can spread out and bite deep into *crostone* (slabs of peasant bread piled with your choice of toppings like a pizza).
>
> **Il Latini** (p. 80) This can be one of the most fun places to eat in Florence—you're seated at communal tables under battalions of hanging ham hocks and treated to huge portions of the Tuscan bounty. No food is too fancy or oddball to offend suspicious young palates, the waiters love to ham it up, and a festive atmosphere prevails.
>
> **Il Pizzaiuolo** (p. 87) When the kids are hankering for a pizza, turn it into a learning experience by visiting the only

Buca dell'Orafo FLORENTINE   A *buca* is a cellar joint with half a dozen crowded tables serving good, basic Florentine fare. Here a few locals hang on every night, but Orafo's years in the guidebooks have made Americans its base of customers—and have jacked its prices above what you'd expect for peasant food. That food is still very well prepared, however, and the location can't be beat. You can't go wrong with the thick *ribollita*. If it's on the menu, go for the *paglia e fieno alla boscaiola* (a "hay and straw" mix of both egg and spinach fettucine in mushroom-meat sauce). Orafo's best secondo is *arista di maiale con patate* (roast pork loin with potatoes), while candied stewed pears round out the meal nicely.

Volta dei Girolami 28r (under the arched alley left of the Ponte Vecchio). © **055/ 213-619.** Reservations strongly recommended (or show up early for spot at a communal table). Primi 8,000L–15,000L (4.15€–8€, $4–$8); secondi 10,000L–25,000L (5€–13€, $5–$13). No credit cards. Tues–Sat noon–2:30pm and 7:30–9:45pm. Bus: 23, 71.

pizza parlor in Florence run by a Neapolitan. The "plain pizza," called *pizza margherita* in Italy, was invented about 100 years ago by a Naples chef who wanted to honor Italy's Queen Margherita with a pizza done in patriotic colors. For the newly created Kingdom of Italy, this meant red (tomatoes), white (mozzarella), and green (fresh basil)—the colors of the new flag. If someone at the table prefers pepperoni, order the pizza with *salame piccante* (hot salami slices); *pepperoni* in Italian are bell peppers.

Ristorante Vecchia Firenze (p. 89) This roomy restaurant has a long menu sure to satisfy everyone's appetites. They love children here, and this was my family's favorite Florentine restaurant when I was 12. The owner, tickled pink one night that a little American boy was struggling to speak Italian, took over our meal, had all the wonders of Tuscan cuisine brought to our table, talked and joked with us in broken English, introduced us to grappa, and kept me up well past my bedtime.

Trattoria da Benvenuto (p. 76) The dishes here are simple and homey—they're sure to have a plate of plain spaghetti and tomato sauce to please finicky youngsters.

I' Cche' c'è c'è ★★ TUSCAN   The name is a dialect variant on "What you see is what you get." What you see is a room with modern art prints and shelves of ancient wine bottles lining the walls. What you get is good Tuscan cooking from Gino Noci, who trained in the kitchens of London before returning here to open a traditional trattoria. The *ravioli rosée* (in creamy tomato sauce) is scrumptious but faces serious competition from the *tagliatelle all boscaiola* (same sauce with giant slices of forest mushrooms added). *Topini* are Florentine potato gnocchi, topped with spinach and cream or four cheeses. You can follow up with the grilled salmon or one of their specialties, *stracotto al chianti* (beef stuffed with celery and carrot and smothered in a chianti gravy served with fried polenta and an artichoke heart).

Via Magalotti 11r (just east of Via Proconsolo, 2 blocks from the Arno). ℂ 055/216-589. Reservations recommended (not available for lunch set-price menu).

Primi 7,000L–15,000L (3.60€–8€, $3.50–$8); secondi 16,000L–20,000L (8€–10€, $8–$10); fixed-price menu without wine 20,000L (10€, $10); tasting menus without wine 50,000L–60,000L (26€–31€, $25–$30). AE, MC, V. Tues–Sun 12:30–2:30pm and 7:30–10:30pm. Closed Aug 10–17. Bus: 23, 71.

MODERATE

Acqua al 2 SLIGHTLY ADVENTUROUS ITALIAN   Under a barrel-vaulted ceiling and dim sconce lights, diners sit elbow to elbow at tightly packed tables to sample this innovative restaurant's *assaggi* (tastings) courses. Acqua al 2 is proud of its almost cultish status, attained through the success of its *assaggio di primi*, which offers you a sampling of five flavorful pastas or *risotti*. The surprise selections might include anything from bow-tie pasta in salmon sauce to rigatoni with eggplant and tomatoes. If you order the *assaggio* for two, you both just may have room left over for a grilled portobello mushroom "steak," one of the many veal dishes, or something more cross-cultural, like *couscous d'agnello* (lamb). They also offer *assaggi* of salads, cheese, and desserts. The place is far from undiscovered, and tour companies have started bringing in tourists by the busload on occasion, but the crowd still remains a good mix of locals and travelers.

Via della Vigna Vecchia 40r (in back of the Bargello). ℭ **055/284-170.** www.acquaal2.it. Reservations strongly recommended. Primi 11,000L–12,000L (6€, $6); secondi 12,000L–28,000L (6€–14€, $6–$14); *assaggio di primi* tasting menu of pastas without wine 13,500L (7€, $7). AE, DC, MC, V. Daily 7:30pm–1am. Closed 1 week in Aug. Bus: 14.

Trattoria da Benvenuto ⊛ 𝓚𝒾𝒹𝓼 TUSCAN HOME COOKING This is a no-nonsense place, simple and good, and Gabriella is a no-nonsense lady who'll get exasperated if you're not ready with your order when she's ready to take it. Da Benvenuto's is basically a neighborhood hangout that somehow found its way into every guidebook over the years. Yet it continues to serve adequate helpings of tasty Florentine home cooking to travelers and locals seated together at long tables in two brightly lit rooms. This is always my first stop on any trip to Florence, where I usually order ravioli or *gnocchi* (potato-dumpling pasta)—both served in tomato sauce— and follow with a *veal scaloppa alla Livornese* or a *frittata* (an omelet filled at the whim of Loriano, Gabriella's husband and cook).

Via Mosca 16r (at the corner of Via dei Neri; walk around the right of the Palazzo Vecchio, under the arch, and it's in front of you after 4 short blocks). ℭ **055/214-833.** Primi 8,000L–18,000L (4.15€–9€, $4–$9); secondi 10,000L–20,000L (5€–10€, $5–$10). No credit cards. Mon–Tues and Thurs–Sat 12:30–3pm and 7:30–midnight. Bus: 23, 71.

INEXPENSIVE

Osteria (Vini e Vecchi Sapori) FLORENTINE/TUSCAN
Within a block of the Palazzo Vecchio squats an authentic *osteria*
with a wood-beamed ceiling, brick floor, the end of a giant chianti
barrel embedded in one wall, and a handwritten menu that starts
Oggi C'è (Today we got . . .). As the sign proudly proclaims, this
one-room joint is devoted to "wine and old flavors," which means
lunch could consist of anything from a rib-sticking stewlike *ribollita* and a *frittata rustica* (a darkly fried omelet thick with potatoes
and vegetables) to an excellent crostini assortment and *scamorza e
speck al forno* (smoked mozzarella melted with ham in a bowl, to
scoop out and slather onto bread). The hours are more guidelines
than set opening and closing times. The paunchy owner will continue pacing back and forth, taking orders, passing around the lone
menu, and welcoming people in off the street until he feels like
going home.

Via dei Magazzini 3r (the alley off Piazza della Signoria to the left of the Palazzo
Vecchio). ✆ **055/293-045.** Primi 8,000L (4.15€, $4); secondi 10,000L–14,000L
(5€–7€, $5–$7). No credit cards. Tues–Sun 9am–11pm. Bus: 14, 23, 71.

4 Near San Lorenzo & the Mercato Centrale

EXPENSIVE

Le Fonticine TUSCAN/BOLOGNESE   Modern paintings carpet the walls like a jigsaw puzzle. Silvano Bruci has taken as much
care over the past 40 years selecting the works of art as his Bologna-
born wife has teaching these Tuscans the finer points of Emilia-
Romagna cuisine. Even with the art, this place still feels a bit like a
country trattoria. If you can, ask to sit *in dietro* (in the back), if only
so you get to walk past the open kitchen and grill. There are so
many good primi it's hard to choose, but you can't go wrong with
lasagne, *penne al prosciutto punte d'asparagi* (stubby pasta with diced
prosciutto and wild asparagus tips), or *ribollita*. Afterward, set to
work on the *cinghiale maremmana cipolline* (stewed wild boar with
caramelized baby onions) or *baccalà alla livornese* (salt cod covered
in tomatoes and served with chickpeas in oil).

Via Nazionale 79r (at Via Ariento, near the station). ✆ **055/282-106.** Reservations
recommended. Primi 12,000L–22,000L (6€–11€, $6–$11); secondi 15,000L–
29,000L (8€–15€, $8–$15). AE, DC, MC, V. Tues–Sat noon–2:30pm and 7–10pm.
Closed July 25–Aug and Dec 22–Jan 6. Bus: 10, 12, 25, 31, 32, 91.

MODERATE

Trattoria Zà-Zà ✿ TUSCAN CASALINGA (HOME COOK-ING) This place serves many of the food market workers from across the way—people who appreciate the importance of using simple, fresh ingredients to make filling dishes. Ask to sit downstairs in the brick barrel vault of the old *cantina* if you want some privacy; if you want company (they make even the small wooden tables communal), sit upstairs, where you can gaze at the racks of chianti flasks and dozens of photos of the restaurant's more (but mostly less) famous patrons. The *antipasto caldo alla Zà-Zà* has a bit of everything. If you don't want *ravioli strascicati* (in creamy ragù), brace yourself for a *tris di minestre* (three soups: *ribollita, pappa al pomodoro,* and *fagioli con farro*). *Bocconcini di vitella alla casalinga con fagioli all'uccelletto* (veal nuggets with tomato-stewed beans) makes an excellent second course; if you're indecisive, try a *grigliata mista al carbone* (mix of charcoal-grilled meats).

Piazza Mercato Centrale 26r (across from market building). ℂ **055/215-411.** Reservations recommended. Primi 7,000L–13,000L (3.60€–7€, $3.50–$7); secondi 14,000L–20,000L (7€–10€, $7–$10); *menù turistico* without wine 25,000L (13€, $13). AE, DC, MC, V. Mon–Sat noon–3pm and 7–11pm. Bus: 10, 12, 25, 31, 32, 91.

INEXPENSIVE

Da Mario FLORENTINE This is down-and-dirty Florentine lunchtime at its best, an *osteria* so basic the little stools don't have backs and a communal spirit so entrenched the waitresses will scold you if you try to take a table all to yourself. Since 1953, their stock in trade has been feeding market workers, and you can watch the kitchen through the glass as they whip out a wipe board menu of simple dishes at lightning speed. Hearty primi include *tortelli di patate al ragù* (ravioli stuffed with potato in ragù), *minestra di farro e riso* (emmer-and-rice soup), and *penne al pomodoro* (pasta quills in fresh tomato sauce). The secondi are basic but good; try the *coniglio arrosto* (roast rabbit) or *girello di vitello ai carciofi* (veal rolled around artichoke hearts, then stewed).

Via Rosina 2r (at the north corner of Piazza Mercato Centrale). ℂ **055/218-550.** Reservations not accepted. Primi 6,000L–6,500L (3.10€–3.35€, $3–$3.25); secondi 8,000L–20,000L (4.15€–10€, $4–$10). No credit cards. Mon–Sat noon–3:30pm. Closed Aug. Bus: 10, 12, 25, 31, 32, 91.

Nerbone FLORENTINE Nerbone has been stuffing stall owners and market patrons with excellent Florentine *cucina povera* ("poor people's food") since the Mercato Centrale opened in 1874. You can try *trippa alla Fiorentina, pappa al pomodoro,* or a plate piled with boiled potatoes and a single fat sausage. But the mainstay here is a *panino con bollito,* a boiled beef sandwich that's *bagnato* (dipped in the meat juices). Grab your glass of wine or beer and either eat standing with the crowd of old men at the side counter or fight for one of the few tables against the wall.

Stall 292 in the Mercato Centrale (enter off Via Ariento; the stall is down to the right). ℰ **055/219-949.** All dishes 5,000L–8,000L (2.60€–4.15€, $2.50–$4). No credit cards. Mon–Sat 7:30am–2:30pm. Closed 2 weeks in Aug and Dec 24–31. Bus: 10, 12, 25, 31, 32, 91.

5 Near Piazza Santa Trínita
VERY EXPENSIVE

Buca Lapi TUSCAN   The vaulted ceiling is carpeted with travel posters, the cuisine is carefully prepared, and the wine comes from the Antinori vineyards (this was once part of their cellars). An interesting start is the *filetto di cinghiale all'olio di rosmarino* (wild boar slices cured like prosciutto and served with rosemary-scented olive oil). One specialty is the *cannelloni gratinati alla Buca Lapi* (pasta canapés stuffed with ricotta and spinach served in a cream sauce of boar and mushrooms). A light secondo could be *coniglio disossato ripieno* (stuffed rabbit), or you can go all out on a masterful *bistecca chianina* (grilled steak, for two only). The desserts are homemade, including a firm and delicate *latte portugese* (a kind of crème caramel) and a richly dense chocolate torte.

Via del Trebbio, 1r (just off Piazza Antinori at the top of Via Tornabuoni). ℰ **055/ 213-768.** Reservations essential. Primi 15,000L–18,000L (8€–9€, $8–$9); secondi 20,000L–45,000L (10€–23€, $10–$23). AE, DC, MC, V. Tues–Sat 12:30–2:30pm; Mon–Sat 7:30pm–10:30pm. Bus: 6, 11, 36, 37, 68.

Cantinetta Antinori FLORENTINE/TUSCAN   The Antinori marchesi started their wine empire 26 generations ago, and, taking their cue from an ancient vintner tradition, installed a wine bar in their 15th-century palazzo 30 years ago. You can sit at the bar staring at dusty racks of venerable vintages in the cork for the perfect vino shopping break or reserve one of the crowded tables set with Ginori china. Most ingredients come fresh from the Antinori farms, as does all the fine wine. Start with the *fettucini all'anatra* (noodles in duck sauce) or the *ribollita* and round out the meal with the *trippa alla Fiorentina* or the *gran pezzo* (thick slab of oven-roasted Chiana beef). If you choose this worthy splurge, skip the second

A Big Step Above Ice Cream: Florentine Gelato

Gelato is a Florentine institution—a creamy, sweet, flavorful food item on a different level entirely from what Americans call "ice cream." Fine Florentine gelato is a craft taken seriously by all except the tourist-pandering spots around major attractions that serve air-fluffed bland "vanilla" and nuclear-waste pistachio so artificially green it glows.

Here's how to order gelato: First, pay at the register for the size of *coppa* (cup) or *cono* (cone) you want, then take the receipt up to the counter to select your flavors (unlike in America, they'll let you stuff multiple flavors into even the tiniest cup). Prices are fairly standardized, with the smallest serving at around 2,000L (1.05€, $1) or 3,500L (1.80€, $1.75) and prices going up in 500L (.25€, 25¢) or 1,000L (.50€, 50¢) increments for six or eight sizes. A warning: Gelato is denser than ice cream and richer than it looks. There's also a concoction called *semifreddo*, somewhere on the far side of the mousse family, in which standard Italian desserts like tiramisu are creamed with milk and then partially frozen.

There are plenty of quality gelaterie besides the one listed here. A few rules of thumb: Look for a sign that

course and order *formaggi misti*, which may include pecorino and mozzarella made fresh that morning. Their *cantucci* (Tuscan biscotti) come from Prato's premier producer.

Palazzo Antinori, Piazza Antinori 3 (at the top of Via Tornabuoni). ⓒ 055/292-234. www.antinori.it. Reservations strongly recommended. Primi 18,000L–25,000L (9€–13€, $9–$13); secondi 25,000L–35,000L (13€–18€, $13–$18); glass of wine 3,500L–20,000L (1.80€–10€, $1.75–$10). AE, DC, MC, V. Mon–Fri 12:30–2:30pm and 7–11:30pm. Closed Aug, Dec 24–Jan 6. Bus: 6, 11, 36, 37, 68.

EXPENSIVE

Il Latini ⓡ *Kids* FLORENTINE   Uncle Narcisso Latini opened this cheap locals' eatin' joint in 1950, though it now gets as many tourists as Florentines. Arrive at 7:30pm to get in the crowd massed at the door, for even with a reservation you'll have to wait as they skillfully fit parties together at the communal tables. In fact, getting proudly proclaims *produzione propria* (homemade) and take a look at the gelato itself—no matter what kind you plan to order, make sure the banana is gray, the egg-based *crema* (egg-based "vanilla," though there's nary a vanilla bean in it) yellow, and the pistachio a natural, pasty pale olive.

The queen of the Florentine gelato parlors, **Vivoli** ⭐⭐⭐, Via Isole delle Stinche 7r, off Via Ghibellina a block before Via Verdi (ⓒ **055/292-334;** www.cosmos.it/ilGelato.Vivoli; Bus: 14, 23, 71), has been the city's best unkept secret since 1929. The regular train of tourists hasn't prompted this place to compromise its premier quality, and you can find a select but delicious range of gelati and semifreddi. The choices change with the seasons, but some inventive creations include the very rummy *croccantina al rhum, araciotti al cioccolato* (candied orange bits in a standard chocolate base), and *agrumi* (somewhere between a sherbet and a gelato flavored with a mélange of citrus fruits). Of course, there's always the old standby: a deceptively pale but dangerously rich *cioccolato* (chocolate). It's open Tuesday to Saturday 8am to midnight and Sunday 10am to midnight.

thrown together with strangers and sharing a common meal is part of the fun here. Under hundreds of hanging prosciutto ham hocks, the waiters try their hardest to keep a menu away from you and serve instead a filling, traditional set meal with bottomless wine. This usually kicks off with *ribollita* and *pappa al pomodoro* or *penne strascicate* (in a ragù mixed with cream). If everyone agrees on the *arrosto misto,* you can get a table-filling platter heaped high with assorted roast meats. Finish off with a round of *cantucci con vin santo* for everyone.

Via del Palchetti 6r (off Via della Vigna Nuova). ⓒ **055/210-916.** Reservations strongly recommended. Primi 10,000L–12,000L (5€–6€, $5–$6); secondi 15,000L–30,000L (8€–16€, $8–$15); unofficial fixed-priced full meal with limitless wine 50,000L–55,000L (26€–28€, $25–$28). AE, DC, MC, V. Tues–Sun 12:30–2:30pm and 7:30–10:30pm. Closed 15 days in Aug and Dec 24–Jan 6. Bus: C, 6, 11, 36, 37, 68.

Osteria No. 1 TUSCAN "Osteria" belies this place's status as a full-fledged restaurant with some of the finer dining in Florence. Well-dressed Italians and Americans sit at well-spaced tables under the vaulted ceilings surrounded by painted coats of arms, musical instruments, and original art. Many opt for a *cocktail di gambereti* (shrimp cocktail) before their first course, which may include *zuppa di fagioli e farro* (bean-and-emmer soup) or the more imaginative *sfogliatine* (giant ravioli stuffed with cheese and carrots in basil-cream sauce). The secondi, all flavorful, range from tasty *sogliola griglia* (grilled sole) and adventurous *cervello* (fried calves' brains with artichokes) to a huge and succulent *bistecca alla Fiorentina*. The wine list is good but overpriced. The one major drawback here is that, though service is friendly it's often hurried, and they tend to rush you through your meal—fine if you're in a rush, but very un-Italian.

Via del Moro 22 (near the Ponte alla Carraia). ☎ **055/284-897**. Reservations recommended. Primi 16,000L–30,000L (8€–16€, $8–$15); secondi 20,000L–35,000L (10€–18€, $10–$18). AE, DC, MC, V. Tues–Sat noon–2:30pm and 7–11pm; Mon 7pm–12:30am. Closed Aug. Bus: A, C, 6, 9, 11, 36, 37, 68.

MODERATE

Coco Lezzone FLORENTINE This tiny trattoria hidden in a tangle of alleys near the Arno consists of long communal tables in a couple of pocket-size rooms wrapped around a cubbyhole of a kitchen whose chef, according to the restaurant's dialect name, is a bit off his rocker. The place is popular with local intellectuals, journalists, and the city soccer team. While enjoying your *ribollita* (known here as a "triumph of humility") or *rigatoni al sugo* (in a chunky ragù), look at where the yellow paint on the lower half of the wall gives way to white: That's how high the Arno flooded the joint in 1966. If you want a *bistecca alla Fiorentina*, call ahead first. Friday is *baccalà* (salt cod) day, and every day their *involtini* (thin veal slice wrapped around vegetables) and *crocchette di filetto* (veal-and-basil meat loaf smothered in tomato sauce) are good.

Via del Parioncino 26r (at the corner of Via Purgatorio). ☎ **055/287-178**. Reservations recommended. Primi 12,000L–25,000L (6€–13€, $6–$13); secondi 15,000L–25,000L (8€–13€, $8–$13). No credit cards. Mon–Sat noon–2:30pm and 7–10pm. Closed late July–Aug and Dec 23–Jan 7. Bus: C, 6, 11, 14, 17.

INEXPENSIVE

Belle Donne FLORENTINE This signless place is easy to miss (look for the potted plants outside). Inside you'll find a single bright room packed with locals, yellowing postcards, the obligatory ropes of garlic, and excellent Florentine home cooking. Try the salad of avocado slices over a nest of julienned zucchini, followed by *zuppa di porri e patate* (leek-and-potato soup) sprinkled with abundant Parmesan. Or, go for the ultratraditional *papardelle cogniglio e porcini* (wide noodles in rabbit/mushroom sauce). The *carpaccio con rucola* (pounded beef disks scattered with arugula) and *bollito misto con salsa verde* (a mix of boiled meats with relish) are respectable secondi. The desserts are nothing special, but the sugar-dusted fruit macedonia is good. Come early to beat the rush and get the dish of your wish—they erase offerings from the menu chalkboard as the kitchen runs out.

Via delle Belle Donne 16r (½ block up from Via del Sole). ✆ 055/238-2609. Reservations recommended. Primi 10,000L (5€, $5); secondi 15,000L (8€, $8). No credit cards. Sept–July Mon–Fri 12:15–2:30pm and 7:15–10:30pm. Bus: 6, 9, 11, 36, 37, 68.

6 Near Santa Maria Novella

MODERATE

Trattoria Guelfa FLORENTINE/TUSCAN   Always crowded and always good, the Guelfa has lots of paintings hanging on its walls and a random trattoria decor—pendulous gourds, wine bottles, and an old oxen yoke rule over the tightly packed noisy tables. The kitchen is very traditional, offering *spaghetti alla rustica* (in a cheesy, creamy tomato sauce) and *risotto ai 4 formaggi* (a gooey rice dish made with four cheeses) as proud primi. For a main course, you can go light with the *pinzimonio di verdure crude* (a selection of seasonally fresh raw veggies with oil to dip them in) or indulge your taste buds with the *petti di pollo alla Guelfa* (a chicken breast rolled around a stuffing of prosciutto, cheese, and truffled cream served with a side of olive oil–drenched oven-roasted potatoes).

Via Guelfa 103r (near the Fortezza, beyond Via Nazionale). ✆ 055/213-306. Reservations strongly recommended. Primi 8,000L (4.15€, $4); secondi 10,000L–22,000L (5€–11€, $5–$11); *menu turistico* with wine 17,000L (9peu], $9). AE, MC, V. Thurs–Tues noon–2:30pm and 7–10:30pm. Bus: 4, 10, 13, 14, 23, 25, 28, 31, 32, 33, 67, 71.

INEXPENSIVE

Trattoria Sostanza FLORENTINE   Sostanza is popularly called Il Troia (the trough) because people have been lining up at the long communal tables since 1869 to enjoy huge amounts of some of the best traditional food in the city. The primi are very simple: pasta in sauce, *tortellini in brodo* (meat-stuffed pasta in chicken broth), and *zuppa alla paesana* (peasant soup ribollita). The secondi don't steer far from Florentine traditions either, with *trippa alla Fiorentina* or their mighty specialty *petti di pollo al burro* (thick chicken breasts lightly fried in butter). It's an extremely unassuming place. The Florentine attitude is so laid-back you may not realize you're meant to be ordering when the waiter wanders over to chat. They also frown on anybody trying to cheat his or her own taste buds out of a full Tuscan meal.

Via Porcellana 25r (near the Borgo Ognissanti end). © 055/212-691. Reservations strongly recommended. Primi 9,000L–10,000L (4.65€–5–, $4.50–$5); secondi 11,000L–28,000L (6€–14€, $6–$14). No credit cards. Mon–Fri noon–2:15pm and 7:30–9:30pm. Closed Aug. Bus: C, 6, 9, 11, 36, 37, 68.

7 Near San Marco & Santissima Annunziata

VERY EXPENSIVE

Taverna del Bronzino FINE TUSCAN   In the 1580 house where Santi di Tito spent the last years of his life here painting, now, polite, efficient, and very accommodating waiters will show you to a table in the vaulted-ceiling dining room or on the arbor-shaded patio. Among the delectable antipasti are *salmone Scozzese selvatica* (wild Scottish salmon) and *petto d'oca affumicato e carciofi* (thin slices of smoked goose breast on a bed of sliced artichokes drowned in olive oil). The *risotto agli asparagi* is a bit light on the asparagus but still very creamy and tasty. You can also try the excellent *ravioli alla Senese* (ricotta and spinach–stuffed pasta in creamy tomato sauce) or *tagliolini ai pesci* (noodles with fish). To stick with the sea you can order *branzino* (sea bass simmered in white wine) next or select the *paillard di vitella all'ortolana* (a grilled veal steak wrapped around cooked vegetables).

Via delle Ruote 27r (between Piazza Indipendenza and San Marco). © 055/ 495-220. Reservations strongly recommended. Primi 15,000L–28,000L (8€–14€, $8–$14); secondi 40,000L–50,000L (21€–26€, $20–$25). AE, DC, MC, V. Mon–Sat 12:30–2:30pm and 7:30–10:30pm. Closed Aug. Bus: 12, 91, anything to San Marco.

INEXPENSIVE

Il Vegetariano VEGETARIAN   Come early to Florence's only vegetarian restaurant and use your coat to save a spot at one of the communal wood tables before heading to the back to get your food. You pay at the start of the meal, after choosing from the daily selections penned on the wipe board, and take your dishes self-service style from the workers behind the counter. The menu changes constantly but includes such dishes as risotto with yellow squash and black cabbage; a soupy, spicy Tunisian-style couscous with vegetables; a quichelike pizza rustica of ricotta, olives, tomatoes, and mushrooms; or a plate with *farro* (emmer) and a hot salad of spinach, onions, sprouts, and bean-curd chunks sautéed in soy sauce. You can mix and match your own salad, and they make a good chestnut flour cake stuffed with hazelnut cream for dessert.

Via delle Ruote 30r (off Via Santa Reparata near Piazza Indipendenza). ✆ 055/ 475-030. Reservations not accepted. Primi 8,000L (4.15€, $4); secondi 10,000L–11,000L (5€–6€, $5–$6). No credit cards. Tues–Fri 12:30–3pm; Tues–Sun 7:30pm–midnight. Closed 2–3 weeks in Aug. Bus: 12, 91, anything to San Marco.

La Mescita SANDWICHES & HOME COOKING   This tiny *fiaschetteria* is immensely popular with local businesspeople and students from the nearby university. Lunch can be a crushing affair, and they have signs admonishing you to eat quickly to give others a chance to sit. You'll be eating with Italians, and it's not for the timid because you have to take charge yourself: securing a seat, collecting your own place setting, and getting someone's attention to give your order before going to sit down. They offer mainly sandwiches, though there are always a few simple meat and pasta dishes ready as well. *Melanzana* (eggplant) is overwhelmingly the side dish of choice, and you can look to the cardboard lists behind the counter to select your wine, although the house wine is very good, and a quarter liter of it is cheaper than a can of soda.

Via degli Alfani 70r (near the corner of Via dei Servi). ✆ 055/239-6400. All sandwiches and dishes 3,500L–9,000L (1.80€–4.65€, $1.75–$4.50). No credit cards. Mon–Sat 8am–9pm. Bus: 6, 31, 32.

8 Near Santa Croce
VERY EXPENSIVE

Cibrèo ✷ REFINED TUSCAN   There's no pasta and no grilled meat—can this be Tuscany? Rest assured that while Benedetta Vitale and Fabio Picchi's culinary creations are a bit out of the ordinary, most are based on antique recipes. The tiny open kitchen rests between the two halves of Cibrèo's split personality—the fan-cooled main restaurant room full of intellectual babble, and the four tables of a tile-walled trattoria entered from around the back, where prices are cut by two-thirds but the selection is smaller. In the restaurant, the elegance is in the substance of the food and the service, not in surface appearances. Waiters pull up a chair to explain the list of daily specials—making each dish sound better than the last—and those garlands of hot peppers hanging in the kitchen window are a hint at the cook's favorite spice. All the food is spectacular, and dishes change regularly, but if they're available try the yellow pepper soup drizzled with olive oil, the soufflé of potatoes and ricotta spiced and served with pecorino shavings and ragù, or the roasted duck stuffed with minced beef, raisins, and pinoli. The wine list is solid, and they make excellent desserts.

Via Andrea del Verrocchio 8r (at the San Ambrogio Market, off Via de' Macchi). ℂ 055/234-1100. Reservations required for restaurant (not accepted at trattoria). Primi 30,000L (16€, $15) at restaurant, 10,000L (5€, $5) at trattoria; secondi with side dish 60,000L (31€, $30) at restaurant, 18,000L (9€, $9) without 6,000L (3.10€, $3) side dish at trattoria. AE, DC, MC, V. Tues–Sat 12:30–2:30pm and 7:30–11:15pm. Closed July 17–Aug and Dec 24–Jan 1. Bus: B, 14.

Ristorante e Vineria alle Murate TUSCAN & CUCINA CREATIVA Soft illumination, soft jazz, and soft pastels rule in this trendy spot owned by chef Umberto Montano. Alle Murate was one of the first places in the city to experiment with nouvelle cuisine. It tries, however, to balance *cucina creativa* with traditional Tuscan techniques and dishes. You could start with *zuppa di fagioli e gamberi* (soup of creamed white beans with shrimp) or the lasagne. The best fish dish is sea bass on a bed of fried potatoes topped with diced tomatoes, and for a main course you could go in for the *anatra disossata alle erbete e scorze di arancia* (duck à l'orange). The *brasato di Chiana* (steak) in Brunello wine, however, was disappointing. For these prices, the portions could be larger and the presentation better, but the food is good and the antipasti, *contorni*, aperitifs, and dessert wines are included in the price of your meal. The *vineria* half—really just a small room off the main one—offers an abbreviated menu at abbreviated prices.

Via Ghibellina 52r (near Borgo Allegri). ℂ 055/240-618. Reservations strongly recommended (specify *vineria* or *ristorante*). Primi 37,000L (19€, $19); secondi 40,000L–45,000L (21€–23€, $20–$23); fixed-price menus without wine 80,000L–100,000L (41€–52€, $40–$50). AE, DC, MC, V. Tues–Sun 7:30–11pm. Bus: 14.

EXPENSIVE

La Baraonda TUSCAN The "hubbub" of this place's name is in full force during lunch, when locals flock here for the superb seasonal food at modest prices—and you can sit outside in summer. At the more expensive dinner, the food is the same but the atmosphere more subdued. The tiny home-baked *schiacciate* with minced black olives gives you a few minutes to mull over the choice between gnocchi in chicken-liver ragù or their specialty risotto with fresh vegetables. Two-star secondi are the *muscolo di manzo* (beef cooked under a pile of caramelized onions) and the other house specialty, *polpettone in umido*, stewed slices of chopped veal that'll change your concept of meat loaf forever. The service is professional yet very friendly; and, as the dishes change monthly with the pickings at the market, they don't bother printing a menu.

Via Ghibellina 67r (at the corner of Borgo Allegri). ☎ 055/234-1171. Reservations strongly recommended. Lunch: Primi 8,000L–10,000L (4.15€–5€, $4–$5); secondi 15,000L (8€, $8). Dinner: Primi 18,000L–20,000L (9€–10€, $9–$10); secondi 25,000L (13€, $13). AE, DC, MC, V. Tues–Sat 12:30–2:30pm and 7:30–10:30pm; Mon 8–10:30pm. Closed Aug and Jan 1–7. Bus: 14.

La Giostra ✸✸✸ ADVENTUROUS TUSCAN   This is one of two restaurants I visit every time I come to town. The chef/owner is Dimitri d'Asburgo Lorena, a Hapsburg prince (with some local Medici blood for good measure) who opened this restaurant merely to indulge his love of cooking. They start you off with a complimentary flute of *spumanti* before you plunge into the tasty *crostini misti* and exquisite primi. Among my favorites are *tortelloni alla Mugellana* (handmade potato-stuffed pasta in ragù), *gnocchetti alla Lord Reinolds* (potato dumplings in a sauce of stilton and Port), homemade *tagliatelle* with tiny wild asparagus spears, and ravioli stuffed with brie in a sauce with thinly sliced, lightly fried artichokes. For an encore, try the *nodino di vitella ai tartufi bianchi* (veal slathered in eggy white truffle sauce with fresh truffle grated on top) or the lighter *spianata alle erbe aromatiche di Maremma* (a huge platter of spiced beef pounded flat and piled with a salad of rosemary sprigs, sage, and other herbs). Don't leave without sampling the sinfully rich Viennese Sachertorte, made from an old Hapsburg family recipe. This place has become (justifiably) popular, and even with a reservation there's often a short wait—laudably, they don't rush anybody to empty up tables—but it's worth it.

Borgo Pinti 10r (off Piazza G. Salvemini). ☎ 055/241-341. Reservations recommended. Primi 20,000L–24,000L (10€–12€, $10–$12); secondi 28,000L–40,000L (14€–21€, $14–$20). AE, DC, MC, V. Daily noon–3pm and 7pm–midnight. Bus: A, B, C, 14, 23, 71, 80.

MODERATE

Il Pizzaiuolo (Kids) ✸ NEAPOLITAN/PIZZA   Despite their considerable skill in the kitchen, Florentines just can't make a decent pizza. It takes a Neapolitan to do that, so business has been booming ever since Naples-born Carmine opened this pizzeria. Even with a reservation, you'll probably have to wait for a spot at a long, crowded, and noisy marble table. You can admire the old photos of Napoli as you wait—with the heavy crowds, the amiable service can get slow. Save the pizza for a main dish; start instead with a Neapolitan first course like *fusilli c'a ricotta* (homemade pasta spirals in creamy tomato-and-ricotta sauce). Of the pizzas, you can't go wrong with a classic *margherita* (mozzarella, tomatoes, and fresh basil), or spice up your evening with a *pizza diavola,* topped with hot salami and olives.

Via de' Macci 113r (near the San Ambrogio market). © 055/241-171. Reservations strongly recommended. Primi 10,000L–18,000L (5€–9€, $5–$9); secondi 12,000L–18,000L (6€–9€, $6–$9); pizza 8,000L–16,000L (4.15€–8€, $4–$8). No credit cards. Mon–Sat 12:30–3pm and 7:30pm–1am. Bus: B, 14.

La Vie en Rose TUSCAN NUOVA CUCINA   The minimalist decor and contemporary music are clues that this isn't your average Tuscan trattoria. This is the cheapest nouvelle cuisine–inspired Tuscan food in town, and they do a good job of it. One of their better antipasti is the *involtini di melanzane* (eggplant slices rolled around a tangy bread crumb paste and served with a salad of sliced pears and sharp pecorino cheese). They were in a pears-and-walnuts phase when I last visited, which produced the quite tasty *ravioli di noci con salsa al pomodoro* (ravioli stuffed with walnuts) with a strangely delicious side salad of pears and arugula in oil. For a second course, it's a toss-up between the baked salmon in hazelnut-butter sauce and the *vitella farcita ai pistacchi* (veal stuffed with pistachios and ham, flavored with rosemary).

Borgo Allegri 68r (on the edge of Piazza dei Ciompi). © 055/245-860. Reservations recommended. Primi 10,000L–12,000L (5€–6€, $5–$6); secondi 12,000L–22,000L (6€–11€, $6–$11). AE, DC, MC, V. Daily noon–midnight. Closed Aug 7–31. Bus: B, 14.

Osteria de' Benci INVENTIVE TUSCAN   This popular trattoria serves enormous portions (especially of secondi) on beautiful hand-painted ceramics under high ceiling vaults echoing with the conversation of Florentine trendoids. The menu changes monthly, but you can always be assured of excellent *salumi*—they come from Falorni, the famed butcher of the Chianti. The *eliche del profeta* are fusiloni tossed with ricotta, olive oil, oregano, and fresh tomatoes sprinkled with *parmigiano.* The unique *spaghetti dell'ubriacone* is bright crimson spaghetti that takes its color from being cooked in red wine, sauced with garlic, pepperoncino, and parsley sautéed in olive oil. And the *cibrèo delle regine* is a traditional rich Florentine dish of chopped chicken livers and gizzards served on toast. While that's indeed better than it sounds, you may prefer the gizzard-less *braciolina piccante,* flame-kissed beef marinated in lemon, parsley, and hot peppers.

Via de' Benci 13r (at the corner of Via de' Neri). ℂ **055/234-4923.** Reservations highly recommended. Primi 10,000L–17,000L (5€–9€, $5–$9); secondi 10,000L–30,000L (5€–16€, $5–$15). AE, DC, MC, V. Mon–Sat 1–2:45pm and 8–10:45pm. Bus: B, 23, 71.

Ristorante Vecchia Firenze ☞ *(Kids* FLORENTINE/TUSCAN

I first dined here with my parents when I was 12, and the place hasn't changed much since. It's set in a 15th-century palazzo, so avoid sitting in the boring front room in favor of the more intimate back rooms or the rowdier stone-lined cantina downstairs full of Florentine students. The *zuppa pavese* is a good vegetable soup, but try the *penne Vecchia Firenze* (pasta quills in a subtle creamy mushroom sauce with tomatoes). By all means order the *bistecca alla Fiorentina,* but if your appetite runs more to *coniglio alla griglia* (grilled rabbit) or *branzino alla griglia* (grilled sea bass), you won't be disappointed.

Borgo degli Albizi 76–78r. ℂ **055/234-0361.** Primi 5,000L–10,000L (2.60€–5€, $2.50–$5); secondi 8,000L–22,000L (4.15€–11€, $4–$11); pizza 10,000L–13,000L (5€–7€, $5–$7); fixed-price menus without wine 24,000L–30,000L (12€–16€, $12–$15). AE, DC, MC, V. Tues–Sun 11am–3pm and 7pm–10pm. Bus: 14, 23, 71.

Trattoria Pallottino FLORENTINE

One long room with a few long tables on the cobblestone floor and a second room on the side are all there is to this local favorite, so reserve early or you won't get a seat. The cook makes a mean *bruschetta al pomodoro* (toasted bread topped with tomatoes over which you are invited to drizzle the olive oil liberally). For a first course, I look no further than the *spaghetti alla fiaccheraia,* with a tomato sauce mildly spiked with hot peppers. You might follow it with the *peposo* (beef stew loaded with black pepper). Skip dessert and pop next door for a Vivoli gelato (see the box, "A Big Step Above Ice Cream: Florentine Gelato," earlier in this section).

Via Isola delle Stinche 1r. ℂ **055/289-573.** Reservations required for dinner. Primi 10,000L–14,000L (5€–7€, $5–$7); secondi 15,000L–25,000L (8€–13€, $8–$13); lunch menu without wine 20,000L (10€, $10; Tues–Sat only). AE, DC, MC, V. Tues–Sun 12:30–2:30pm and 7:30–10:30pm. Closed Aug 5–21. Bus: 14, 23, 71.

INEXPENSIVE

Antico Noè SANDWICHES & WINE   A *fiaschitteria* with superior sandwiches masquerading as a regular bar, the Antico Noè is popular with students and shopkeepers for its well-stuffed *panini* and cheap glasses of quaffable wine—perfect for a light lunch on the go or a snack. The place is rather hidden, but you'll know you've found it when you see a small crowd gathered around a door in the shade of a covered alley. You can order your sandwich from the list, invent your own, or (better yet) let them invent one for you. They surprised me on my last trip with a rather tasty combination of stuffed chicken and sliced porcini mushrooms topped with a slightly spicy creamy tomato spread. They've recently opened up a sit-down osteria next door serving simple Tuscan dishes.

Volta di San Piero 6r (the arched alley off Piazza San Pier Maggiore). ✆ **055/ 234-0838.** Sandwiches 4,000L–8,000L (2.05€–4.15€, $2–$4); wine 1,000L– 2,500L (.50€–1.30€, $.50–$1.25) per glass; primi 10,000L–20,000L (5€–10€, $5–$10); secondi 14,000L–20,000L (7€–10€, $7–$10). No credit cards. Mon–Sat 8am–midnight (often open Sun, too). Bus: B, 14, 23, 71.

9 In the Oltrarno

EXPENSIVE

Osteria Santo Spirito NOUVELLE TUSCAN   Opened in late 1996, this place offers some of the hippest dining in town. Two deep-red rooms with undulating track lighting are stacked on top of each other, and funk and dance music pounds from the speakers as they serve up excellent dishes with a modern twist. You can start with a salad like *pollo pinoli e uvetta con dressing* (chicken, pine nut, and raisin), or for pasta try *orecchiette Santo Spirito* (pasta in spicy tomato sauce with ricotta) or *gnocchi di patate gratinati* (oven-baked gnocchi swimming in a bubbling hot mix of soft cheeses flavored with truffle). Afterward, fill up on *filetto di manzo à tartufo* (beef filet with truffles) or the *coscie d'anatre con la panna* (very meaty roasted duck in cream sauce with carrots and bacon).

Piazza Santo Spirito 16r. ✆ **055/238-2383.** Reservations recommended. Primi 10,000L–18,000L (5€–9€, $5–$9); secondi 22,000L–40,000L (11€–21€, $11–$20). AE, DC, MC, V. Wed–Mon 12:45–2:30pm and 7:45–11:30pm. Bus: B, 11, 36, 37, 68.

MODERATE

Alla Vecchia Bettola FLORENTINE   Founded by the owners of Nerbone in the Mercato Centrale (see review earlier in this chapter), this simple room right on the piazza may not look it, but it's one of the premier restaurants in town for ultratraditional Florentine food. It fills up very early with food-loving Florentines, who choose from an always-changing menu that may include *penne alla Bettola* in spicy cream tomato sauce, rigatoni dressed with crushed olives, or *riso sulle testicciole d'agnello* (a "local's" rice dish cooked in a halved sheep's head). Secondi range from *anatra ripiena* *tartufata* (stuffed duck in truffle sauce) to the superlative *carpaccio con rucola*—pounded disks of beef piled high with arugula and tissue-thin slices of pecorino cheese. As far as wine goes, you simply pay for however much you finish of the light and tangy house wine on the table.

Viale L. Ariosto 32–34r (on Piazza Tasso). (C) **055/224-158.** Reservations required. Primi 9,000L–13,000L (4.65€–7€, $4.50–$7); secondi 13,000L–18,000L (7€–9€, $7–$9). No credit cards. Tues–Sat noon–2:30pm and 7:30–10:30pm. Closed 3 weeks in Aug, Dec 23–Jan 2, Easter. Bus: 12, 13.

Il Cantinone ⭑ *Kids* TUSCAN   With tourists and large groups of locals all seated at long tables under the low arc of a brick ceiling, the convivial noise can sometimes get a bit overwhelming. But the feeling of having walked into a party is part of the charm of this place. The specialty is *crostini,* slabs of peasant bread that act as vehicles for toppings like prosciutto, tomatoes, mozzarella, and sausage. The wine list is excellent—due perhaps to this locale's past incarnation as a chianti cellar—and the best way to sample it is through the *degustazione.* You and your companion get an antipasto, two primi (usually pasta dishes), and a secondo, which might be a tender and tasty wild boar stew. With each course you get a different wine, building from something like a light Orvieto *secco* through a well-chosen chianti to a brawny Brunello for the meat dish.

Via Santo Spirito 6r (the first right across the Santa Trinita bridge). (C) **055/ 218-898.** Reservations recommended. Primi 6,000L–18,000L (3.10€–9€, $3–$9); secondi 14,000L–40,000L (7€–21€, $7–$20); *menu degustazione* (tastings of wine and food, for 2 only) 40,000L (21€, $20) per person. AE, DC, MC, V. Tues–Sun 12:30–2pm and 7:30–10:30pm. Bus: 6, C, 11, 36, 37, 68.

I Raddi TUSCAN   This trattoria hidden in the heart of the Oltrarno is a true find—excellent cooking at reasonable prices in a city rapidly overpricing itself. The beamed ceiling and Tuscan standbys on the menu give it a grounding in tradition while the young staff and light touch in the kitchen lend a fresh Bohemian air. The specialty is *tagliolini ardiglione* (with sausage and aromatic herbs), but they also make a mean *crespelle alla Fiorentina* (pasta crepes layered with cheese). They do a fine *cibrèo,* a tasty *peposo alla fornacina con spinaci* (beef baked in wine with lots of pepperoncino and served with spinach), and a spicy *fagioli all'uccelleto con salsiccia.*

Via Ardiglione 47r (off Via dei Serragli, near Piazza delle Carmine). (C) **055/ 211-072.** Reservations recommended. Primi 12,000L (6€, $6); secondi 16,000L–25,000L (8€–13€, $8–$13). AE, MC, V. Mon–Sat noon–3pm and 7–11pm. Closed 10 days in Feb and 10 days in mid-Aug. Bus: D, 11, 36, 37, 68.

La Casalinga FLORENTINE   Their recent expansion sadly removed the last wisps of Renaissance aura from La Casalinga, replacing it with a crowded, almost cafeterialike feeling—but the home cooking of its name is still some of the most genuine in town. The ribollita is thick, the *ravioli al sugo di coniglio* (in a rabbit sauce) rich, and the *pasta della nonna* (short, hollow pasta in a sauce of tomatoes, sausage, and onions) excellent. Don't expect anything fancy in the secondi department either, just solid favorites like *bollito misto* (a mix of boiled meats with green sauce), *trippa alla Fiorentina,* and *galletto ruspante al forno* (half a young oven-baked chicken). The starving artists and local artisans have been all but driven out by the tourist hordes, but if you want to stuff yourself on huge portions of Oltrarno workman's food, this is the place to come.

Via dei Michelozzi 9r (just off Piazza Santo Spirito). © **055/218-624.** Reservations recommended. Primi 6000L–7,500L (3.10€–3.85€, $3–$3.75); secondi 8,000L–17,000L (4.15€–9€, $4–$9). AE, DC, MC, V. Mon–Sat noon–2:30pm and 7–9:45pm. Closed 3 weeks in Aug. Bus: B, 11, 36, 37, 68.

Osteria del Cinghiale Bianco TUSCAN   Massimo Masselli will sooner turn people away at the door than rush you through your meal. The place does a good repeat business of locals (including cooks from other restaurants) and tourists alike who come for the delicious *taglierini* (wide noodles) with pesto or the famous *strozzapreti* ("priest-chokers" made of the spinach-and-ricotta mix normally found inside ravioli, served with melted butter). You can't go wrong ordering anything made of the restaurant's namesake *cinghiale* (wild boar)—from the cold boar slices as an appetizer to *cinghiale con polenta* (wild boar stew cozied up to creamy, firm polenta) as a main course. For the romantically inclined, there are a few private niches with single tables, including one perched above the wall between the two main rooms. Set in the base of a 12th-century tower, this place milks its medieval look with exposed stone, odd iron implements hanging everywhere, and lights hidden in suspended cauldrons or the pigeon-holed walls.

Borgo Sant' Jacopo 43r. © **055/215-706.** Reservations required on weekends. Primi 9,000L–18,000L (4.65€–9€, $4.50–$9); secondi 20,000L–25,000L (10€–13€, $10–$13). No credit cards. Thurs–Mon noon–2:30pm and 7–10:30pm. Closed July 13–Aug 5. Bus: C, 6, 11, 36, 37, 68.

INEXPENSIVE

EnotecaBar Fuori Porta ENOTECA/CROSTONI   You can dine outside in nice weather or sit on the benches at tiny wooden tables inside to taste the excellent pizzalike crostini here. Start with an appetizer; the selection changes daily but could include *pappa al pomodoro* or gnocchi with broccoli rabe and sausage. The *crostoni* are divided by cheese—mozzarella, sharp pecorino, creamy goat-cheese *caprino*—along with a list of the toppings to accompany them. My fave is *caprino con prosciutto arrosto e pomodori secchi* (with cooked prosciutto and sun-dried tomatoes). The wine is a key part of your meal (order by the glass or quarter carafe); the list draws from the more interesting vineyards in Tuscany and beyond, while the dessert wines represent the best from all Italy. This place is a bit out of the way but worth the trip.

Via del Monte alle Croci 10r (near San Niccolò, through the gate at Via San Miniato). ℂ **055/234-2483.** Sandwiches and appetizers 3,000L–12,000L (1.55€–6€, $1.50–$6). AE, MC, V. Mon–Sat 12:30–3:30pm and 7pm–1am. Bus: C.

10 In the Hills

Trattoria le Cave di Maiano ⚑ TUSCAN This converted farmhouse is the countryside restaurant of choice for Florentines wishing to escape the city heat on a summer Sunday afternoon. You can enjoy warm-weather lunches on the tree-shaded stone terrace with a bucolic view. In cooler weather, you can dine inside several large rustic rooms with haphazard paintings scattered on the walls. The *antipasto caldo* of varied *crostini* and fried polenta is a good way to kick off a meal, followed by a *misto della casa* (for two only) that gives you a sampling of primi. This may include *penne strascicate* (stubby pasta in cream sauce and tomato ragù), or *riso allo spezzacamino* (rice with beans and black cabbage). The best secondo is the *pollastro al mattone* (chicken roasted under a brick with pepper) or the *lombatina di vitello alla griglia* (grilled veal chop).

Via Cave di Maiano 16 (in Maiano, halfway between Florence and Fiesole east of the main road). ℂ **055/59-133.** Reservations required. Primi 10,000L–15,000L (5€–8€, $5–$8); secondi 18,000L–30,000L (9€–15€, $9–$16). AE, DC, MC, V. Tues–Sun 12:30–3:30pm and 7:30–midnight. Bus: 7 (get off at Villa San Michele, then walk ¾ mile (1km) back up the side road past the Pensione Benecistà); a taxi is a better idea.

5

Exploring Florence

Florence is the Renaissance city—home to Michelangelo's *David*, Botticelli's *Birth of Venus,* and Raphael's Madonnas, where Fra' Angelico painted delicate *Annunciations* in bright primary colors and Giotto frescoed monks wailing over the *Death of St. Francis.* The city is so dense in art, history, and culture that even a short visit can wear out the best of us. Take a hint from that great pragmatist Mark Twain, who, after acknowledging the genius of Michelangelo, said "I do not want Michelangelo for breakfast—for luncheon—for dinner—for tea—for supper—for between meals. I like a change occasionally."

Don't necessarily pass up the Uffizi or take a rain check on *David* and the Accademia, but do take the time to enjoy the simple pleasures of Florence—wander the medieval streets in Dante's old neighborhood, sip a cappuccino on Piazza della Signoria and people-watch, haggle for a leather jacket at the street market around San Lorenzo, or spend a morning immersed in the greenery of the Boboli Gardens or an afternoon wandering the countryside that begins just a 15-minute stroll from the major sights.

1 On Piazza Del Duomo

The cathedral square is filled with tourists and caricature artists during the day, strolling crowds in the early evening, and knots of students strumming guitars on the Duomo's steps at night. Though it's always crowded, the piazza's vivacity and the glittering facades of the cathedral and the baptistery doors keep it an eternal Florentine sight.

At the corner of busy pedestrian main drag Via Calzaiuoli sits the pretty little **Loggia del Bigallo** (1351–58). Inside is a small museum of 14th-century works, which is unfortunately almost always closed. Call ✆ **055/215-440** if you're interested in trying to make an appointment to get in to see the 1342 *Madonna della Misericordia* by the school of Bernardo Daddi, which features the earliest known cityscape view of Florence.

Note that just south of the Duomo, hidden in the tangle of medieval streets toward Piazza della Signoria, is a 14th-century Florentine house restored and converted into the **Casa di Dante (Dante's House)** (© **055/219-416**), a small museum chronicling the life and times of the great poet. But, this isn't likely the poet's actual house. The entrance is up the side alley of Via Santa Margherita, and it's open Monday and Wednesday to Saturday 10 am to 6pm (to 4pm in winter) and Sunday 10am to 2pm. Admission is 5,000L (2.60€, $2.50) adults and free for those under 10.

Duomo (Cathedral of Santa Maria dei Fiori) 🏛🏛   For centuries, people have commented that Florence's cathedral is turned inside out, its exterior boasting Brunelleschi's famous dome, Giotto's bell tower, and a festive cladding of white, green, and pink marble, but its interior left spare, almost barren.

By the late 13th century, Florence was feeling peevish: Its archrivals Siena and Pisa sported huge new Duomos filled with art while it was saddled with the tiny 5th- or 6th-century Santa Reparata as a cathedral. So, in 1296, the city hired Arnolfo di Cambio to design a new Duomo, and he began raising the facade and the first few bays before his death in 1302. Work continued under the auspices of the Wool Guild and architects Giotto di Bondone (who concentrated on the bell tower) and Francesco Talenti (who finished up to the drum of the dome and in the process greatly enlarged Arnolfo's

---

ⓘ Tips The Best Times to Sightsee

Museums Open on Mondays: Palazzo Vecchio, Museo Bardini, Museo di Firenze Com'Era, Museo di Santa Maria Novella, Raccolta della Ragione, Casa Buonarroti, Casa di Dante, Opera di Santa Croce, Museo dell'Opera dell Duomo, Campanile di Giotto, Duomo's cupola, Opificio Pietre Dure, Museo Stibbert, Instituto e Museo di Storia di Scienza, Palazzo Medici-Riccardi, Museo Horne, Cappella Brancacci, Synagogue, Spedale degli Innocenti, Roman Amphitheater, and Museo Archeologico (Fiesole).

   Sights Open During Il Riposo (1–4pm): Uffizi, Accademia, Palazzo Vecchio, Duomo and its cupola, Museo dell'Opera dell Duomo, Campanile di Giotto, Baptistery, Palazzo Vecchio, Santa Croce, Galleria Palatina (Pitti Palace), Forte di Belvedere and Boboli Gardens, Cappella Brancacci, Roman Amphitheater, and Museo Archeologico (Fiesole).

Florence Attractions

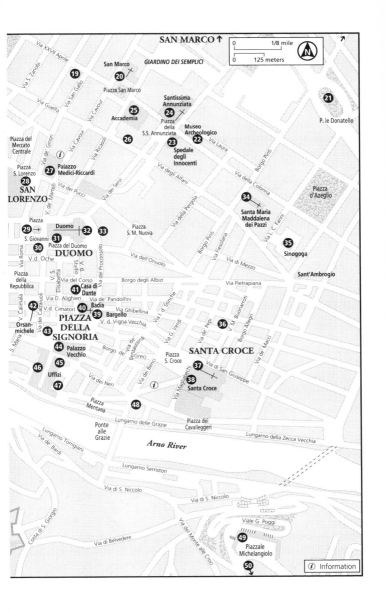

SAN MARCO ↑

0   1/8 mile
0   125 meters

Via XXVII Aprile

Via S. Zanobi

San Marco

19

20

GIARDINO DEI SEMPLICI

Piazza San Marco

21

P. le Donatello

Via Guelfa

Via San Gallo

Via Cavour

Santissima
Annunziata

25
Accademia

24
Piazza
della
S.S. Annunziata

Museo
Archeologico
22

Piazza del
Mercato
Centrale

26

23
Spedale
degli
Innocenti

Via Laura

Borgo Pinti

Piazza
d'Azeglio

Piazza
S. Lorenzo

27 Palazzo
Medici-Riccardi

28
**SAN
LORENZO**

Via de' Pucci

Via dei Servi

Via degli Alfani

Via della Colonna

34

Santa Maria
Maddalena
dei Pazzi

Piazza

29

30
S. Giovanni

31
Piazza del Duomo
DUOMO

Duomo **32**
33

Piazza
S. M. Nuova

Via della Pergola

Borgo Pinti

Via Fiesolana

35

Sinogoga

Via L.C. Farini

Via d.Oche

Via Roma

V.S.
Via del Corso
**V.S.
Elisabetta**

Via dell'Oriuolo

Via di Mezzo

Sant'Ambrogio

Piazza
della
Repubblica

41 Casa di
Dante
Via D. Alighieri

42
V.d. Cimatori **40** Badia
PIAZZA
DELLA
SIGNORIA
Orsan-
michele **43**

Borgo degli Albizi

Via de' Pandolfini

Via Ghibellina
39 Bargello
V.d. Vigna Vecchia

Via Pietrapiana

Via G. Verdi

Via de' Pepi

V.M. Buonarroti

Borgo Allegri

36

Via de' Macci

44 Palazzo
Vecchio

Via de' Cerchi

Via dei Cimatori

45

46
Uffizi

47

Borgo de' Greci

Via de' Benci

SANTA CROCE

Piazza
S. Croce

37

38
Santa Croce

Via di San Giuseppe

Via dei Neri

Piazza
Mentana

48

Lungarno delle Grazie

Piazza dei
Cavalleggeri

Lungarno della Zecca Vecchia

Ponte
alle
Grazie

Arno River

Lungarno Serristori

Via de' Bardi

Costa di S. Giorgio

Via di S. Niccolo

Via di S. Niccolo

Viale G. Poggi

Via di Belvedere

Via del Monte alle Croci

49
Piazzale
Michelangiolo

50
↓

ⓘ Information

original plan). The facade we see today is a neo-Gothic composite designed by Emilio de Fabris and built from 1871 to 1887 (for its story, see the Museo dell'Opera dell Duomo, later in this chapter).

The Duomo's most distinctive feature is its enormous **dome** ⍟⍟⍟, which dominates the skyline and is a symbol of Florence itself. The raising of this dome, the largest in the world in its time, was no mean architectural feat, tackled admirably by Filippo Brunelleschi between 1420 and 1436. You can climb up between the two shells of the cupola for one of the classic panoramas across the city. At the base of the dome, just above the drum, Baccio d'Agnolo began adding a balcony in 1507. One of the eight sides was finished by 1515, when someone asked Michelangelo—whose artistic opinion was by this time taken as cardinal law—what he thought of it. The master reportedly scoffed, "It looks like a cricket cage." Work was immediately halted, and to this day the other seven sides remain rough brick.

The Duomo was actually built around **Santa Reparata** so it could remain in business during construction. For more than 70 years, Florentines entered their old church through the freestanding facade of the new one, but then in 1370 the original was torn down when the bulk of the Duomo, except the dome, was finished. Ever the fiscal conservatives, the citizens started clamoring to see some art as soon as the new facade's front door was completed in the early 1300s—to be sure their investment would be more beautiful than rival cathedrals. Gaddo Gaddi was commissioned to mosaic an *Enthronement of Mary* in the lunette above the inside of the main door, and the people were satisfied. The stained-glass windows set in the facade were designed by Lorenzo Ghiberti, and Paolo Uccello, a painter obsessed by the newly developed perspective, frescoed the huge *hora italica* clock with its four heads of Prophets in 1443.

At a right-aisle pier are steps leading down to the excavations of the old Santa Reparata. In 1972, a tomb slab inscribed with the name Filippo Brunelleschi was discovered down there (visible through a gate). Unless you're interested in the remains of some ancient Roman houses and parts of the paleo-Christian mosaics from Santa Reparata's floor, the admission price isn't worth it.

Against the left-aisle wall are the only frescoes besides the dome in the Duomo. The earlier one to the right is the greenish ***Memorial to Sir John Hawkwood*** ⍟ (1436), an English *condottiere* (mercenary commander) whose name the Florentines mangled to Giovanni Acuto when they hired him to rough up their enemies.

Before he died, or so the story goes, the mercenary asked to have a bronze statue of him riding his charger to be raised in his honor. Florence solemnly promised to do so but, in typical tightwad style, after Hawkwood's death hired the master of perspective and illusion Paolo Uccello to paint an equestrian monument instead—much cheaper than casting a statue in bronze. Andrea Castagno copied this painting-as-equestrian-statue idea 20 years later when he frescoed a *Memorial to Niccolò da Tolentino* next to Uccello's work. Near the end of the left aisle is Domenico di Michelino's *Dante Explaining the Divine Comedy* (1465). If that's Hell on the left and the mountain of Purgatory in the middle, then 15th-century Florence on the right, featuring the cathedral's brand-new dome, must be Paradise.

In the back left corner of the sanctuary is the **New Sacristy.** Lorenzo de' Medici was attending Mass in the Duomo one April day in 1478 with his brother Giuliano when they were attacked in the infamous Pazzi Conspiracy. The conspirators, egged on by the pope and led by a member of the Pazzi family, old rivals of the Medici, fell on the brothers at the ringing of the sanctuary bell. Giuliano was murdered on the spot—his body rent with 19 wounds—but Lorenzo vaulted over the altar rail and sprinted for safety into the New Sacristy, slamming the bronze doors behind him. Those doors were cast from 1446 to 1467 by Luca della Robbia, his only significant work in the medium. Earlier, Luca had provided a lunette of the *Resurrection* (1442) in glazed terra cotta over the door, as well as the lunette Ascension over the south sacristy door. The interior of the New Sacristy is filled with beautifully inlaid wood cabinet doors.

The frescoes on the **interior of the dome** were designed by Giorgio Vasari but mostly painted by his less-talented student Frederico Zuccari by 1579. The frescoes were subjected to a thorough cleaning completed in 1996, which many people saw as a waste of restoration lire when there are so many more important works to be salvaged throughout the city. The scrubbing did, however, bring out Zuccari's only saving point—his innovative color palette.

Piazza del Duomo. ℂ **055/230-2885.** Admission to church free; Santa Reparata excavations 3,000L (1.55€, $1.50); cupola 10,000L (5€, $5), under 6 free. Church: Mon–Fri 10am–5pm; 1st Sat of month 10am–3:30pm, other Sat 10am–4:45pm; Sun 1–5pm. Free tours every 40 min. daily, 10:30am–noon and 3–4:20pm. Cupola: Mon–Fri 8:30am–6:20pm; Sat 8:30am–5pm (first Sat of month to 3:20pm). Bus: 1, 6, 17, 14, 22, 23, 36, 37, 71.

Battistero (Baptistery) ⟨★★★⟩   In choosing a date to mark the beginning of the Renaissance, art historians often seize on 1401, the year Florence's powerful wool merchant's guild held a contest to decide who'd receive the commission to design the **North Doors** ⟨★⟩ of the Baptistery to match the Gothic **South Doors** cast 65 years earlier by Andrea Pisano. The era's foremost Tuscan sculptors each designed and cast a bas-relief bronze panel depicting his own vision of The Sacrifice of Isaac. Twenty-two-year-old Lorenzo Ghiberti, competing against the likes of Donatello, Jacopo della Quercia, and Filippo Brunelleschi, won hands down. He spent the next 21 years casting 28 bronze panels and building his doors. Although limited by his contract to design the scenes within Gothic frames as on Pisano's doors, Ghiberti infused his figures and compositions with an unmatched realism and classical references that helped define Renaissance sculpture. (Ghiberti stuck a self-portrait in the left door, the fourth head from the bottom of the middle strip, wearing a turban.)

The result so impressed the merchant's guild—not to mention the public and Ghiberti's fellow artists—they asked him in 1425 to do the **East Doors** ⟨★★★⟩, facing the Duomo, this time giving him the artistic freedom to realize his Renaissance ambitions. Twenty-seven years later, just before his death, Ghiberti finished 10 dramatic life-like Old Testament scenes in gilded bronze, each a masterpiece of Renaissance sculpture and some of the finest low-relief perspective in Italian art. The panels now mounted here are excellent copies; the originals are displayed in the Museo dell'Opera dell Duomo (see below). Ghiberti's modest bald head shows up again here, this time the fifth from the bottom of the left door's middle strip of busts. Years later, Michelangelo was standing before these doors and someone asked his opinion. His response sums up Ghiberti's life accomplishment as no art historian ever could: "They are so beautiful that they would grace the entrance to Paradise." They've been called the Gates of Paradise ever since.

The Baptistery is one of Florence's oldest, most venerated buildings. Florentines long believed it was originally a Roman temple, but it most likely was raised somewhere between the 4th and 7th centuries on the site of a Roman palace. The octagonal drum was rebuilt in the 11th century, and by the 13th century it had been clad in its characteristic green-and-white Romanesque stripes of marble and capped with its odd pyramidlike dome.

The interior is ringed with columns pilfered from ancient Roman buildings and is a spectacle of mosaics above and below. The floor was inlaid in 1209, and the ceiling was covered between 1225 and the early 1300s with glittering **mosaics** 🦌🦌. Most were crafted by Venetian or Byzantine-style workshops, which worked off designs drawn by the era's best artists. Coppo di Marcovaldo drew sketches for the over 26-foot- (7.8m-) high, ape-toed Christ in Judgment and the Last Judgment that fills over a third of the ceiling.

To the right of the altar is the 1425 wall **tomb of Antipope John XXIII,** designed by Michelozzo and Donatello, who cast the bronze effigy of the deceased, deposed pontiff.

Piazza di San Giovanni. ✆ **055/230-2885.** Admission 5,000L (2.60€, $2.50), under 6 free. Mon–Sat noon–6:30pm; Sun 8:30am–1:30pm. Bus: 1, 6, 17, 14, 22, 23, 36, 37, 71.

Campanile di Giotto (Giotto's Bell Tower) 🦌🦌   In 1334, Giotto started the cathedral bell tower (clad in the same three colors of marble gracing the Duomo) but completed only the first two levels before his death in 1337. He was out of his league with the engineering aspects of architecture, and the tower was saved from falling in on itself by Andrea Pisano, who doubled the thickness of the walls. Andrea, a master sculptor of the Pisan Gothic school, also changed the design to add statue niches—he even carved a few of the statues himself—before quitting the project in 1348. Francesco Talenti finished the job between 1350 and 1359—he exchanged the heavy solidness of the base for a much lighter, airier effect by using sets of two-light windows and a single final massive three-light window on each side.

The **reliefs** and **statues** in the lower levels—by Andrea Pisano, Donatello, and others—are all copies, the weather-worn originals now housed in the Museo dell'Opera del Duomo (see below). You can climb the 414 steps to the top of the tower. What makes the 25-foot- (84m-) high view different from what you get out of the more popular climb up the cathedral dome, besides a cityscape vista, are great views of the Baptistery as you ascend and the best close-up shot in the whole city of Brunelleschi's dome.

Piazza del Duomo. ✆ **055/230-2885.** Admission 10,000L (5€, $5). Apr–Oct daily 9am–6:50pm; Nov–Mar daily 9am–4:20pm. Bus: 1, 6, 17, 14, 22, 23, 36, 37, 71.

Museo dell'Opera dell Duomo (Duomo Works Museum) 🦌
This museum exists mainly to house the sculptures removed from the niches and doors of the Duomo group for restoration and

preservation out of the elements. The dusty old museum was completely rearranged from 1998 to 2000.

The first small rooms house **Gothic sculptures** from the exteriors of the baptistery and Duomo, and speak of the fate of the cathedral's facade. The half-finished 14th-century face was covered in the statues seen here, which came from the chisels of Donatello, Nanni di Banco, and the first cathedral architect, Arnolfo di Cambio, who used some unusual techniques to achieve a kind of realism in his flattened figures, including giving his *Madonna* faintly disturbing glass eyes.

The courtyard has now been enclosed so as to show off—under natural daylight, as they should be seen—Lorenzo Ghiberti's original gilded bronze panels from the Baptistery's **Gates of Paradise** *(★★★*, which are being displayed as they're slowly restored. Ghiberti devoted 27 years to this project (1425–52), and you can now admire up close his masterpiece of *schiacciato* (squished) relief—using the Donatello technique of almost sketching in perspective to create the illusion of depth in low relief.

On the way up the stairs, you pass **Michelangelo's *Pietà*** *(★* (1548–55), his second and penultimate take on the subject, which the sculptor probably had in mind for his own tomb. The face of Nicodemus is a self-portrait, and Michelangelo most likely intended to leave much of the statue group only roughly carved, just as we see it. Art historians inform us that the polished figure of Mary Magdalene on the left was finished by one of Michelangelo's students, while storytellers relate that part of the considerable damage to the group was inflicted by the master himself when, in a moment of rage and frustration, he took a hammer to it.

The top floor of the museum houses the **Prophets** carved for the bell tower, the most noted of which are the remarkably expressive figures carved by Donatello: the drooping aged face of the *Beardless Prophet;* the sad fixed gaze of *Jeremiah;* and the misshapen ferocity of the bald ***Habakkuk*** *(★* (known to Florentines as *Lo Zuccone*—pumpkin head—and M.I.A. for restoration as we go to press). Mounted on the walls above are two putti-encrusted marble ***cantorie* (choir lofts).** The slightly earlier one (1431) on the entrance wall is by Luca della Robbia. His panels (the originals now displayed down at eye level, with plaster casts set in the actual frame above) are in perfect early Renaissance harmony, both within themselves and with each other, and they show della Robbia's mastery of creating great depth within a shallow piece of stone. Across the room,

Donatello's *cantoria* ✿ (1433–38) takes off in a new artistic direction as his singing cherubs literally break through the boundaries of the "panels" to leap and race around the entire *cantoria* behind the mosaicked columns.

The room off the right stars one of Donatello's more morbidly fascinating sculptures, a late work in polychrome wood of *The Magdalene* ✿ (1453–55), emaciated and veritably dripping with penitence. Surrounding it are small embroidered panels from priestly Dalmatic robes designed by Antonio del Pollaiolo, and an ornate silver **Altar Front,** commissioned for the Baptistery in 1366 and not finished until 1480, over which time the city's best and brightest gold- and silversmiths all had a whack at it, including Andrea del Verrocchio, Antonio del Pollaiolo, and Michelozzo di Bartolommeo (who did the large central saint).

Out the other end of the Prophets room you'll find Andrea Pisano's **panels** from the first few levels of the bell tower (early 14th c.), possibly made to Giotto's designs.

The new exit corridor leading off here houses some of the **machines** used to build the cathedral dome, **Brunelleschi's death mask** as a grisly reminder of its architect, and the **wooden model proposals** for the cupola's drum and for the facade. The original Gothic facade was destroyed in 1587 to make room for one done in High Renaissance style, but the patron behind the work—Grand Duke Francesco de' Medici—died before he could choose from among the submissions by the likes of Giambologna and Bernardo Buontalenti. The Duomo remained faceless until purses of the 18th century heavy with money and relentless bad taste gave it the neo-Gothic facade we see today.

Piazza del Duomo 9 (directly behind the dome end of the cathedral). ✆ **055/ 230-2885.** Admission 10,000L (5€, $5), under 6 free. Mon–Sat 9am–7:30pm; Sun 9am–1:40pm. Bus: B, 14, 23, 71.

2 Around Piazza della Signoria

When the medieval Guelf party finally came out on top of the Ghibellines, they razed part of the old city center to build a new palace for civic government. It's said the Guelfs ordered architect Arnolfo di Cambio to build what we now call the Palazzo Vecchio in the corner of this space, but to be careful that not one inch of the building sat on the cursed former Ghibelline land. This odd legend was probably fabricated to explain Arnolfo's quirky off-center architecture, where even the building's basic outline doesn't have many right angles.

The space around the palazzo became the new civic center of town, the L-shaped **Piazza della Signoria** ⟨★★⟩, named after the oligarchic ruling body of the medieval city. Today, it's an outdoor sculpture gallery, teeming with tourists and full of postcard stands, horses-and-buggies, and a few outdoor cafes.

The statuary on the piazza is particularly beautiful, starting on the far left (as you're facing the Palazzo Vecchio) with Giambologna's equestrian statue of *Grand Duke Cosimo I* (1594). To its right is one of Florence's favorite sculptures to hate, the *Fontana dei Neptuno (Neptune Fountain;* 1560–75), created by Bartolomeo Ammannati as a tribute to Cosimo I's naval ambitions but nicknamed by the Florentines *Il Biancone,* "Big Whitey." Michelangelo, to whom many a Renaissance quip is attributed, took one look at it and shook his head, moaning "Ammannato, Ammannato, what a beautiful piece of marble you've ruined." The highly mannerist bronzes surrounding the basin are much better, probably because a young Giambologna had a hand in most of them.

Note the **porphyry plaque** set in the ground in front of the fountain. This marks the site where puritanical monk Savonarola held the Bonfire of the Vanities: With his fiery apocalyptic preaching, he whipped the Florentines into a reformist frenzy, and hundreds filed into this piazza, arms loaded with paintings, clothing, and other effects that represented their "decadence." They consigned it all to the flames of a roaring pile. However, after a few years the pope (not amused by Savonarola's criticisms) excommunicated first the monk and then the entire city for supporting him. On May 23, 1498, the Florentines decided they'd had enough of the rabid-dog monk, dragged him and two followers to the torture chamber, pronounced them heretics, and led them into the piazza for one last day of fire and brimstone. In the very spot where they once burnt their luxurious belongings, they put the torch to Savonarola himself. The event is commemorated by an anonymous painting kept in Savonarola's old cell in San Marco and by the plaque here.

To the right of the Neptune Fountain is a long, raised platform fronting the Palazzo Vecchio known as the *arringheria,* from which soapbox speakers would lecture to crowds before them (we get our word "harangue" from this). On its far left corner is a copy (original in the Bargello) of Donatello's ***Marzocco,*** symbol of the city, with a Florentine lion resting his raised paw on a shield emblazoned with the city's emblem, the *giglio* (lily). To its right is another Donatello replica, ***Judith Beheading Holofernes*** (original inside the Palazzo Vecchio). Farther down is a man who needs little introduction,

Michelangelo's *David,* a 19th-century copy of the original now in the Accademia. Near enough to David to look truly ugly in comparison is Baccio Bandinelli's *Heracles* (1534). Poor Bandinelli was trying to copy Michelangelo's muscular male form but ended up making his Heracles merely lumpy. He caught nothing but flak over this hack job—Cellini wrote it off as a "sack of melons."

At the piazza's south end, beyond the long U that opens down the Uffizi, is one of the square's earliest and prettiest embellishments, the **Loggia dei Lanzi** ✸✸ (1376–82), named after the Swiss guard of lancers (*lanzi*) Cosimo de' Medici stationed here. The airy loggia was probably built on a design by Andrea Orcagna—spawning another of its many names, the Loggia di Orcagna (another is the Loggia della Signoria). The three huge arches of its simple, harmonious form were way ahead of the times, an architectural style that really belongs to the Renaissance. This open arcade is filled with statuary, though as we go to press half of it is encased in big wooden boxes as they restore the pieces. At the front left corner stands Benvenuto Cellini's masterpiece in bronze, *Perseus* ✸✸ (1545), holding out the severed Medusa's head before him, restored from 1996 to 2000. On the far right of the loggia has stood Giambologna's *Rape of the Sabines* ✸✸, one of the most successful mannerist sculptures in existence, a piece you must walk all the way around to appreciate, catching the action and artistry from different angles. Sadly, once boxed and examined for restoration, authorities determined that the outdoors had wreaked intolerable damage, and the original statue will be removed to the Accademia (to take the place of its plaster model long anchoring the museum's first room) with a marble copy to take its place here.

⌒Tips **Reserving Tickets for the Uffizi & Other Museums**

Finally, you can bypass the hours-long ticket line at the **Uffizi Galleries** by reserving a ticket and an entry time in advance by calling ℭ **055/294-883** or checking on the Web at **www.arca.net/uffizi/reservation.htm**. By March, entry times can already be booked over a week in advance. You can also reserve for the **Accademia Gallery** (another interminable line, to see *David*), as well as the **Galleria Palatina** in the Pitti Palace, the **Bargello,** and several others. They charge a nominal fee (worth every penny), and you can pay by credit card.

Across the piazza, on the north end at no. 5, is the **Raccolta della Ragione** (© **055/283-078**), a gallery of mainly late-19th- and 20th-century art with some nice second-story views over the piazza. It's open Wednesday to Saturday 9am to 4pm and Sunday 8am to 1pm; admission is 4,000L (2.05€, $2).

Gallerie degli Uffizi (Uffizi Galleries) ★★★ The Uffizi is one of the world's great museums, the single best introduction to Renaissance painting, with works by Giotto, Masaccio, Paolo Uccello, Sandro Botticelli, Leonardo da Vinci, Perugino, Michelangelo, Raphael Sanzio, Titian, Caravaggio, and the list goes on. The museum is deceptively small. What looks like a small stretch of gallery space can easily gobble up half a day—many rooms suffer the fate of containing nothing but masterpieces.

Know before you go that the Uffizi regularly shuts down rooms for crowd-control reasons—especially in summer, when the bulk of the annual 1.5 million visitors stampedes the place. Of the more than 3,100 artworks in the museum's archives, only about 1,700 were on exhibit in 1999. As they restore the building from the 1993 bombing, they're also making new exhibition spaces available.

The painting gallery is housed in the structure built to serve as the offices (*uffizi* is Florentine dialect for *uffici,* or "offices") of the Medici, commissioned by Cosimo I from Giorgio Vasari in 1560— perhaps his greatest architectural work. The painting gallery was started by Cosimo I as well and is now housed in the second-floor rooms that open off a long hall lined with ancient statues and frescoed with grotesques.

The first room off to your left after you climb Vasari's monumental stairs (**Room 2;** Room 1 is perennially closed) presents you with a crash course in the Renaissance's roots. It houses three huge altarpieces by Tuscany's greatest late-13th-century masters. On the right is Cimabue's *Santa Trínita Maestà* (1280), still very much rooted in the Byzantine traditions that governed painting in the early Middle Ages—gold-leaf crosshatching in the drapery, an Eastern-style inlaid throne, spoonlike depressions above the noses, highly posed figures, and cloned angels with identical faces stacked up along the sides. On the left is Duccio's *Rucellai Maestà* (1285), painted by the master who studied with Cimabue and eventually founded the Sienese school of painting. The style is still thoroughly medieval but introduces innovations into the rigid traditions. Gone are the cross-hatchings, replaced by an idiosyncratic golden hem that crinkles around the Madonna's lap to the floor. There's a little

Tips for Seeing the Uffizi

If you have the time, make two trips to the museum. On your first, concentrate on the first dozen or so rooms and pop by the Greatest Hits of the 16th Century, with works by Michelangelo, Caravaggio, Raphael, and Titian. Return later for a brief recap and continue with the rest of the gallery.

Be aware that the **gift shop** at the end of the galleries closes 20 minutes before the museum. You can visit it without reentering the museum at any time; if you plan to stay in the collections until closing, go down to the shop earlier during your visit and get the guards' attention before you pass through the exit turnstile, so they'll know you're just popping out to buy a few postcards and will recognize you when you ask to be let back in.

more weight to the Child she holds, and the Madonna's face has a more human, somewhat sad, expression.

In the center of the room is Giotto's incredible ***Ognissanti Maestà*** 🟊🟊🟊 (1310), by the man who's generally credited as the founding father of Renaissance painting. It's sometimes hard to appreciate just how much Giotto changed when he junked half the traditions of painting to go his own way. It's mainly in the very simple details, the sorts of things we take for granted in art today, such as the force of gravity, the display of basic emotions, the individual facial expressions, and the figures who look like they have an actual bulky body under their clothes. Giotto's Madonna has actual knees forming a real lap on which the Christ child perches. She sways slightly to one side, the fabric of her off-white shirt pulling realistically against her breasts as she twists. Instead of floating in mysterious space, Giotto's saints and angels stand on solid ground.

Room 3 pays homage to the 14th-century Sienese school with several delicately crafted works by Simone Martini and the Lorenzetti brothers. Here is Martini's ***Annunciation*** 🟊 (1333). Note that Mary, who in so much art both before and after this period is depicted as meekly accepting her divine duty, looks reluctant, even disgusted, at the news of her imminent Immaculate Conception. Pietro and Ambrogio Lorenzetti helped revolutionize Sienese art and the Sienese school before succumbing to the Black Death in 1348. Of their work here, Ambrogio's 1342 *Presentation at the Temple* is the finest, with a rich use of color and a vast architectural space created to open up the temple in the background.

The Uffizi

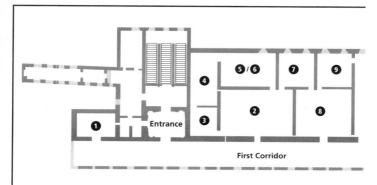

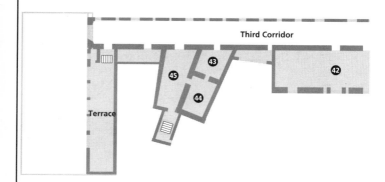

1	Archaeological Room	**15**	Leonardo da Vinci
2	Giotto & 13th-Century Paintings	**16**	Geographic Maps
3	Sienese Paintings (14th Century)	**17**	Ermafrodito
4	Florentine Paintings (14th Century)	**18**	The Tribune
5/6	International Gothic	**19**	Perugino & Signorelli
7	Early Renaissance	**20**	Dürer & German Artists
8	Filippo Lippi	**21**	Giovanni Bellini & Giorgione
9	Antonio del Pollaiolo	**22**	Flemish & German Paintings
10/14	Botticelli & Ghirlandaio	**23**	Mantegna & Correggio

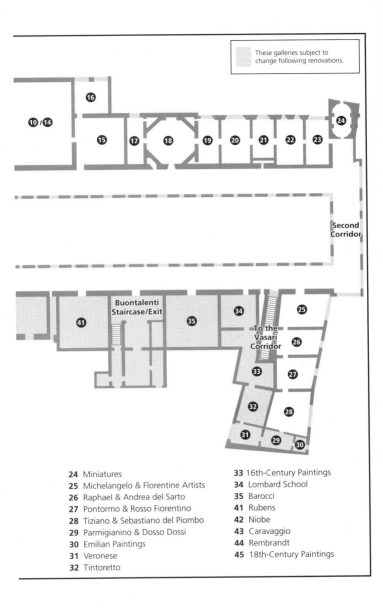

These galleries subject to change following renovations.

10/14
16
15 **17** **18** **19** **20** **21** **22** **23**
24

Second Corridor

Buontalenti Staircase/Exit

41 **35** **34** **25**

To the Vasari Corridor

26

33 **27**

32 **28**

31 **29** **30**

Room 4 houses the works of the 14th-century Florentine school, where you can clearly see the influence Giotto had on his contemporaries. **Rooms 5 and 6** represent the dying gasps of the International Gothic style, still grounded in medievalism but admitting a bit of the emergent naturalism and humanist philosophy into their works. Lorenzo Monaco's *Coronation of the Virgin* (1413) is particularly beautiful, antiquated in its styling but with a delicate suffused coloring. Gentile da Fabriano was one of the most talented of the era, caring little for foreshortening or other newfangled perspective devices and more about dense storytelling.

In **Room 7,** the Renaissance proper starts taking shape, driven primarily by the quest of two artists, Paolo Uccello and Masaccio, for perfect perspective. On the left wall is Uccello's *Battle of San Romano* (1456), famously innovative but also rather ugly. This painting depicts one of Florence's great victories over rival Siena, but for Uccello it was more of an excuse to explore perspective—with which this painter was, by all accounts, positively obsessed. One knight at the bottom right has, in the immortal words of art historian Frederick Hartt, "even managed to die in perspective."

In the far corner is the only example of Masaccio's art here (he died at 27), the *Madonna and Child with St. Anne,* which he helped his master, Masolino, paint in 1424. Masaccio's earthy realism and sharp light are evident in the figures of Mary and the Child, as well as in the topmost angel peeking down. In the center of the room is Piero della Francesca's **Portrait of Frederico da Montefeltro and Battista Sforza** 🏵️🏵️, painted around 1465 or 1470 and the only work by this remarkable Sansepolcran artist to survive in Florence. The fronts of the panels depict the famous duke of Urbino and his wife, while on the backs are horse-drawn carts symbolic of the pair's respective virtues. Piero's incredibly lucid style and modeling and the detailed Flemish-style backgrounds need no commentary, but do note he purposefully painted the husband and wife in full profile—without diluting the realism of a hooked nose and moles on the duke—and mounted them face to face, so they'll always gaze into each other's eyes.

In Fra' Angelico's *Coronation of the Virgin* (1435), the colorful amphitheater of saints gives the work great volume. Here too is Domenico Veneziano's 1445 *Madonna Enthroned with Saints,* painted with a careful geometry of architecture that nonetheless mimics the old-fashioned gold frames of medieval triptychs.

Room 8 is devoted to Filippo Lippi, with more than half a dozen works by the lecherous monk who turned out rich religious paintings with an earthy quality and a three-dimensionality that make them immediately accessible. His most famous painting here is the *Madonna and Child with Two Angels* (1455–66). Also here are a few works by Filippo's illegitimate son, Filippino. **Room 9** is an interlude of virtuoso paintings by Antonio del Pollaiolo, plus a number of large Virtues by his less-talented brother, Piero. These two masters of anatomical verisimilitude greatly influenced the young Botticelli, three of whose early works reside in the room. This introduction to Botticelli sets us up for the next room, invariably crowded with tour-bus groups.

The walls separating **Rooms 10 to 14** were knocked down in the 20th century to create one large space to accommodate the resurgent popularity of Sandro Filipepi—better known by his nickname, Botticelli ("little barrels")—master of willowy women in flowing gowns. Fourteen of his paintings line the walls, along with works by his pupil (and illegitimate son of his former teacher) Filippino Lippi and Domenico Ghirlandaio, Michelangelo's first artistic master. But everybody flocks here for just two paintings, Botticelli's *Birth of Venus* and his *Primavera* (*Allegory of Spring*). Though in later life Botticelli was influenced by the puritanical preachings of Savonarola and took to cranking out boring Madonnas, the young painter began in grand pagan style. Both paintings were commissioned between 1477 and 1483 by a Medici cousin for his private villa, and they celebrate not only Renaissance art's love of naturalism but also the humanist philosophy permeating 15th-century Florence, a neo-Platonism that united religious doctrine with ancient ideology and mythological stories.

In the ***Birth of Venus*** ⟨★★⟩, the love goddess is born of the sea on a half shell, blown to shore by the Zephyrs. Ores, a goddess of the seasons, rushes to clothe her. Some say the long-legged goddess was modeled on Simonetta Vespucci, a renowned Florentine beauty, cousin to Amerigo (the naval explorer after whom America is named) and not-so-secret lover of Giuliano de' Medici, Lorenzo the Magnificent's brother). The ***Primavera*** ⟨★★⟩ is harder to evaluate, because contemporary research indicates it may not actually be an allegory of spring influenced by the humanist poetry of Poliziano but rather a celebration of Venus, who stands in the center, surrounded by various complicated references to Virtues through mythological characters. Zephyr chases Chloris on the right, from whose union will arise Flora (scattering her flowers); the three Graces on the left are about to be struck by Cupid's blind arrows as they dance next to Mercury, who's reaching up with his caduceus stick to shoo away a miniature storm brewing. More than 500 species of plant life carpet the ground. Also check out Botticelli's *Adoration of the Magi,* where the artist painted himself in the far right side, in a great yellow robe and golden curls.

Room 15 boasts Leonardo da Vinci's ***Annunciation*** ✸✸✸, which the young artist painted in 1472 or 1475 while still in the workshop of his master, Andrea del Verrocchio; however, he was already fully developed as an artist. The solid yet light figures and *sfumato* airiness blurring the distance render remarkably life-like figures somehow suspended in a surreal dreamscape. Leonardo helped Verrocchio on the *Baptism of Christ*—most credit the artist-in-training with the angel on the far left as well as the landscape, and a few art historians think they see his hand in the figure of Jesus as well. The *Adoration of the Magi,* which Leonardo didn't get much beyond the sketching stage, shows how he could retain powerful compositions even when creating a fantasy landscape of ruinous architecture and incongruous horse battles. The room also houses works by Lorenzo di Credi and Piero di Cosimo, fellow 15th-century maestros, and a *Pietà* that shows Perugino's solid plastic style of studied simplicity. (This Umbrian master would later pass it on to his pupil Raphael.) Piero della Francesca's student Luca Signorelli painted a *Crucifixion* (ca. 1500) that has a similar modeled reality, with bits of inspired realism in the foreshortened arms of the wildly gesturing Mary Magdalene and the skull at the base of the Cross.

Uffizi officials use **Room 18, the Tribune,** as a crowd-control pressure valve. You may find yourself stuck shuffling around it slowly, staring at the mother-of-pearl discs lining the domed ceiling; studying the antique statues, such as the famous *Medici Venus* (a 1st-century B.C. Roman copy of a Greek original); and scrutinizing the Medici portraits wallpapering the room. The latter include many by the talented early baroque artist Agnolo Bronzino, whose portrait of ***Eleonora of Toledo*** ✸, wife of Cosimo I, with their son Giovanni de' Medici (1545), is particularly well worked. It shows her in a satin dress embroidered and sewn with velvet and pearls. When the Medici tombs were opened in 1857, her body was found buried in this same dress (it's now in the Pitti Palace's costume museum).

Also here is an idealized posthumous *Portrait of Cosimo il Vecchio* (1518–20) done in waxy colors by mannerist master Pontormo; the *Madonna and Child with St. John* (1527), also in this room, is more typical of his hyperrealized style. Be on the lookout also for Raphael's late *St. John the Baptist in the Desert* (1518) and mannerist Rosso Fiorentino's 1522 Angel Musician, where an insufferably cute little *putto* (cherub) plucks at an oversized lute—it's become quite the Renaissance icon in the recent spate of angel mania.

Room 19 is devoted to both Perugino, who did the luminous *Portrait of Francesco delle Opere* (1494), and Luca Signorelli, whose *Holy Family* (1490–95) was painted as a tondo set in a rectangle, with allegorical figures in the background and a torsion of the figures that were to influence Michelangelo's version (in a later room). **Room 20** is devoted to Dürer, Cranach, and other German artists who worked in Florence, while **Room 21** takes care of 16th-century Venetians Giovanni Bellini, Giorgione, and Carpaccio. In **Room 22** are Flemish and German works by Hans Holbein the Younger, Hans Memling, and others, and **Room 23** contains Andrea Mantegna's triptych of the *Adoration of the Magi, Circumcision,* and *Ascension* (1463–70), showing his excellent draftsmanship and fascination with classical architecture. Emilian artist Correggio painted three of the pieces in this room, including a *Rest on the Flight into Egypt* (1515) and the late masterpiece *Adoration of the Child* (1524).

Now we move into the west wing, still in throes of restoration following the bombing. **Room 25** is overpowered by Michelangelo's *Holy Family* 🟊🟊🟊 (1506–08), one of the few panel paintings by the great master. The glowing colors and shocking nudes in the background seem to pop off the surface, and the torsion of the figures was to be taken up as the banner of the mannerist movement. Michelangelo also designed the elaborate frame.

Room 26 is devoted to Andrea del Sarto and High Renaissance darling Raphael. Of Raphael we have the *Madonna of the Goldfinch* (1505), a work he painted in a Leonardesque style for a friend's wedding, and several important portraits, including *Pope Leo X with Cardinals Giulio de' Medici and Luigi de' Rossi* and *Pope Julius II,* as well as a famous *Self-portrait.* Del Sarto was the most important painter in Florence in the early 16th century, while Michelangelo and Raphael were off in Rome. His consciously developed mannerist style is evident in his masterful *Madonna of the Harpies* (1515–17).

Room 27 is devoted to works by Del Sarto's star mannerist pupils, Rosso Fiorentino and Pontormo, and by Pontormo's adopted son, Bronzino. Fiorentino's ***Moses Defends the Daughters of Jethro*** ✦ (1523) owes much to Michelangesque nudes but is also wholly original in the use of harsh lighting that reduces the figures to basics shapes of color.

As this book went to press, the rooms beyond this point were still being repaired and rearranged, and the exhibits may not be returned to their original order by the time you visit (consequently, the floor plan may be incorrect). Be on the lookout, though, for these masterpieces. Later mannerists such as Il Parmigianino carried the movement to its logical extremes with the almost grotesquely elongated bodies of the ***Madonna of the Long Neck*** ✦ (1534). Of the great Venetian Titian you'll see a warm full-bodied ***Flora*** ✦✦ and a poetic ***Venus of Urbino*** ✦ languishing on her bed. There's a *Death of Adonis* and *Portrait of a Woman* by the Sienese High Renaissance painter Sebastiano del Piombo, plus several works of Tintoretto, Rubens, and Rembrandt, including two *Self-portraits* by the latter, one as a youth and the other as an old man.

Caravaggio was the baroque master of *chiaroscuro*—painting with extreme harsh light and deep shadows. The Uffizi preserves his painting of the severed head of *Medusa,* a *Sacrifice of Isaac,* and his famous ***Bacchus*** ✦✦. Caravaggio's work influenced a generation of artists, including Artemisia Gentileschi, the only female painter to make a name for herself in the late Renaissance/early baroque. Artemisia was eclipsed in fame by her slightly less talented father, Orazio, and she was the victim and central figure in a sensational rape trial brought against Orazio's one-time collaborator. Among her work here is the violent *Judith Slaying Holofernes.*

Cosimo I de' Medici, after he moved to the Pitti Palace across the river in the Oltrarno, needed a way to get to and from his home and his office without mingling with the peons on the streets. So he had Giorgio Vasari build him the **Corridorio Vasariano (Vasarian Corridor)** in 1565. It took only 5 months to complete this above-ground tunnel running along the Arno, across the tops of the Ponte Vecchio shops, and then zigzagging its way to the Pitti. The corridor, hung with paintings and poked through with lots of windows, was open to visitors prior to the bombing but has since been closed for restoration and rearrangement. When it reopens, it'll probably become a showcase for all the gallery's portraits. Meanwhile, you can sometimes get permission to enter it by reserving ahead (call to get more information).

Piazzale degli Uffizi 6 (off Piazza della Signoria). ⓒ **055/23-885;** reserve tickets at
ⓒ 055/294-883. Admission 15,000L (8€, $8). Summer: Tues–Wed
8:30am–9:45pm; Thurs–Sat 8:30am–11:15pm; Sun 8:30am–7:15pm. Winter:
Tues–Sat 8:30am–9:45pm; Sun 8:30am–7:15pm. Ticket window closes 45 min.
before museum. Bus: A, B, 23, 71.

Palazzo Vecchio 🍇   Florence's imposing fortresslike town hall
was built from 1299 to 1302 on the designs of Arnolfo di Cambio,
Gothic master builder of the city. Arnolfo managed to make it solid
and impregnable-looking yet still graceful, with thin-columned
Gothic windows and two orders of crenellations—square for the
main rampart and swallow-tailed on the 313-foot- (94m) high bell
tower.

The palace was once home to the various Florentine republican
governments (and today to the municipal government). Cosimo I
and his ducal Medici family moved to the palazzo in 1540 and
engaged in massive redecoration. Michelozzo's 1453 **courtyard** just
through the door was left architecturally intact but frescoed by
Vasari with scenes of Austrian cities to celebrate the 1565 marriage
of Francesco de' Medici and Joanna of Austria. The fountain in the
middle is a facsimile of a putto holding a (very small) dolphin by
Verrocchio, who also cast the bronze weather vane being scaled by a
lion that once topped off the bell tower (replaced by a copy outside)
under the vaults leading to the ticket office.

The grand staircase leads up to the **Sala dei Cinquecento,** named
for the 500-man assembly that met here in the pre-Medici days of
the Florentine Republic and site of the greatest fresco cycle that ever
wasn't. Leonardo da Vinci was commissioned in 1503 to paint one
long wall with a battle scene celebrating a famous Florentine victory.
He was always trying new methods and materials and decided to
mix wax into his pigments. Leonardo had finished painting part of
the wall, but it wasn't drying fast enough, so he brought in braziers
stoked with hot coals to try to hurry the process. As others watched
in horror, the wax in the fresco melted under the intense heat and
the colors ran down the walls to puddle on the floor. Michelangelo
never even got past making the preparatory drawings for the fresco
he was supposed to paint on the opposite wall—Pope Julius II called
him to Rome to paint the Sistine Chapel, and the master's sketches
were destroyed by eager young artists who came to study them and
took away scraps. Eventually, the bare walls were covered by Vasari
and assistants in 1563–65 with blatantly subservient frescoes exalt-
ing Cosimo I de' Medici and his dynasty.

Buying Discount Sightseeing Coupons

For 15,000L (8€, $8), the city sells a "carnet" of 10 coupons (good for 6 months) that comes with a guidebook. Each coupon gets you 50% off admission to one of the following: Palazzo Vecchio, Museo di Santa Maria Novella, Museo Bardini, Museo di Firenze Com'Era, Cenacolo di Santo Spirito, Raccolta della Ragione, Cappella Brancacci, Museo Stibbert, and Museo Marino Marini.

Off the corner of the room (to the right as you enter) is the **Studiolo di Francesco I,** a claustrophobic study in which Cosimo's eldest son and heir performed his alchemy and science experiments and where baroque paintings hide secret cupboards. Against the wall of the Sala dei Cinquecento, opposite the door you enter, is Michelangelo's statue of *Victory* ✸, carved from 1533 to 1534 for the Julius II tomb but later donated to the Medici. Its extreme torsion—the way the body twists and spirals upward—was to be a great influence on the mannerist movement.

The first series of rooms on the second floor is the **Quartiere degli Elementi,** again frescoed by Vasari. The **Terrazza di Saturno,** in the corner, has a view over the Uffizi to the hills across the Arno. A small room nearby contains the original Verrocchio *Putto Holding a Dolphin* statue removed from the fountain in the courtyard. Crossing the balcony overlooking the Sala dei Cinquecento, you enter the **Apartments of Eleonora di Toledo,** decorated for Cosimo's Spanish wife. Her small private chapel is a masterpiece of mid-16th-century painting by Bronzino. Farther on, under the sculpted ceiling of the **Sala dei Gigli,** are Domenico Ghirlandaio's fresco of *St. Zenobius Enthroned* with ancient Roman heroes, and Donatello's original *Judith and Holofernes* ✸ bronze (1455), one of his last works. Next door to the Cancelleria, Machiavelli's old office, is the **Guardaroba,** painted from 1563 to 1565 with surprisingly accurate (for the time) maps of every corner of the known world by Fra' Egnazio Danti.

During the summer evening hours, the following sections, normally closed, are open: the **Loeser Collections,** with paintings by Pietro Lorenzetti and Bronzino and sculptures by Tino di Camaino and Jacopo Sansovino, and, perhaps more fun, the outdoor **Balustrade** running around the roof behind the crenellations—it offers a unique panorama of the city and the piazza below.

Piazza della Signoria. © **055/276-8465** or 055/276-8325. Admission 11,000L (6€, $6). Fri–Sat and Mon–Wed 9am–7pm; Thurs 9am–2pm; Sun 8am–1pm. June–Sept also sometimes Mon, Wed, and Fri–Sat 8–11pm (sections normally closed are open, so admission is about 15,000L, 8€, $8). Bus: A, B, 23, 71.

Ponte Vecchio (Old Bridge) 🛠🛠🛠   The oldest and most famous bridge across the Arno, the Ponte Vecchio we know today was built in 1345 by Taddeo Gaddi to replace an earlier version. The characteristic overhanging shops have lined the bridge at least since the 12th century. In the 16th century, it was home to butchers until Cosimo I moved into the Palazzo Pitti across the river. He couldn't stand the stench as he crossed the bridge from on high in the Corridorio Vasariano (see above) every day, so he evicted the meat cutters and moved in the classier gold- and silversmiths, tradesmen who occupy the bridge to this day.

A bust of the most famous Florentine goldsmith, the swashbuckling autobiographer and *Perseus* sculptor Benvenuto Cellini, stands off to the side of the bridge's center, in a small piazza overlooking the Arno. From this vantage point Mark Twain, spoiled by the Mighty Mississippi, once wryly commented, "It is popular to admire the Arno. It is a great historical creek, with four feet in the channel and some scows floating about. It would be a very plausible river if they would pump some water into it. They call it a river, and they honestly think it is a river . . . . They even help out the delusion by building bridges over it. I do not see why they are too good to wade."

The Ponte Vecchio's fame saved it in 1944 from the Nazis, who had orders to blow up all the bridges before retreating out of Florence as Allied forces advanced. They couldn't bring themselves to reduce this span to rubble—so they blew up the ancient buildings on either end instead to block it off. The Arno flood of 1966 wasn't so discriminating, however, and severely damaged the shops. Apparently, a private night watchman saw the waters rising alarmingly and called many of the goldsmiths at home, who rushed to remove their valuable stock before it got washed away.

Via Por Santa Maria/Via Guicciardini. Bus: B, D.

Museo di Storia della Scienza (Science Museum) 🛠   The mainframe computer and multifunction calculator don't hold a candle to this collection's beautifully engraved intricate mechanical instruments. Galileo and his ilk practiced a science that was an art form of the highest aesthetic order. The cases display such beauties as a mechanical calculator from 1664—a gleaming bronze sandwich of engraved disks and dials—and an architect's compass and plumb disguised as a dagger, complete with sheath.

In the field of astronomy, the museum has the lens with which Galileo discovered four of the moons of Jupiter (which he promptly and prudently named after his Medici patrons) and, alongside telescopes of all sizes and complexity, a tiny "lady's telescope" made of ivory that once came in a box of beauty products. There's also a somewhat grisly room devoted to medicine, with disturbingly realistic wax models of just about everything that can go wrong during childbirth.

Other scientific oddities include a perpetual-motion machine and an automatic writer; dual portraits that show either husband or wife, depending on your angle of view; and watch-sized sundials a la Fred Flintstone. And what Italian institution would be complete without a holy relic? In this case, it's the middle finger of Galileo's right hand, swiped while he was en route to reinterment in Santa Croce. He was allowed burial in a Christian church only in the 18th century, after he was posthumously vindicated against the Inquisition for supporting a heliocentric view of the universe.

Piazza dei Giudici 1 (next to the Uffizi at the Arno end of Via dei Castellani). ℭ **055/239-8876.** Admission 12,000L (6€, $6) adults, 7,500L (3.90€, $3.75) ages 15–25, 5,000L (2.60€, $2.50) ages 6–14 and over 65, under 6 free. Mon–Sat 9:30am–1pm; Mon, Wed, and Fri 2–5pm. Bus: B, 23, 71.

Orsanmichele ✶✶   This tall structure halfway down Via dei Calzaiuoli looks more like a Gothic warehouse than a church—which is exactly what it was, built as a granary/grain market in 1337. After a miraculous image of the Madonna appeared on a column inside, however, the lower level was turned into a chapel. The city's merchant guilds each undertook the task of decorating one of the outside nichelike Gothic tabernacles around the lower level with a statue of their guild's patron saint. Masters like Ghiberti, Donatello, Verrocchio, and Giambologna all cast or carved masterpieces to set here. Since 1984, these have been removed and are being replaced by casts as the originals are slowly cleaned and exhibited up on the second story (see below).

In the chapel's dark interior (emerged in 1999 from a long restoration and entered around the "back" side on Via dell'Arte della Lana) are recently restored 14th- to 16th-century paintings by the likes of Lorenzo di Credi and Il Poppi. The elaborate Gothic *Tabernacle* ✶ (1349–59) by Andrea Orcagna looks something like a miniature church, covered with statuettes, enamels, inset colored marbles and glass, and reliefs. It protects a luminous 1348 *Madonna and Child* painted by Giotto's student Bernardo Daddi. The prominent statue of the *Madonna, Child, and St. Anne* to its left is by Francesco da Sangallo (1522).

Across Via dell'Arte della Lana from the Orsanmichele's main entrance is the 1308 Palazzo dell'Arte della Lana. This Gothic palace was home to medieval Florence's most powerful body, the guild of wool merchants, which employed about one-third of Florence in the 13th and 14th centuries. Up the stairs inside you can cross over the hanging walkway to the first floor (American second floor) of Orsanmichele. These are the old granary rooms, now housing a **museum of the statues** 𝒢 that once surrounded the exterior. A few are still undergoing restoration, but eight of the original sculptures are here, well labeled, including Donatello's marble *St. Mark* (1411–13); Ghiberti's bronze *St. John the Baptist* (1413–16), the first life-size bronze of the Renaissance; and Verrocchio's *Incredulity of St. Thomas* (1473–83). Upstairs are some nifty city views and 40 decaying medieval statuettes from the Gothic pinnacles outside.

Via Arte della Lana 1/Via de' Calzaiuoli. ℭ 055/284-944. Free admission. Church: daily 9am–noon and 4–6pm. Museum: daily 9–9:45am, 10–10:45am, and 11–11:45am. Both closed the 1st and last Mon of month. Bus: A.

Museo Nazionale del Bargello (Bargello Museum) 𝒢𝒢

Inside this 1255 Gothic palazzo is Florence's premier sculpture museum, with works by Michelangelo, the della Robbias, and Donatello. The palace was built as civic offices, then used as the home of the Capitano del Popolo and then the city's *podestà* (a minor noble brought in from a different town to rule Florence for a set period of time), and later became the city's prison.

In the old **armory** are 16th-century works, including some of Michelangelo's earliest sculptures. Carved by a 22-year-old Michelangelo while he was visiting Rome, ***Bacchus*** 𝒢𝒢 (1497) was obviously inspired by the classical antiquities he studied there but is also imbued with his own irrepressible Renaissance realism—here is a (young) God of Wine who's actually drunk, reeling back on unsteady knees and holding the cup aloft with a distinctly tipsy wobble. Michelangelo polished and finished this marble in the traditional manner, but in 1503–05, soon after finishing his famous *David* with a high polish, he carved the ***Pitti Tondo*** 𝒢 here, a *schiacciato* Madonna and Child scene in which the artist began using the textures of the partially worked marble itself to convey his artistic message. One of his weaker works here is the so-called *Apollo-David* (art historians can't agree on which hero the unfinished work was meant to be), but the master is back in top form with the bust of *Brutus* (ca. 1539). Some people like to see in this sculpture an idealized portrait of Michelangelo himself; a more accurate and less contentious representation sits nearby, the famous and oft-cast bronze bust of *Michelangelo* by his pupil Daniele da Volterra. Also in this room are works by Benvenuto Cellini, including a battered *Narcissus* and his first cast bronze, a portrait bust of *Cosimo I* (1545–48). Seek out Giambologna's *Flying Mercury* (ca. 1564), looking for all the world as if he's on the verge of taking off from the ground—justifiably one of this mannerist's masterpieces.

The palazzo's inner **courtyard**—one of the few medieval cortile in Florence to survive in more-or-less its original shape—is studded with the coats of arms of various past *podestà* and other notables. The grand stairwell leads up to a second-story loggia filled with a flock of whimsical bronze birds cast by Giambologna for the Medici's gardens. The doorway leads into the old **Salone del Consiglio Generale (General Council Room)** , a vast space with a high ceiling filled with glazed terra-cotta Madonnas by Luca della Robbia and his clan, and some of the most important sculptures of the early Renaissance.

Donatello dominates the room, starting with a mischievously smiling *Cupid* (ca. 1430–40). Nearby is his polychrome bust of *Niccolò da Uzzano,* a bit of hyperrealism next to two much more delicate busts of elfin-featured characters by Desiderio da Settignano. Donatello sculpted the *Marzocco,* lion symbol of the Florentine Republic, out of pietra serena between 1418 and 1420. The marble *David* (1408) is an early Donatello, but the bronze **David** (1440–50) beyond it is a much more mature piece, the first freestanding nude since antiquity. The figure is a nubile, almost erotic youth, with a shy, detached air that has little to do with the giant severed head at his feet. Against the far wall is **St. George** , carved in 1416 for a niche of Orsanmichele. The relief below it of the saint slaying his dragon is an early example of the sculptor's patented *schiacciato* technique, using thinly etched lines and perspective to create great depth in a very shallow space.

In the back right corner of this room are two bronze relief panels by Brunelleschi and Ghiberti of the *Sacrifice of Isaac,* finalists in the famous 1401 competition for the commission to cast the Baptistery's doors. Ghiberti's panel won for the greater dynamism and flowing action in his version.

Out the other end of the room is the **Islamic Collection,** a testament to Florence's wide and profitable trade network. Decorative arts from the Roman era through the 16th century fill the long corridor, at the end of which is the small **Cappella Maddalena,** where condemned prisoners spent their last moments praying for their souls; it was frescoed by Giotto's studio. A perpendicular corridor houses the largest collection of ivories in the world, from the 5th to 17th centuries. Next to the staircase at the end is a room of 16th-century **majolica porcelain** from Urbino, Faenza, and Florence, and Moorish ceramics from Spain.

Upstairs are rooms with glazed terra cottas by Andrea and Giovanni della Robbia and another room devoted to the sculptural production of Leonardo da Vinci's teacher Verrocchio, including yet another *David* (1465), a haughty youth with a tousle of hair inspired by the Donatello version downstairs. Off the Andrea della Robbia room is a hall filled with hundreds of small bronzes by Antonio del Pollaiolo, Baccio Bandinelli, and especially Giambologna, who was a master of this fashion in High Renaissance art.

Via del Proconsolo 4. ☎ 055/238-8606; reserve tickets at ☎ 055/294-883. Admission 8,000L (4.15€, \$4). Daily 8:30am–1:50pm. Closed 2nd and 4th Mon and 1st, 3rd, and 5th Sun of each month. Bus: A, 14, 23.

Badia Fiorentina   The slender pointed bell tower of this Benedictine abbey founded in A.D. 978 is one of the landmarks of the Florentine skyline. Sadly, the bells Dante wrote of in his *Paradiso* no longer toll the hours. Serious structural problems have silenced the tower, though the thick scaffolding in which it has been wrapped for several years is coming down. Arnolfo di Cambio was responsible for a late Romanesque overhaul of the church in 1284 to 1310, but Matteo Segaloni completely reconstructed the interior in the 17th century.

In the now-baroque interior, some say Dante first laid eyes on his beloved Beatrice, and Boccaccio, of *Decameron* fame, used to lecture on Dante's Divine Comedy here. The church's most arresting sight is a 1485 Filippino Lippi painting of the *Madonna Appearing to St. Bernard.* The box to shed light on it parcels out a measly 10 seconds for each coin, so feed it only 50L pieces. For a 1,000L, .50€, (50¢) "donation," the sacristan will throw on the lights to the trompe-l'oeil ceiling.

Via Dante Alighieri and Via del Proconsolo. ☎ **055/287-389.** Free admission. Thurs–Tues 5–7pm (sometimes also in the morning). Bus: A, 14, 23.

Santa Trínita ⟡ Beyond Bernardo Buontalenti's late-16th-century **facade** lies a dark church, rebuilt in the 14th century but founded by the Vallombrosans before 1177. The third chapel on the right has what remains of the detached frescoes by Spinello Aretino (pushbutton light), which were found under Lorenzo Monaco's excellent 1422 frescoes covering the next chapel down.

In the right transept, Domenico Ghirlandaio frescoed the **Cappella Sassetti** ⟡ in 1483 with a cycle on the *Life of St. Francis* (coin-op lights), but true to form he set all the scenes against Florentine backdrops and peopled them with portraits of the notables of the day. The most famous is *Francis Receiving the Order from Pope Honorius,* which in this version takes place under an arcade on the north side of Piazza della Signoria—the Loggia dei Lanzi is featured in the middle, and on the left is the Palazzo Vecchio. (The Uffizi between them hadn't been built yet.) It's also full of contemporary portraits: In the little group on the far right, the unhandsome man with the light red cloak is Lorenzo the Magnificent.

The chapel to the right of the main altar houses the miraculous **Crucifix** that once hung in San Miniato al Monte. One day the nobleman Giovanni Gualberto was storming up the hillside in a rage, on his way to wreak revenge on his brother's murderer. Gualberto paused at San Miniato and after some reflection decided to pardon the assassin, whereupon this crucifix bowed its head in approval. Gualberto went on to found the Vallombrosan order of monks, who later established this church. In the second chapel to the left of the altar is a **tomb** carved by Luca della Robbia (1454–57).

The granite column on the **piazza** outside came from the Baths of Caracalla in Rome. The south end of the piazza leads to the **Ponte Santa Trínita,** one of Italy's most graceful bridges. In 1567, Ammannati built a span here that was set with four 16th-century statues of the seasons in honor of the marriage of Cosimo II. After the Nazis blew up the bridge in 1944, it was rebuilt, and all was set into place again—save the head on the statue of Spring, which remained lost until a team dredging the river in 1961 found it by accident. From the bridge you get a great view upriver of the Ponte Vecchio and downriver of the **Ponte alla Carraia** (another postwar reconstruction), where in 1304 so many people gathered to watch a floating production of Dante's *Inferno* that it collapsed and all were drowned. Florentine wits were quick to point out that all the people who went to see Hell that day found what they were looking for.

Piazza Santa Trínita. ℂ **055/216-912.** Free admission. Mon–Sat 8am–noon; daily 4–7pm. Bus: A, B, 6, 11, 36, 37, 68.

3 Around San Lorenzo & the Mercato Centrale

The church of San Lorenzo (below) is practically lost behind the leather stalls and souvenir carts of Florence's vast **San Lorenzo street market** (see chapter 6, "Shopping"). In fact, the hawking of wares and bustle of commerce is what characterizes all the streets of this neighborhood, centered around both the church and the nearby **Mercato Centrale food market.** This is a colorful scene, but one of the most pickpocket-happy in the city, so be wary.

San Lorenzo ⟨⟨   A rough brick anti-facade and the undistinguished stony bulk of a building surrounded by the stalls of the leather market hide what is most likely the oldest church in Florence, founded in A.D. 393. San Lorenzo was the city's cathedral until the bishop's seat moved to Santa Reparata (later to become the Duomo) in the 7th century. More important, it was the Medici family's parish church, and as those famous bankers began to accumulate their vast fortune, they started a tradition of lavishing it on this church that lasted until the clan died out in the 18th century. Visiting the entire church complex at once is tricky: Though interconnected, the church proper, the Old Sacristy, and the Laurentian Library have different open hours. The Medici tombs, listed separately below, have a separate entrance around the back of the church and have still different hours.

The first thing Giovanni di Bicci de' Medici, founder of the family fortune, did for the church was hire Brunelleschi to tune up the **interior,** rebuilding according to the architect's plans in 1426. The second chapel on the right aisle contains a mannerist *Marriage of the Virgin* by Rosso Fiorentino. At the end of the aisle is a Desiderio da Settignano marble tabernacle that's a mastery of *schiacciato* relief and carefully incised perspective. Across the aisle is one of the two bronze 1460 **pulpits** ⟨⟨⟨⟨—the other is across the nave—that were Donatello's last works. His patron and the first great consolidator of Medici power, which at this early stage still showed great concern for protecting the interests of the people, was Cosimo il Vecchio, Lorenzo the Magnificent's grandfather. Cosimo, whose wise behind-the-scenes rule made him popular with the Florentines, died in 1464 and is buried in front of the high altar. The plaque marking the spot is simply inscribed "Pater Patriae"—father of his homeland.

Off the left transept is the **Sagrestia Vecchia (Old Sacristy)** ⟨⟨, one of Brunelleschi's purest pieces of early Renaissance architecture. The terra-cotta tondo decorations were all designed by Donatello, who may also have done the bronze doors with figures of the

Apostles and Martyrs (though some now believe Michelozzo to be the sculptor). In the center of the chapel Cosimo il Vecchio's parents, Giovanni di Bicci de' Medici and his wife, Piccarda Bueri, rest in peace.

The transept chapel to your right as you exit this sacristy holds an *Annunciation* by Filippo Lippi and a neoclassical monument to Donatello, who died in 1466 and, according to his final wishes, is buried in the vault below, near his old friend and patron Cosimo il Vecchio.

Around the corner, on the wall of the left aisle, expands Bronzino's huge fresco of the ***Martyrdom of San Lorenzo*** ✿. The 3rd-century namesake saint of this church, San Lorenzo was a flinty early Christian and the treasurer of the Roman church. When commanded by the Romans to hand over the church's wealth, Lorenzo appeared before Emperor Valerian's prefect with "thousands" of sick, poor, and crippled people saying "Here is all the church's treasure." The Romans weren't amused and decided to martyr him on a gridiron over hot coals. Feisty to the last, at one point while Lorenzo lay there roasting he called out to his tormentors through gritted teeth, "Turn me over, I'm done on this side."

Near this fresco is the entrance to the cloister and just inside it a stairwell to the right leading up to the **Biblioteca Laurenziana (Laurentian Library)** ✿✿, closed indefinitely in 1999 until "urgent maintenance" is completed. Michelangelo designed this in 1524 to house the Medici's manuscript collection, and it stands as one of the most brilliant works of mannerist architecture. The vestibule is a whacked-out riff on the Renaissance, all *pietra serena* and white plaster walls like a good Brunelleschi piece, but turned inside out. There are phony piers running into each other in the corners, pilaster strips that support nothing, and brackets that exist for no reason. On the whole, however, it manages to remain remarkably coherent. Its star feature is a *pietra serena* flight of curving stairs flowing out from the entrance to the reading room. Michelangelo designed the latter as well, right down to the decorative details, but kept it a much more sober composition. Out the other end of the reading room, a small set of rooms displays some of the old Medici manuscripts.

Piazza San Lorenzo. 𝄪 **055/216-634.** Free admission. Church: daily 7am–noon and 3:30–6:30pm. Old Sacristy: (usually) Sept–July Mon, Wed, Fri, and Sat 10–11:45am; Tues and Thurs 4–5:45pm. Laurentian Library: Mon–Sat 9am–1pm. Bus: 1, 6, 7, 11, 14, 17, 23, 67, 68, 70, 71.

Cappelle Medicee (Medici Chapels) 🕊🕊 When Michelangelo built the New Sacristy (see below) between 1520 and 1533 (finished by Vasari in 1556), it was to be a tasteful monument to Lorenzo the Magnificent and his generation of fairly pleasant Medici. When work got underway on the Chapel of the Princes in 1604, it was to become one of the world's most god-awful and arrogant memorials, dedicated to the grand dukes, some of Florence's most decrepit tyrants. The **Cappella dei Principi (Chapel of the Princes)** 🕊 is an exercise in bad taste, a mountain of cut marbles and semiprecious stones—jasper, alabaster, mother-of-pearl, agate, and the like—slathered onto the walls and ceiling with no regard for composition and still less for chromatic unity. The pouring of ducal funds into this monstrosity began in 1604 and lasted until the rarely conscious Gian Gastone de' Medici drank himself to death in 1737 without an heir—but teams kept doggedly at the thing, and they were still finishing the floor in 1962. The tombs of the grand dukes in this massive marble mistake were designed by Pietro Tacca in the 17th century, and off to the left and right of the altar are small treasuries full of gruesome holy relics in silver-bedecked cases. The dome of the structure, seen from the outside, is one of Florence's landmarks, a kind of infant version of the Duomo's.

Michelangelo's **Sagrestia Nuova (New Sacristy)** 🕊🕊, built to jibe with Brunelleschi's Old Sacristy in San Lorenzo proper, is much calmer. (An architectural tidbit: The windows in the dome taper as they get near the top to fool you into thinking the dome is higher.) Michelangelo was supposed to produce three tombs here (perhaps four) but ironically got only the two less important ones done. So Lorenzo de' Medici the Magnificent—wise ruler of his city, poet of note, grand patron of the arts, and moneybags behind much of the Renaissance—ended up with a mere inscription of his name next to his brother Giuliano's on a plain marble slab against the entrance wall. Admittedly, they did get one genuine Michelangelo sculpture to decorate their slab, a *Madonna and Child* that's perhaps the master's most beautiful version of the theme (the other two statues are later works by less talented sculptors).

On the left wall of the sacristy is Michelangelo's ***Tomb of Lorenzo*** 🕊, duke of Urbino (and Lorenzo the Magnificent's grandson), whose seated statue symbolizes the contemplative life. Below him on the elongated curves of the tomb stretch *Dawn* (female) and *Dusk* (male), a pair of Michelangelo's most famous sculptures, where he uses both high polish and rough cutting to impart strength, texture, and psychological suggestion to the allegorical works. This pair mirrors the similarly fashioned and equally important *Day* (male) and *Night* (female) across the way. The latter two lounge underneath the statue of *Giuliano, duke of Nemours*, a son of Lorenzo the Magnificent whose effigy symbolizes the active life. One additional point *Dawn* and *Night* brings out is that Michelangelo really wasn't too adept at the female body—he just produced softer, less muscular men with slightly elongated midriffs and breasts sort of tacked on at funny angles.

Piazza Madonna degli Aldobrandini (behind San Lorenzo, where Via Faenza and Via del Giglio meet). ✆ **055/238-8602.** Admission 11,000L (6€, $6). Daily 8:30am–1:50pm. Closed 1st, 3rd, and 5th Mon and 2nd and 4th Sun of each month. Bus: 1, 6, 7, 11, 14, 17, 23, 67, 68, 70, 71.

Palazzo Medici-Riccardi ✦   The Palazzo Medici-Riccardi was built by Michelozzo in 1444 for Cosimo de' Medici il Vecchio; it's the prototype Florentine palazzo, on which the more overbearing Strozzi and Pitti palaces were later modeled. It remained the Medici private home until Cosimo I more officially declared his power as duke by moving to the city's traditional civic brain center, the Palazzo Vecchio. A door off the right of the entrance courtyard leads up a staircase to the **Cappella dei Magi,** the oldest chapel to survive from a private Florentine palace; its walls are covered with gorgeously dense and colorful Benozzo Gozzoli **frescoes** (1459–63). Rich as tapestries, the walls depict an extended *Journey of the Magi* to see the Christ child, who's being adored by Mary in the altarpiece (a 15th-century copy of the Filippo Lippi original, which is now in Berlin).

Gozzoli is at his decorative best here, inheriting an attention to minute detail in plants and animals from his old teacher Fra' Angelico, adding in a liberal supply of Giottesque rock outcroppings and crazy Dr. Seussian trees, and painting in portraits of just about any contemporary figure he could think of. The last magus, a young pup in gold with flaxen locks, is a highly idealized portrait of Lorenzo the Magnificent.

Another door on the right of the entrance corridor leads up to an anteroom with a soft and touching painting of the *Madonna and Child* by Filippo Lippi. Beyond this is a baroque gallery whose ceiling was trompe-l'oeil frescoed by Luca Giordano with an *Apotheosis of the Second Medici Dynasty.*

Via Cavour 1. ✆ **055/276-0340.** Admission 8,000L (4.15€, $4) adults, 5,000L (2.60€, $2.50) ages 6–12. Thurs–Tues 9am–7pm. Number of visitors limited; arrive early or call to book a time to visit. Bus: 1, 6, 7, 11, 14, 17, 23, 67, 68, 70, 71.

4 On or Near Piazza Santa Maria Novella

Piazza Santa Maria Novella boasts patches of grass and a central fountain. The two squat obelisks, resting on the backs of Giambologna tortoises, once served as the turning posts for the "chariot" races held here from the 16th to the mid–19th century. However, these days the piazza sees more action as a roving ground for the few Gypsies picking tourists' pockets in Florence and the hangout for the city's economically depressed small immigrant population and even smaller cache of itinerants. Several bars and pubs have tried to infuse the area with some life, but the night still leans toward the seedy around here.

Santa Maria Novella 🏛🏛   Of all Florence's major churches, the home of the Dominicans is the only one with an original **facade** 🏛 that matches its era of greatest importance. The lower Romanesque half was started in the 14th century by architect Fra' Jacopo Talenti, who had just finished building the church itself (started in 1246). Leon Battista Alberti finished the facade, adding a classically inspired Renaissance top that not only went seamlessly with the lower half but also created a Cartesian plane of perfect geometry.

The church's interior underwent a massive restoration in the late 1990s, returning Gioto's restored *Crucifix* to pride of place, hanging in the nave's center—and becoming the first church in Florence to charge admission. Against the second pillar on the left of the nave is the pulpit from which Galileo was denounced for his heretical theory that Earth revolved around the Sun. Just past the pulpit, on the left wall, is **Masaccio's *Trinità*** 🏛🏛🏛 (ca. 1428), the first painting in the world to use perfect linear mathematical perspective. Florentine citizens and artists flooded in to see the fresco when it was unveiled, many remarking in awe that the coffered ceiling seemed to punch a hole back into space, creating a chapel out of a flat wall.

The transept is filled with spectacularly frescoed chapels. The far right **Cappella dei Bardi** is a bit confusing, with 14th-century frescoes covering over parts of earlier ones. The lunette frescoes of the *Madonna,* however, were probably painted in 1285 by Cimabue. The chapel to the right of the high altar is the **Cappella di Filippo Strozzi.** Strozzi commissioned Filippino Lippi to fresco it in 1486, but the artist didn't finish until 1502, after a trip to Rome that heavily influenced him toward an increased classicism—consequently, these works have an odd, almost antique look.

The **sanctuary** ⚿ behind the main altar was frescoed after 1485 by Domenico Ghirlandaio with the help of his assistants and apprentices, probably including a very young Michelangelo. The left wall is covered with a cycle on *The Life of the Virgin* and the right wall with the *Life of St. John the Baptist.* The works have a highly polished decorative quality and are less biblical stories than snapshots of the era's fashions and personages, full of portraits of the Tornabuoni family who commissioned them.

The **Cappella Gondi** to the left of the high altar contains the *Crucifix* carved by Brunelleschi to show his buddy Donatello how it should be done (see the review on Santa Croce later in this chapter for the story). The chapel next to it (also named the Cappella Gondi) is a disconcerting switch over to the late Renaissance, with a cupola frescoed by Alessandro Allori and a painting by Bronzino over the altar. At the end of the left transept is a different **Cappella Strozzi,** covered with restored **frescoes** ⚿ (1357) by Nardo di Cione, early medieval casts of thousands where the Saved mill about Paradise on the left and the Damned stew in a Dantean inferno on the right.

Piazza Santa Maria Novella. ✆ 055/215-918. 5,000L (2.60€, $2.50) adults, 3,000L (1.55€, $1.50) ages 12–18. Mon–Thurs and Sat 9:30am–5pm; Fri and Sun 1–5pm. Bus: A, 6, 11, 12, 36, 37, 68.

Museo di Santa Maria Novella ⚿   The cloisters of Santa Maria Novella's convent are open to the public as a museum. The **Chiostro Verde,** with a cypress-surrounded fountain and chirping birds, is named for the greenish tint in the pigment used by Paolo Uccello in his **frescoes** ⚿⚿. His works line the right wall of the first walkway; the most famous is the confusing, somewhat disturbing first scene you come to, where the *Flood and Recession of the Flood and the Drunkenness and Sacrifice of Noah* (1446) are all squeezed onto one panel as the story lines are piled atop one another and Noah appears several times. The two giant wooden walls on either side are meant to be the Ark, shown both before and after the Flood, seen in extreme, distorting perspective.

The **Cappella degli Spagnoli (Spanish Chapel)** ⚿ got its name when it became the private chapel of Eleonora of Toledo, recently arrived in Florence to be Cosimo de' Medici's bride. The pretty chapel was entirely frescoed by Andrea da Firenze and his assistants in a kind of half Florentine–half Sienese style around 1365. On the right wall is a complex scene showing an *Allegory of the Dominican Order,* at the base of which St. Dominic lets loose black-and-white spotted dogs to attack wolves and foxes (representing heretics). The dogs are a kind of inside joke: The Dominicans wore piebald robes, and their name could be written in Latin as *Domini canes*, or "hounds of the Lord." On the far left of the scene is a huge artists' conception of how the finished Duomo would appear—considering this was 55 years before Brunelleschi even started his dome, Andrea's guess wasn't far off the mark.

Piazza Santa Maria Novella (entrance to the left of the church facade). ℂ **055/ 282-187.** Admission 5,000L (2.60€, $2.50). Sat and Mon–Thurs 9am–2pm, Sun 8am–1pm; June–Sept sometimes also Tues 8–11pm (with live Gregorian chant and Renaissance choir music; admission 10,000L, 5€ $5). Bus: A, 6, 11, 12, 36, 37, 68.

Ognissanti ⋩   Founded in 1256 by the Umiliati, a wool-weaving sect of the Benedictines whose trade helped establish this area as a textile district, the present Ognissanti was rebuilt by its new Franciscan owners in the 17th century. It has the earliest baroque **facade** in Florence, designed by Matteo Nigetti in 1627 and rebuilt in travertine in 1872.

Ognissanti was the parish church of the Vespucci family, agents of the Medici bank in Seville. A young Domenico Ghirlandaio portrayed several of the family members in his *Madonna della Misericordia* (1470) on the second altar to the right. The lady under the Madonna's left hand may be Simonetta Vespucci, renowned beauty of her age, mistress of Giuliano de' Medici (Lorenzo's brother), and the possible model for Venus in Botticelli's *Birth of Venus*. The young man with black hair to the Madonna's right is said to be Amerigo Vespucci (1454–1512), whose letters about exploring the New World in 1499 and again from 1501 to 1502 would become so popular that a cartographer used a corruption of Amerigo's name on an influential set of maps to describe the newly discovered continent. Sorry, Columbus. The family tombstone (America's namesake rests in peace underneath) is to the left of this altar.

Between the third and fourth altars is Botticelli's fresco of a pensive *St. Augustine in His Study* (1480), a much more intense work

---

⌒ Tips Seeing David

The wait to get in to see *David* can be up to an hour if you didn't reserve ahead. Try getting there before the museum opens in the morning or an hour or two before closing time.

than its matching *St. Jerome in His Study* by Ghirlandaio across the nave. Botticelli, whose real name was Sandro Filipepi, is buried under a round marker in the second chapel in the right transept. Most of the rest of the church is a baroque mess of precious stonework, but in the left transept's second chapel is the habit St. Francis was wearing when he received the stigmata. You can enter the convent to the left of the church facade at Borgo Ognissanti 42. In the refectory here is Domenico Ghirlandaio's **Last Supper** 𝕮, painted in 1480 with a background heavy on Christian symbols.

Piazza Ognissanti. © 055/239-8700. Free admission. Church: daily 8am–noon and 4–6:30pm. Convent: Mon, Tues, and Sat 9am–noon. Bus: B, D, 12.

5 Near San Marco & Santissima Annunziata

Galleria dell'Accademia (Academy Gallery) 𝕮𝕮 Though tour-bus crowds flock here just for Michelangelo's *David,* anyone with more than a day in Florence can take the time to peruse some of the Accademia's paintings as well.

The first long hall is devoted to Michelangelo and, though you pass his *Slaves* and the entrance to the painting gallery, most visitors are immediately drawn down to the far end, a tribune dominated by the most famous sculpture in the world: **Michelangelo's David** 𝕮𝕮𝕮. A hot young sculptor fresh from his success with the *Pietà* in Rome, Michelangelo offered in 1501 to take on a slab of marble that had already been worked on by another sculptor (who had taken a chunk out of one side before declaring it too strangely shaped to use). The huge slab had been lying around the Duomo's workyards so long it earned a nickname, *Il Gigante* (the Giant), so it was with a twist of humor that Michelangelo, only 29 years old, finished in 1504 a Goliath-size David for the city.

There was originally a vague idea that the statue would become part of the Duomo, but Florence's republican government soon wheeled it down to stand on Piazza della Signoria in front of the Palazzo Vecchio to symbolize the defeated tyranny of the Medici, who had been ousted a decade before (but would return with a vengeance). During a 1527 anti-Medicean siege on the palazzo, a bench thrown at the attackers from one of the windows hit David's left arm, which reportedly came crashing down on a farmer's toe. (A young Giorgio Vasari came scurrying out to gather all the pieces for safekeeping, despite the riot going on around him, and the arm was later reconstituted.) Even the sculpture's 1873 removal to the Accademia to save it from the elements (a copy stands in its place) hasn't kept it entirely safe—in 1991, a man threw himself on the statue and began hammering at the right foot, dislodging several toes. The foot was repaired, and *David*'s Plexiglas shield went up.

The hall leading up to *David* is lined with perhaps Michelangelo's most fascinating works, the four famous *nonfiniti* ("unfinished") **Slaves,** or **Prisoners** ✶✶✶. Like no others, these statues symbolize Michelangelo's theory that sculpture is an "art that takes away superfluous material." The great master saw a true sculpture as something that was already inherent in the stone, and all it needed was a skilled chisel to free it from the extraneous rock. That certainly seems to be the case here, as we get a private glimpse into Michelangelo's working technique: how he began by carving the abdomen and torso, going for the gut of the sculpture and bringing that to life first so it could tell him how the rest should start to take form. Whether he intended the statues to look the way they do now or in fact left them only half done has been debated by art historians to exhaustion. The result, no matter what the sculptor's intentions, is remarkable, a symbol of the master's great art and personal views on craft as his Slaves struggle to break free of their chipped stone prisons.

Nearby, in a similar mode, is a statue of **St. Matthew** ✶✶ Michelangelo began carving (1504–08) as part of a series of Apostles he was at one point going to complete for the Duomo. (The *Pietà* at the end of the corridor on the right is by one of Michelangelo's students, not the master as was once thought.)

Off this hall of *Slaves* is the first wing of the painting gallery, which includes a panel, possibly from a wedding chest, known as the **Cassone Adimari** ✶, painted by Lo Scheggia in the 1440s. It shows the happy couple's promenade to the Duomo, with the green-and-white marbles of the Baptistery prominent in the background. Also here are an *Adoration of the Child* (1480–90) by Lorenzo di Credi that exhibits a strong Flemish influence and a famous *Virgin of the Sea* (1475–80) by Botticelli or someone in his bottega (perhaps Filippino Lippi).

The final large room of this gallery (formerly the first room of the museum) is centered on Giambologna's final plaster model for the *Rape of the Sabines*—though rumor has it the actual, final statue, recently removed from the Logia dei Lanzi for restoration, will eventually be placed here. A classic mannerist sculpture, its spiraling figures invite you to walk all the way around the figure—you're presented with new scenes at every angle. In fact, Giambologna designed the work so you literally can't appreciate it fully from one viewpoint alone. Also in this room are Perugino's *Assumption* (1500), featuring a couple of pregnant-looking angels, and a *Descent from the Cross,* on which he collaborated with Filippino Lippi. From here, return to *David.*

In the wings off *David's* tribune are large paintings by Michelangelo's contemporaries, mannerists over whom he had a very strong influence—they even say Michelangelo provided the original drawing from which Pontormo painted his amorous *Venus and Cupid.* Off the end of the left wing is a long 19th-century hall crowded wall to wall and stacked floor to ceiling with **plaster casts** of hundreds of sculptures and busts—the Accademia, after all, is what it sounds like: an academy for budding young artists, founded in 1784 as an offshoot of the Academy of Art Design that dates from Michelangelo's time (1565).

As you move toward the exit, you'll pass the three **Byzantine Rooms** of the painting gallery, where hangs Pacino da Buonaguida's complexly theological *Tree of the Cross* (ca. 1310). Upstairs are more paintings, including Andrea Orcagna's *Pentecost,* a 16th-century Russian panel covered with tiny thumbnail portraits of hundreds of saints, and the violently disturbing colors of a 15th-century *Coronation of the Virgin* by Straus, the so-called Master of the Madonna. The museum is busy installing a collection of antique musical instruments featuring violins made by Stradivarius.

Via Ricasoli 60. © **055/238-8612** or 055/238-8609; reserve tickets at © **055/ 294-883**. Admission 12,000L (6€, $6). Tues–Sat 8:30am–6:50pm; Sun 8:30am–1:50pm. Bus: 1, 6, 7, 10, 11, 17, 20, 25, 31, 32, 33, 67, 68, 70.

San Marco ⭒⭒   In 1437, Cosimo de' Medici il Vecchio, grandfather of Lorenzo the Magnificent, had Michelozzo convert a medieval monastery here into a new home for the Dominicans, in which Cosimo also founded Europe's first public library. From 1491 until he was burned at the stake on Piazza della Signoria in 1498, this was the home base of puritanical preacher Girolamo Savonarola. The monastery's most famous friar, though, was early Renaissance painter Fra' Angelico, and he left many of his finest works, devotional images painted with the technical skill and minute detail of a miniaturist or an illuminator but on altarpiece scale. While his works tended to be transcendently spiritual, Angelico was also prone to filling them with earthy details with which any peasant or stone mason could identify.

The museum rooms are entered off a pretty cloister. The old Pilgrim's Hospice has been converted into a **Fra' (Beato) Angelico Gallery** 🏛🏛, full of altarpieces and painted panels. Also off the cloister is the **Reffetorio Grande (Great Refectory),** with 16th- and 17th-century paintings, and the **Sala del Capitolo (Chapter House),** frescoed from 1441 to 1442 with a huge *Crucifixion* by Fra' Angelico and his assistants. The door next to this leads past the stair-case up to the Dormitory (see below) to the **Sala del Cenacolo (Small Refectory),** with a long fresco of the *Last Supper* by Domenico Ghirlandaio.

The **Dormitorio (Dormitory)** 🏛🏛 of cells where the monks lived is one of Fra' Angelico's masterpieces and perhaps his most famous cycle of frescoes. In addition to the renowned *Annunciation* 🏛🏛 at the top of the stairs to the monk's rooms, Angelico painted the cells themselves with simple works to aid his fellow friars in their meditations. One of these almost anticipates surrealism—a Flagellation where disembodied hands strike at Christ's face and a rod descends on him from the blue-green back-ground. Angelico's assistants carried out the repetitious Crucifixion scenes in many of the cells. At the end of one of the corridors is the suite of cells occupied by Savonarola when he was here prior. In the first are two famous portraits of him by his devout follower and tal-ented painter Fra' Bartolomeo, along with an anonymous 16th-century painting of *Savonarola Burned at the Stake* on Piazza della Signoria. The **Biblioteca (Library)** off the corridor to the right of the stairs was designed by Michelozzo in 1441 and contains beauti-fully illuminated choir books. At the end of this hall, off to the right, is a two-cell suite used by Cosimo il Vecchio as a retreat; it's frescoed with an *Adoration of the Magi* by Benozzo Gozzoli and Fra' Angelico.

In the **church of San Marco**—entered from the piazza outside and open afternoons and on Mondays, unlike the museum—there's a 14th-century fresco of the *Annunciation* on the entrance wall. The second altarpiece on the right aisle is a Sacred Conversation by Fra' Bartolomeo. On the next altar is an 8th-century Byzantine mosaic of the *Madonna in Prayer* from Constantinople. (You can see where it was sawed in half when it was first shipped to Rome.) A small *Crucifix* by Fra' Angelico was recently placed over the altar.

Piazza San Marco 1. ℂ **055/238-8608.** Admission 8,000L (4.15€, $4). Daily 8:30am–1:50pm. Closed 1st, 3rd, and 5th Sun and 2nd and 4th Mon of each month. Bus: 1, 6, 7, 10, 11, 17, 20, 25, 31, 32, 33, 67, 68, 70.

Cenacolo di Sant'Apollonia 𝕣   There are no lines at this former convent and no crowds. Few people even know to ring the bell at the nondescript door. What they're missing is an entire wall covered with the vibrant colors of Andrea del Castagno's masterful *Last Supper* (ca. 1450). Castagno used his paint to create the rich marble panels that checkerboard the trompe-l'oeil walls and broke up the long white tablecloth with the dark figure of Judas the Betrayer, whose face is painted to resemble a satyr, an ancient symbol of evil.

Via XXVII Aprile 1. ⓒ **055/238-8607.** Free admission. Daily 8:30am–1:50pm. Closed 1st, 3rd, and 5th Sun and 2nd and 4th Mon of each month. Bus: 1, 6, 7, 10, 11, 17, 20, 25, 31, 32, 33, 67, 68, 70.

Santissima Annunziata   In 1230, seven Florentine nobles had a spiritual crisis, gave away all their possessions, and retired to the forests to contemplate divinity. They returned to what were then the fields outside the city walls and founded a small oratory, proclaiming they were Servants of Mary, or the Servite Order. The oratory was enlarged by Michelozzo (1444–81) and later baroqued. Under the facade's **portico,** you enter the **Chiostro dei Voti (Votice Cloister),** designed by Michelozzo with Corinthian-capitaled columns and decorated with some of the city's finest mannerist frescoes (1465–1515). Rosso Fiorentino provided an *Assumption* (1513) and Pontormo a *Visitation* (1515) just to the right of the door, but the main works are by their master, Andrea del Sarto, whose ***Birth of the Virgin*** 𝕣 (1513) in the far right corner is one of his finest works. To the right of the door into the church is a damaged but still fascinating *Coming of the Magi* (1514) by del Sarto, who included a self-portrait at the far right, looking out at us from under his blue hat.

The **interior** is excessively baroque. Just to the left as you enter is a huge tabernacle hidden under a mountain of flowers and *ex votos* (votive offerings). It was designed by Michelozzo to house a small painting of the *Annunciation.* Legend holds that this painting was started by a friar who, vexed that he couldn't paint the Madonna's face as beautifully as it should be, gave it up and took a nap. When he awoke, he found an angel had filled in the face for him. Newlywed brides in Florence don't toss their bouquets—they head here after the ceremony to leave their flowers at the shrine for good luck.

The large circular **tribune** was finished for Michelozzo by Leon Battista Alberti. You enter it from its left side via the left transept, but first pause to pay your respects to Andrea del Sarto, buried under a floor slab at the left-hand base of the great arch. Of the eight rounded chapels off the tribune, the one to the left as you enter has a *Madonna and Saints* recently attributed to Umbrian master Perugino. Beyond it is a chapel with Bronzino's Resurrection. At the back of the tribune, in the center, is a chapel squared off by mannerist sculptor Giambologna and filled with bronze plaques and statues by him to serve as his tomb. (His protégé Pietro Tacca is buried here as well.)

From the left transept, a door leads into the **Chiostro dei Morti (Cloister of the Dead;** track down a sacristan to open it), where over the entrance door is another of Andrea del Sarto's greatest frescoes, the *Madonna del Sacco* ❀, and, a *Rest on the Flight into Egypt* scene that got its name from the sack Joseph is leaning against to do a little light reading. (If you can't find someone with the key, you can get a glimpse of the fresco by peering through the grimy window in the small chapel recessed to the door's left.) Also off this cloister is the **Cappella di San Luca (Chapel of St. Luke),** evangelist and patron saint of painters. It was decorated by late Renaissance and mannerist painters, including Pontormo, Alessandro Allori, Santi di Tito, and Giorgio Vasari. Luca Giordano frescoed the ceiling with the *Vision of St. Bernard* to hang over the floor under which are interred artists Benvenuto Cellini, Pontormo, Franciabigio, and others. Back in the church, the fourth chapel on the left aisle houses a Perugino *Assumption,* and the first two chapels contain beautiful works by Andrea del Castagno.

On the **piazza** ❀❀ outside, flanked by elegant porticos (see Spedale degli Innocenti, below), is an equestrian statue of *Grand Duke Ferdinando I,* Giambologna's last work; it was cast in 1608 after his death by his student Pietro Tacca, who also did the two little fountains of fantastic mermonkey-monsters. The piazza's beauty is somewhat ruined by the car and bus traffic routed through both ends, but it's kept lively by students from the nearby university, who sit on the loggia steps for lunch and hang out here in the evenings.

Piazza Santissima Annunziata. ✆ **055/239-8034.** Free admission. Daily 7:30am–12:30pm and 4–6:30pm. Bus: 6, 31, 32.

Spedale degli Innocenti   Europe's oldest foundling hospital, opened in 1445, is still going strong as a convent orphanage, though times have changed a bit. The lazy Susan set into the wall on the left end of the arcade—where people would once leave unwanted babies, swivel it around, ring the bell, and run—has since been blocked up. The colonnaded **portico** ❀ (built 1419–26) was designed by Filippo Brunelleschi when he was still an active gold-smith. It was his first great achievement as an architect and helped define the new Renaissance style he was developing. Its repetition by later artists in front of other buildings on the piazza makes it one of the most exquisite squares in all Italy. The spandrels between the arches of Brunelleschi's portico are set with glazed **terra-cotta reliefs** of swaddled babes against rounded blue backgrounds—hands-down the masterpieces of Andrea della Robbia.

Many of the **cloisters** inside the convent were also designed by Brunelleschi, and while the first-floor gallery of High Renaissance art is closed for lack of staff, the **Pinacoteca (Picture Gallery)** in a long hall upstairs is still open. Here are kept a 15th-century Neri di Bicci *Coronation of the Virgin*, the *Madonna and Child with Angel* (painted by Botticelli when he was 20 years old and copied from a work by his master Filippo Lippi), and a *Madonna and Child* in glazed terra cotta by Luca della Robbia. Nearby is Domenico Ghirlandaio's colorful *Adoration of the Magi*, with a Massacre of the Innocents going on in the background.

Piazza Santissima Annunziata 12. ⓒ 055/249-1708. Admission 5,000L (2.60€, $2.50). Thurs–Tues 8:30am–2pm. Bus: 6, 31, 32.

Museo Opificio delle Pietre Dure

In the 16th century, Florentine craftsmen perfected the art of *pietre dure*, piecing together cut pieces of precious and semi-precious stones in an inlay process, and the Medici-founded institute devoted to the craft has been in this building since 1796. Long ago misnamed a "Florentine mosaic" by the tourism industry, this is a highly refined craft in which skilled artisans (artists, really) create scenes and boldly colored intricate designs in everything from cameos and tabletops to never-fade stone "paintings." Masters are adept at selecting, slicing, and polishing stones so that the natural grain or color gradations in the cross sections will, once cut and laid in the design, become the contours, shading, and molding that give good *pietre dure* scenes their depth and illusion of three-dimensionality. The collection in this museum is small, but the pieces are uniformly excellent. Souvenir shops all over town sell modern *pietre dure* items—much of it mass-produced junk, but some very nice. The best contemporary *maestro* is Ilio de Filippis, whose workshop is called Pitti Mosaici (see chapter 6, "Shopping").

Via degli Alfani 78. ⓒ 055/265-1357; 055/294-883 for ticket reservations (not necessary). Admission 4,000L (2.05€, $2), under 6 free. Mon–Sat 9am–2pm. Bus: 6, 31, 32.

Museo Archeologico (Archaeological Museum) 𝒜𝒜   This embarrassingly rich collection is often overlooked by visitors in full-throttle Renaissance mode. It conserves Egyptian artifacts, Roman remains, many Attic vases, and an important Etruscan collection. Parts of it have been undergoing restoration and rearrangement for years and are closed indefinitely, including the garden. The relics to be on the lookout for start in the first ground-floor room with an early-4th-century B.C. bronze **Chimera** 𝒜𝒜, a mythical beast with a lion's body and head, a goat head sprouting from its back, and a serpent for a tail (the tail was incorrectly restored in 1785). The beast was found near Arezzo in 1553 and probably made in a Chiusi or an Orvieto workshop as a votive offering. The legend that claims Benvenuto Cellini recast the left paws is hogwash; the feet did have to be reattached, but they had the originals to work with. Ground-floor room III contains a **silver amphora** studded with concave medallions, a work from Antioch (ca. A.D. 380).

In room III on the upper floor is an extraordinarily rare **Hittite wood-and-bone chariot** from the 14th century B.C. Room XIV upstairs has a cast bronze *Arringatore,* or orator, found near Perugia. It was made in the 1st century B.C. and helps illustrate how Roman society was having a great influence on the Etruscan world—not only in the workmanship of the statue but also in the fact that the Etruscan orator Aule Meteli is wearing a Roman toga. Room XIII contains the museum's most famous piece, the *Idolino* 𝒜. The history of this nude bronze lad with his outstretched hand is long, complicated, and in the end a bit mysterious. The current theory is that he's a Roman statue of the Augustan period (around the time of Christ), with the head perhaps modeled on a lost piece by the Greek master Polycleitus. The rub: *Idolino* was originally probably part of a lamp stand used at Roman banquets. The male torso displayed here was fished out of the sea near Livorno. It was made in Greece around 480 to 470 B.C.—the earliest known Greek bronze cast using the lost wax method. The horse's head also in this room once belonged to the Medici, as did much of this museum's collections, and tradition holds that it was a source of inspiration for Verrocchio and Donatello as they cast their own equestrian monuments. It was probably once part of a Hellenistic sculpture from the 2nd or 1st century B.C.

Via della Colonna 38. ☎ **055/23-575.** Admission 8,000L (4.15€, $4). Mon–Sat 9am–2pm; 2nd and 4th Sun of month 9am–1pm. Closed 2nd and 4th Mon of month. Bus: 6, 31, 32.

Cimitero degli Inglesi (Protestant Cemetery)   When this plot of green was nestled up against the city's medieval walls, it was indeed a quiet, shady, and reflective spot. When those walls were demolished in the late 19th century and the boulevard Viale put in their place, it became a traffic circle instead. We can only hope that frail and gentle Elizabeth Barrett Browning can block out the noise from her tomb off the left of the main path. The **sepulcher** was designed by her husband and fellow poet Robert Browning after her death in Florence in 1861.

Piazzale Donatello 38. ℂ **055/582-608.** Free admission (ring at the gate). Mon–Sat 9am–noon. Bus: 8, 33, 70, 80.

6 Around Piazza Santa Croce

Piazza Santa Croce is pretty much like any in Florence—a nice bit of open space ringed with souvenir and leather shops and thronged with tourists. It's most unique feature (aside from the one time a year it's covered with dirt and violent Renaissance soccer is played on it) is the **Palazzo Antellisi** on the south side. This well-preserved, 16th-century patrician house (its ground floor recessed under wood corbels and facade painted with fading frescoes and grotesques by Giovanni di Ser Giovanni), is owned by a contessa who rents out a bunch of peachy apartments.

Santa Croce 🌟🌟   The center of the Florentine Franciscan universe was begun in 1294 by Gothic master Arnolfo di Cambio in order to rival the huge church of Santa Maria Novella being raised by the Dominicans across the city. The church wasn't completed and consecrated until 1442, and even then it remained faceless until the neo-Gothic **facade** was added in 1857 (and cleaned in 1998–99). The cloisters are home to Brunelleschi's Cappella de' Pazzi (see the Museo dell'Opera, below), the convent partially given over to a famous leather school (see chapter 6, "Shopping"), and the church itself a shrine of 14th-century frescoes and a monument to notable Florentines, whose tombs and memorials litter the place like an Italian Westminster. The best artworks, such as the Giotto frescoes, are guarded by lire-gobbling lightboxes; bring plenty of 500L (.25€, 25¢) pieces.

The Gothic **interior** is wide and gaping, with huge pointed stone arches creating the aisles and an echoing nave trussed with wood beams, in all feeling vaguely barnlike (an analogy the occasional fluttering pigeon only enforces). The floor is paved with worn tombstones—because being buried in this hallowed sanctuary got you one step closer to Heaven, the richest families of the day paid big bucks to stake out small rectangles of the floor. On the right aisle is the first tomb of note, a mad Vasari contraption (currently under restoration) containing the bones of the most venerated of Renaissance masters, **Michelangelo Buonarroti,** who died of a fever in Rome in 1564 at the ripe age of 89. The pope wanted him buried in the Eternal City, but Florentines managed to sneak his body back to Florence. Past Michelangelo is a pompous 19th-century cenotaph to Florentine **Dante Alighieri,** one of history's greatest poets, whose *Divine Comedy* codified the Italian language. He died in 1321 in Ravenna after a long and bitter life in exile from his hometown (on trumped-up embezzlement charges), and that Adriatic city has never seen fit to return the bones to Florence, the city that would never readmit the poet when he was alive.

Against a nave pillar farther up is an elaborate **pulpit** (1472–76) carved by Benedetto di Maiano with scenes from the life of St. Francis. Next comes a wall monument to **Niccolò Machiavelli,** the 16th-century Florentine statesman and author whose famous book *The Prince* was the perfect practical manual for a powerful Renaissance ruler.

Past the next altar is an *Annunciation* (1433) carved in low relief of *pietra serena* and gilded by Donatello. Nearby is Antonio Rossellino's 1446 tomb of the great humanist scholar and city chancellor **Leonardo Bruni** (d. 1444). Beyond this architectural masterpiece of a tomb is a 19th-century knockoff honoring the remains of **Gioacchino Rossini** (1792–1868), composer of the *Barber of Seville* and the *William Tell Overture.*

Around in the right transept is the **Cappella Castellani** frescoed by Agnolo Gaddi and assistants, with a tabernacle by Mino da Fiesole and a *Crucifix* by Niccolò Gerini. Agnolo's father, Taddo Gaddi, was one of Giotto's closest followers, and the senior Gaddi is the one who undertook painting the **Cappella Baroncelli** (1332–38) at the transept's end. The frescoes depict scenes from the Life of the Virgin, and to the left of the window is an *Angel Appearing to the Shepherds* that constitutes the first night scene in Italian fresco. The altarpiece *Coronation of the Virgin* is by Giotto. To the left of this chapel is a doorway, designed by Michelozzo, leading to the *sagrestia* (sacristy) past a huge *Deposition* (1560) by Alessandro Allori that had to be restored after it incurred massive water damage when the church was inundated during the 1966 flood. In the sacristy are frescoes by Spinello Aretino (*Way to*

Calvary), Taddeo Gaddi (*Crucifixion*), and Niccolò Gerini (*Resurrection*). Past the gift shop is a leather school and store.

In the right transept, Giotto frescoed the two chapels to the right of the high altar. The frescoes were whitewashed over during the 17th century but uncovered from 1841 to 1852 and inexpertly restored. The **Cappella Peruzzi** 👁👁 on the right is a late work and not in the best shape. The many references to antiquity in the styling and architecture of the frescoes reflect Giotto's trip to Rome and its ruins. His assistant Taddeo Gaddi did the altarpiece. Even more famous, if only as the setting for a scene in the film *A Room with a View,* is the **Cappella Bardi** 👁👁 immediately to the right of the high altar. The key panels here include the *Trial by Fire Before the Sultan of Egypt* on the right wall, full of telling subtlety in the expressions and poses of the figures. One of Giotto's most well-known works is the lower panel on the left wall, the *Death of St. Francis,* where the monks weep and wail with convincing pathos. Alas, big chunks of the scene are missing from when a tomb was stuck on top of it in the 18th century. Most people miss seeing *Francis Receiving the Stigmata,* which Giotto frescoed above the outside of the entrance arch to the chapel.

Agnolo Gaddi designed the stained-glass windows, painted the saints between them, and frescoed a *Legend of the True Cross* cycle on the walls of the rounded **sanctuary** behind the high altar. Over the altar hangs a *Crucifix* by the "Master of Filigne," once wrongly identified as Giotto. At the end of the left transept is another Cappella Bardi, this once housing a legendary *Crucifix* 👁 by Donatello. According to Vasari, Donatello excitedly called his friend Filippo Brunelleschi up to his studio to see this *Crucifix* when he had finished carving it. The famed architect, whose tastes were aligned with the prevailing view of the time that refinement and grace were much more important than realism, criticized the work with the words, "Why Donatello, you've put a peasant on the cross!" Donatello sniffed, "If it was as easy to make something as it is to criticize, my Christ would really look to you like Christ. So you get some wood and try to make one yourself." Secretly, Brunelleschi did just that, and one day he invited Donatello to come over to his studio for lunch. Donatello arrived bearing the food gathered up in his apron. Shocked when he beheld Brunelleschi's elegant *Crucifix,* he let the lunch drop to the floor, smashing the eggs, and after a few moments turned to Brunelleschi and humbly offered, "Your job is making Christs and mine is making peasants." Tastes change, and to modern eyes this "peasant" stands as the stronger work. If you want to see how Brunelleschi fared with his Christ, visit it at Santa Maria Novella.

Past a door as you head back down the left aisle is a 16th-century ***Deposition*** by Bronzino. A bit farther along, against a pier, is the roped-off floor tomb of Lorenzo Ghiberti, sculptor of the baptistery doors. Against the wall is an altarpiece of the *Incredulity of St. Thomas* by Giorgio Vasari. The last tomb on the right is that of **Galileo Galilei** (1564–1642), the preeminent Pisan scientist who figured out everything from the action of pendulums and the famous law of bodies falling at the same rate (regardless of weight) to discovering the moons of Jupiter and asserting that Earth revolved around the Sun. This last one got him in trouble with the church, which tried him in the Inquisition and—when he wouldn't recant—excommunicated him. At the urging of friends frightened his obstinacy would get him executed as a heretic, Galileo eventually kneeled in front of an altar and "admitted" he'd been wrong. He lived out the rest of his days under house arrest near Florence and wasn't allowed a Christian burial until 1737. Giulio Foggini designed this tomb for him, complete with a relief of the solar system—the sun, you'll notice, is at the center. The pope finally got around to lifting the excommunication in 1992. Italians still bring him fresh flowers.

Piazza Santa Croce. ⓒ **055/244-619.** Free admission. Easter to early Oct Mon–Sat 8am–6:30pm, Sun 3–6pm; winter Mon–Sat 8am–12:30pm and 3–6:30pm, Sun 3–6pm. Bus: B, 13, 23, 71.

Museo dell'Opera di Santa Croce ⓡ   Part of Santa Croce's

convent has been set up as a museum, mainly to harbor artistic victims of the 1966 Arno flood, which buried the church under tons of mud and water. You enter through a door to the right of the church facade, which spills into an open-air courtyard planted with cypress and filled with bird song. On the grass are seated Baccio Bandinelli's *God* in marble and a Henry Moore bronze.

At the end of the path is the **Cappella de' Pazzi** ⓡ, one of Filippo Brunelleschi's architectural masterpieces (faithfully finished after his death in 1446). Giuliano di Maiano probably designed the porch that now precedes the chapel, set with glazed terra cottas by Luca della Robbia. The rectangular chapel is one of Brunelleschi's signature pieces and a defining example of (and model for) early Renaissance architecture. Light gray *pietra serena* is used to accent the architectural lines against smooth white plaster walls, and the only decorations are della Robbia roundels of the *Apostles*

(1442–52). The Evangelists surrounding the dome may have been designed by Donatello or Brunelleschi himself before being produced by the della Robbia workshop. The chapel was barely finished by 1478, when the infamous Pazzi Conspiracy got the bulk of the family, who were funding this project, either killed or exiled.

Through a doorway to the right of the chapel is another Brunelleschi contribution, the second cloister, planted with rose bushes. From back in the first cloister you can enter the museum proper via the long hall of the **refectory.** On your right as you enter is the painting that became emblematic of all the artworks damaged during the 1966 flood, Cimabue's *Crucifix* ✿, one of the masterpieces of the artist who began bridging the gap between Byzantine tradition and Renaissance innovation, not the least by teaching Giotto to paint. At the room's end is an entire wall frescoed in the late–14th century by Taddeo Gaddi with a *Last Supper* and above it the *Tree of the Cross* surrounded by scenes of saints. Also here is a huge gilded bronze St. Louis of Toulouse by Donatello.

Piazza Santa Croce 16. ✆ **055/244-619.** Admission 8,000L (4.15€, $4). Mar–Sept Thurs–Tues 10am–12:30pm and 2:30–6:30pm; Oct–Feb Thurs–Tues 10am–12:30pm and 3–5pm. Bus: B, 13, 23, 71.

Museo Horne Of the city's several small once-private collections, the one formed by Englishman Herbert Percy Horne and left to Florence in his will has perhaps the best individual pieces, though the bulk of it consists of mediocre paintings by good artists. In a 15th-century palazzo designed by Cronaca (not Sangallo, as had once been believed), the collections are left, unlabeled, as Horne arranged them; the reference numbers on the handout they give you correspond to the stickers on the wall, not the numbers on the frames. The best works are a *St. Stephen* by Giotto and Sienese mannerist Domenico Beccafumi's weirdly colored tondo of the *Holy Family.*

Via dei Benci 6. ✆ **055/244-661.** Admission 8,000L (4.15€, $4). Mon–Sat 9am–1pm; in summer also Tues 8:30–11pm. Bus: B, 13, 23, 71.

Casa Buonarroti Though Michelangelo Buonarroti never actually lived in this modest palazzo, he did own the property and left it to his nephew Lionardo. Lionardo named his own son after his famous uncle, and this younger Michelangelo became very devoted to the memory of his namesake, converting the house into a museum and hiring artists to fill the place with frescoes honoring the genius of his great uncle.

Upstairs is the good stuff, starting with a display case regularly rotating pages from the museum's collection of original drawings. In the first room off the landing are Michelangelo's earliest sculptures: the *Madonna of the Steps,* carved before 1492 when he was a 15- or 16-year-old student in the Medici sculpture garden. A few months later, the child prodigy was already finished carving another marble, a confused tangle of bodies known as the *Battle of the Centaurs and Lapiths.* The sculptural ideals that were to mark his entire career are already evident here: a fascination with the male body to the point of ignoring the figures themselves in pursuit of muscular torsion and the use of rough "unfinished" marble to speak sculptural volumes.

Another room contains the wooden model for the facade of San Lorenzo he designed (never built), as well as a clay-and-wood *Torso* that was a model for a river god intended to be incorporated into the Medici Chapels. A second room off the landing houses the small wooden *Crucifix* discovered in Santo Spirito in 1963 and soon hailed as a long-lost early piece. The Christ here, though in true Michelangelo *contraposto* positioning, is so slight he looks like he could blow away at any minute. This is so unlike the more robust, vigorous Michelangelo we're used to that not everyone buys its authenticity.

Via Ghibellina 70. ℂ **055/241-698.** www.casabuonarroti.it. Admission 12,000L (6€, $6) adults, 8,000L (4.15€, $4) students and seniors over 65. Wed–Mon 9:30am–1:30pm. Bus: 14, 23.

Santa Maria Maddalena dei Pazzi The entrance to this church is an unassuming, unnumbered door on Borgo Pinti that opens onto a pretty cloister designed in 1492 by Giuliano da Sangallo, open to the sky and surrounded by large *pietra serena* columns topped with droopy-eared Ionic capitals. The interior of the 13th-century church was remodeled in the 17th and early 18th centuries and represents the high baroque at its restrained best. At the odd hours listed above, you can get into the chapter house to see the church's hidden main prize, a wall-filling fresco of the **Crucifixion and Saints** ✸ (1493–96) by Perugino, grand master of the Umbrian school. Typical of Perugino's style, the background is drawn as delicately in blues and greens as the posed figures were fleshed out in full-bodied volumes of bright colors. The *Christ on the Cross* here was painted by his workshop.

Next to Borgo Pinti 58. ℂ **055/247-8420.** Admission to church free. Perugino Crucifixion: 1,000L (.50€, 50¢) "donation." Church: daily 9am–noon; Mon–Fri 5–5:20pm and 6–6:50pm; Sat 5–6:20pm; Sun 5–6:50pm. Perugino Crucifixion: ring bell at no. 58 9–10am or enter through sacristy (knock at the last door on the right inside the church) at 5pm or 6:15pm. Bus: A, 6, 14, 23, 31, 32, 71.

Sinagoga (Synagogue) and Jewish Museum The center of the 1,000-strong Jewish community in Florence is this imposing Moorish-Byzantine synagogue, built in the 1870s. In an effort to create a neo-Byzantine building, the architects ended up making it look rather like a church, complete with a dome, an apse, a pulpit, and a pipe organ. The intricate polychrome arabesque designs, though, lend it a distinctly Eastern flavor, and the rows of prayer benches facing each other, and the separate areas for women, hint at its Orthodox Jewish nature. Though the synagogue is technically Sephardic, the members of the Florentine Jewish community are Italian Jews, a Hebrew culture that has adapted to its Italian surroundings since the 1st century B.C. when Jewish slaves were first brought to Rome. (The Florentine community dates from the 14th century.) Upstairs, the small museum is most interesting for its photographic chronicle of the ghetto's history.

Via Farina 4. ✆ **055/234-6654**. Admission 6,000L (3.10€, $3) adults, 4,000L (2.05€, $2) students. Sun–Fri 10am–1pm; Sun–Thurs 2–4pm (to 5pm in summer); obligatory 45-min. guided tours every 25 min. Bus: 6, 31, 32.

7 In the Oltrarno

Santa Felícita The 2nd-century Greek sailors who lived in this neighborhood brought Christianity to Florence with them, and this little church was probably the second to be established in the city, the first edition of it rising in the late–4th century. The current version was built in the 1730s. The star works are in the first chapel on your right, paintings by mannerist master Pontormo (1525–27). *The Deposition* and frescoed *Annunciation* are rife with his garish color palette of oranges, pinks, golds, lime greens, and sky blues. The four round paintings of the *Evangelists* surrounding the dome are also by Pontormo, except for the *St. Mark* (with the angel), which was probably painted by his pupil Bronzino. For some older works, ask to visit the sacristy off the right transept, with paintings by Taddeo Gaddi and Niccolò Gerini and a glazed terra cotta *Madonna and Child* by Luca della Robbia.

Piazza Santa Felícita (2nd left off Via Guicciardini across the Ponte Vecchio). ✆ **055/213-018**. Free admission. Daily 8am–noon and 3:30–6:30pm. Bus: B, D.

Palazzo Pitti & Giardino Boboli (Pitti Palace & Boboli Gardens) ✦✦✦ Though the original, much smaller Pitti Palace was a Renaissance affair probably designed by Filippo Brunelleschi, that palazzo is completely hidden by the enormous mannerist mass we see today. Inside are Florence's most extensive set of museums,

---

Buying a Pitti Cumulative Ticket

In 2001, you could buy a 20,000L (10€, $10) cumulative ticket (15,000L, 8€, $8 after 4pm) good for the Galleria Palatina, Giardino Boboli, Galleria d'Arte Moderna, and Museo degli Argenti. Whether this deal will remain available is anybody's guess.

---

including the Galleria Palatina, a huge painting gallery second in town only to the Uffizi, with famous works by Raphael, Andrea del Sarto, Titian, and Rubens. When Luca Pitti died in 1472, Cosimo de' Medici's wife, Eleonora of Toledo, bought this property and unfinished palace to convert into the new Medici home—she hated the dark, cramped spaces of the family apartments in the Palazzo Vecchio. They hired Bartolomeo Ammannati to enlarge the palazzo, which he did starting in 1560 by creating the courtyard out back, extending the wings out either side, and incorporating a Michelangelo architectural invention, "kneeling windows," on the ground floor of the facade. (Rather than being visually centered between the line of the floor and that of the ceiling, kneeling windows' bases extend lower to be level with the ground or, in the case of upper stories, with whatever architectural element delineates the baseline of that story's first level.) Later architects finished the building off by the 19th century, probably to Ammannati's original plans, in the end producing the oversize rustication of its outer walls and overall ground plan that make it one of the masterpieces of Florentine mannerist architecture.

The ticket office for the painting gallery—the main, and for many visitors, most interesting of the Pitti museums—is off Ammannati's excellent **interior courtyard** ✦ of gold-tinged rusticated rock grafted onto the three classical orders.

Galleria Palatina ✦✦✦ If the Uffizi represents mainly the earlier masterpieces collected by the Medici, the Pitti Palace's painting gallery continues the story with the High Renaissance and later eras, a collection gathered by the Medici, and later the Grand Dukes of Lorraine. The works are still displayed in the old-world fashion, which hung paintings according to aesthetics—how well, say, the Raphael matched the drapes—rather than that boring academic chronological order. In the first long **Galleria delle Statue (Hall of Statues)** are an early Peter Paul Rubens's *Risen Christ*, Caravaggio's *Tooth-puller* ✦, and a 19th-century tabletop inlaid in *pietre dure*, an exquisite example of the famous Florentine mosaic craft. The next five rooms made up the Medici's main apartments, frescoed by Pietro da Cortona in the 17th-century baroque style—they're home to the bulk of the paintings.

The **Sala di Venere (Venus Room)** is named after the neoclassical *Venus,* which Napoléon had Canova sculpt in 1810 to replace the *Medici Venus* the Emperor had appropriated for his Paris digs. Four masterpieces by the famed early-16th-century Venetian painter Titian hang on the walls. Art historians still argue whether *The Concert* 🎨 was wholly painted by Titian in his early 20s or by Giorgione, in whose circle he moved. However, most now attribute at most the fop on the left to Giorgione and give the rest of the canvas to Titian. There are no such doubts about Titian's *Portrait of Julius II,* a copy of the physiologically penetrating work by Raphael in London's National Gallery (the version in the Uffizi is a copy Raphael himself made), or the *Portrait of a Lady (La Bella).* Titian painted the *Portrait of Pietro Aretino* for the writer/thinker himself, but Aretino didn't understand the innovative styling and accused Titian of not having completed the work. The painter, in a huff, gave it to Cosimo I as a gift. The room also contains Rubens's *Return from the Hayfields,* famous for its classically harmonious landscape.

The **Sala di Apollo (Apollo Room)** has another masterful early *Portrait of an Unknown Gentleman* by Titian as well as his sensual, luminously gold ***Mary Magdalene*** 🎨, the first in a number of takes on the subject the painter was to make throughout his career. There are several works by Andrea del Sarto, whose late *Holy Family* and especially *Deposition* display the daring chromatic experiments and highly refined spatial compositions that were to influence his students Pontormo and Rosso Fiorentino as they went about mastering mannerism. The latter painted the *Madonna and Child Enthroned with Saints* here. Guido Reni's *Cleopatra* with her snake is a late work in which is fully evident the classicism that, through this artist (revered up there with Michelangelo until about 100 years ago but currently quite unfashionable), would help define the later European baroque.

The **Sala di Marte (Mars Room)** is dominated by Rubens, including the enormous ***Consequences of War*** 🎨🎨, which an aged Rubens painted for his friend Sustermans at a time when both were worried that their Dutch homeland was on the brink of battle. Rubens's ***The Four Philosophers*** 🎨 is a much more lighthearted work, in which he painted himself at the far left, next to his seated brother Filippo.

The star of the **Sala di Giove (Jupiter Room)** is Raphael's *La Velata* ⚘⚘, one of the crowning achievements of his short career and a summation of what he had learned about color, light, naturalism, and mood. It's probably a portrait of his Roman mistress called La Fornarina, a baker's daughter who sat for many of his Madonnas. The sharply lit study of wrinkles in the small *St. Jerome* here has been variously attributed to Piero di Pollaiolo and Verrocchio. There are some more influential paintings by Andrea del Sarto, as well as Fra' Bartolomeo's last work, a *Deposition* whose recent restoration revealed two saintly figures in the background. Nearby is the *Madonna del Sacco* by Umbrian painter Perugino, whose tinkering with the spatial relationships between the figures and the background influenced his student Raphael and other High Renaissance artists.

Raphael is the focus of the **Sala di Saturno (Saturn Room)** ⚘⚘, where the transparent colors of his *Madonna*s and probing portraits show the strong influence of both Leonardo da Vinci (the *Portrait of Maddalena Strozzi Doni* owes much to the *Mona Lisa*) and Raphael's old master Perugino, whose *Deposition* and a *Mary Magdalene* hang here as well. The **Sala dell'Iliade (Illiad Room)** has another Raphael portrait, this time of a ***Pregnant Woman*** ⚘, along with some more Titian masterpieces. Don't miss *Mary Magdalene* and ***Judith*** ⚘, two paintings by one of the only female artists of the late Renaissance era, Artemesia Gentileschi, who often turned to themes of strong biblical women.

From here, you enter a series of smaller rooms with smaller paintings. The **Sala dell'Educazione di Giove (Room of Jupiter's Education)** has two famous works: one a 1608 ***Sleeping Cupid*** ⚘⚘ Caravaggio painted while living in exile from Rome (avoiding murder charges) on the island of Malta; and the other Cristofano Allori's ***Judith with the Head of Holofernes*** ⚘, a Freudian field day where the artist depicted himself in the severed head, his lover as Judith holding it, and her mother as the maid looking on. The small **Sala della Stufa** off the left was frescoed by Pietro da Cortona and retains its 1640 majolica tiled floor. Past **Napoléon's bathroom** are a series of rooms with less-distinguished works.

Apartamenti Reali ⚘   The other wing of the *piano nobile* is taken up with the Medici's private apartments, which were reopened in 1993 after being restored to their late-19th-century appearance when the kings of the House of Savoy, rulers of the Unified Italy, used the suites as their Florentine home. The over-the-top sumptuous fabrics, decorative arts furnishings, stuccoes, and frescoes reflect the neo-baroque and Victorian tastes of the Savoy kings. Amid the general interior-decorator flamboyance are some thoroughly appropriate baroque canvases, plus some earlier works by Andrea del Sarto and Caravaggio's *Portrait of a Knight of Malta* 😊. From January to May, you can visit the apartments only by guided tour Tuesday and Saturday (and sometimes Thursday) hourly 9 to 11am and 3 to 5pm (reserve ahead at © **055/238-8614;** inquire about admission fees).

Galleria d'arte Moderna 😊 Modern art isn't what draws most people to the capital of the Renaissance, but the Pitti's collection includes some important works by the 19th-century Tuscan school of art known as the Macchiaioli, who painted a kind of Tuscan Impressionism, concerned with the *macchie* (marks of color on the canvas and the play of light on the eye). Most of the scenes are of the countryside or peasants working, along with the requisite lot of portraits. Some of the movement's greatest talents are here, including Silvestro Lega, Telemaco Signorini, and Giovanni Fattori, the genius of the group. Don't miss his two white oxen pulling a cart in *The Tuscan Maremma* 😊.

Galleria del Costume & Museo Degli Argenti These aren't the most popular of the Pitti's museums, and the **Museo degli Argenti** has what seems like miles of the most extravagant and often hideous *objets d'art* and housewares the Medici and Lorraines could put their hands on. If the collections prove anything, it's that as the Medici became richer and more powerful, their taste declined proportionally. Just be thankful their **carriage collection** has been closed for years. The **Costume Gallery** is more interesting. The collections concentrate on the 18th to 20th centuries but also display outfits from back to the 16th century. The dress in which Eleonora of Toledo was buried, made famous by Bronzino's intricate depiction of its velvety embroidered silk and in-sewn pearls on his portrait of her in the Uffizi, is usually on display.

Giardino Boboli (Boboli Gardens) 😊😊 The statue-filled park behind the Pitti Palace is one of the earliest and finest Renaissance gardens, laid out mostly between 1549 and 1656 with box hedges in geometric patterns, groves of ilex, dozens of statues, and rows of cypress. In 1766, it was opened to the Florentine public, who still come here with their families for Sunday-morning strolls. Just above the entrance through the courtyard of the Palazzo Pitti is an oblong **amphitheater** modeled on Roman circuses. Today, we see in the middle a **granite basin** from Rome's Baths of Caracalla and an **Egyptian obelisk** of Ramses II, but in 1589 this was the setting for the wedding reception of Ferdinando de' Medici's marriage to Christine of Lorraine. For the occasion, the Medici commissioned entertainment from Jacopo Peri and Ottavio Rinuccini, who decided to set a classical story entirely to music and called it *Dafne*—the world's first opera. (Later, they wrote a follow-up hit *Erudice*, performed here in 1600; it's the first opera whose score has survived.)

Around the park, don't miss the rococo **Kaffehaus,** with bar service in summer, and near the top of the park the **Giardino del Cavaliere,** the Boboli's prettiest hidden corner—a tiny walled garden of box hedges with private views over the wooded hills of Florence's outskirts. At the north end of the park, down around the end of the Pitti Palace, are some fake caverns filled with statuary, attempting to invoke some vaguely classical sacred grotto. The most famous, the **Grotta Grande,** was designed by Giorgio Vasari, Bartolomeo Ammannati, and Bernardo Buontalenti between 1557 and 1593, dripping with phony stalactites and set with replicas of Michelangelo's unfinished *Slave* statues. (The originals were once placed here before being moved to the Accademia.) All the grottoes are being restored, but you can visit them by appointment by calling ✆ **055/218-741.** Near the exit to the park is a Florentine postcard fave, the *Fontana di Bacco* (Bacchus Fountain; 1560), a pudgy dwarf sitting atop a tortoise. It's actually a portrait of Pietro Barbino, Cosimo I's potbellied dwarf court jester.

Piazza Pitti. **Galleria Palatina:** ✆ 055/238-8614; reserve tickets at ✆ 055/294-883; admission 12,000L (6€, $6); Easter–Oct Tues–Sat 8:30am–10pm, Sun 8:30am–8pm; winter Tues–Sat 8:30am–6:50pm, Mon 8:30am–1:50pm. **Galleria d'Arte Moderna:** ✆ 055/238-8616; admission 8,000L (4.15€, $4); daily 9am–2pm, closed 1st, 3rd, and 5th Mon and 2nd and 4th Sun of each month. **Galleria del Costume:** ✆ 055/238-8713; admission 8,000L (4.15€, $4); Tues–Sun 9am–2pm. **Museo degli Argenti:** ✆ 055/238-8710; admission 15,000L (8€, $8); daily 8:30am–1:50pm, closed 1st, 3rd, and 5th Mon and 2nd and 4th Sun of each month. **Giardino Boboli:** ✆ 055/265-1816; admission 4,000L (2.05€, $2); daily 9am–sunset, closed 1st and last Mon of each month. Bus: D, 11, 36, 37, 68.

Santo Spirito ✿   One of Filippo Brunelleschi's masterpieces of architecture, this 15th-century church doesn't look like much from the outside (no true facade was ever built), but the **interior** ✿ is a marvelous High Renaissance space—an expansive landscape of proportion and mathematics worked out in classic Brunelleschi style, with coffered vaulting, tall columns, and the stacked perspective of arched arcading. Good late Renaissance and baroque paintings are scattered throughout, but the best stuff lies up in the transepts and in the east end, surrounding the extravagant **baroque altar** with a ciborium inlaid in *pietre dure* around 1607.

The **right transept** begins with a *Crucifixion* by Francesco Curradi. Against the back wall of the transept, the first chapel holds an early-15th-century *Madonna del Soccorso* of uncertain authorship. Two chapels down is one of Filippino Lippi's best works, a *Madonna and Child with Saints and Donors.* The background seen through the classical arches was painted with an almost Flemish exacting detail. In the east end of the church, the center two chapels against the back wall contain Alessandro Allori altarpieces: *The Martyred Saints* (1574) on the right has a predella view of what the Palazzo Pitti looked like before its enlargement; and the *Christ and the Adulteress* on the left is extremely advanced in style, already almost a work of the late baroque. In the **left transept,** the first chapel on the right side is a late-15th-century *Madonna Enthroned with Child and Saints.* Next to this is the highly skilled *St. Monica and Augustinian Nuns,* an almost monochrome work of black and pale yellow, faintly disturbing in its eerie monotony and perfection of composition. It's now usually attributed to the enigmatic Andrea del Verrocchio, one-time master of Leonardo da Vinci. The second chapel on the back wall of this transept has a marble altarpiece sculpted by Andrea Sansovino, next door to which is a late-15th-century painting of the *Trinity with Saints Mary Magdalene and Catherine,* attributed to the same anonymous master who did the *Madonna Enthroned* in this transept.

The famed **piazza** outside is one of the focal points of the Oltrarno, shaded by trees and lined with trendy cafes that see some bar action in the evenings. It's not quite the pleasant hangout it once was, however—especially since the heroin set moved in a few years ago, making it a less than desirable place to be after midnight (though early evening is still fine). Stop by Bar Ricci at no. 9r, where more than 300 facade designs for faceless Santo Spirito line the walls, the product of a fun-loving contest the bar held in 1980.

Piazza Santo Spirito. Ⓒ **055/210-030.** Free admission. Daily 8am–noon; Thurs–Tues 4–6pm. Bus: D, 6, 11, 36, 37, 68.

Cenacolo di Santo Spirito Museum   The dark and haphazard museum in the church's old refectory (entrance to the left of Santo Spirito's facade) has a gathering of Romanesque and paleo-Christian stone sculptures and reliefs. The main reason to drop by is the end wall frescoed by Andrea Orcagna and his brother Nardo di Cione in 1360 with a *Last Supper* (of which only 1.5 apostles and a halo are left) and above it a beautiful *Crucifixion,* one of 14th-century Florence's masterpieces.

Piazza Santo Spirito 29. ⓒ **055/287-043.** Admission 4,000L (2.05€, $2). Tues–Sat 9am–2pm; Sun 8am–1pm. Bus: D, 6, 11, 36, 37, 68.

Santa Maria della Carmine ✹✹✹   Following a 1771 fire that destroyed everything but the transept chapels and sacristy, this Carmelite church was almost entirely reconstructed and decorated in high baroque style. Ever since a long and expensive restoration of the famous frescoes of the **Cappella Brancacci** in the right transept, they've blocked off just that chapel and you have to enter through the cloisters (doorway to the right of the church facade) and pay admission. The frescoes were commissioned by an enemy of the Medici, Felice Brancacci, who in 1424 hired Masolino and his student Masaccio to decorate it with a cycle on the life of St. Peter. Masolino probably worked out the cycle's scheme and painted a few scenes along with his pupil before taking off for 3 years to serve as court painter in Budapest, during which time Masaccio kept painting, quietly creating one of his masterpieces and some of the early Renaissance's greatest frescoes. Masaccio left for Rome in 1428, where he died at age 27. The cycle was completed between 1480 and 1485 by Filippino Lippi, who faithfully imitated Masaccio's technique.

Even before Lippi's intervention, though, the frescoes had been an instant hit. People flocked from all over the city to admire them, and almost every Italian artist of the day came to sketch and study Masaccio's mastery of perspective, bold light and colors, and unheard-of touches of realism. Even later masters like Leonardo da Vinci and Michelangelo came to learn what they could from the young artist's genius. A 1980s restoration cleaned off the dirt and dark mold that had grown in the egg-based pigments used to "touch up" the frescoes in the 18th century and removed additions like the prudish ivy leaves trailing across Adam and Eve's privates.

Masolino was responsible for the *St. Peter Preaching,* the upper panel to the left of the altar, and the two top scenes on the right wall, which shows his fastidiously decorative style in a long panel of

St. Peter Healing the Cripple and *Raising Tabitha,* and his *Adam and Eve.* Contrast this first man and woman, about to take the bait offered by the snake, with the ***Expulsion from the Garden*** 👁️👁️ across from it painted by Masaccio. Masolino's figures are highly posed models, expressionless and oblivious to the temptation being offered. Masaccio's Adam and Eve, on the other hand, burst with intense emotion and forceful movement. The top scene on the left wall is also by Masaccio, and it showcases both his classical influences and another of his innovations, perfect linear perspective. On the end wall, Masaccio painted the lower scene to the left of the altar of *St. Peter Healing the Sick with His Shadow,* unique at the time for its realistic portrayal of street beggars and crippled bodies. The two scenes to the right of the altar are Masaccio as well, with the *Baptism of the Neophytes* taking its place among his masterpieces. Most of the rest of the frescoes were painted by Filippino Lippi, who also touched up the long lower panel on the left wall with *St. Peter Raising the Son of Theophilus* and *St. Peter Enthroned.* This panel was started by Masaccio, but either left unfinished or damaged when Medici supporters scratched out the portraits of the Brancacci family, which were most likely once painted into the crowd.

The interior of the rest of the church has trompe-l'oeil ceilings by Domenico Staggi and Giuseppe Romei. The left transept chapel, which isn't blocked off, is one of Florence's most harmonious examples of the baroque (1675–83), with a ceiling painted by Luca Giordano.

Piazza della Carmine. ✆ **055/238-2195.** Admission to church free; Brancacci chapel 5,000L (2.60€, $2.50). **Church:** daily 9am–noon and 4:30–6pm. **Brancacci chapel:** Wed–Sat and Mon 10am–5pm; Sun 1–5pm. Bus: D, 6, 11, 36, 37, 68.

Museo Zoologico La Specola

Italy has very few zoos, but this is the largest zoological collection, rooms full of insects, crustaceans, and stuffed birds and mammals—everything from ostriches and apes to a rhinoceros. The museum was founded here in 1775, and the collections are still displayed in the style of an old-fashioned natural sciences museum, with specimens crowded into beautiful old wood-and-glass cases. The last 10 rooms contain an important collection of human anatomical wax models crafted between 1775 and 1814 by Clemente Susini for medical students. The life-size figures are flayed, dissected, and disemboweled to varying degrees and are truly disgusting, but fascinating.

Via Romana 17. ✆ **055/228-8251.** www.specola.unifi.it. Admission 8,000L (4.15€, $4). Thurs–Tues 9am–1pm. Bus: D, 11, 36, 37, 68.

8 In the Hills

Piazzale Michelangiolo ⍟   This panoramic piazza is a required stop for every tour bus. The balustraded terrace was laid out in 1885 to give a sweeping vista of the entire city, spread out in the valley below and backed by the green hills of Fiesole beyond. The monument to Michelangelo in the center of the piazza is made up of bronze replicas of *David* and his Medici chapel sculptures.

Viale Michelangelo. Bus: 12, 13.

San Miniato al Monte ⍟⍟   High atop a hilltop, its gleaming white-and-green facade visible from the valley below, San Miniato is one of the few ancient churches of Florence to survive the centuries virtually intact. San Miniato was an eastern Christian who settled in Florence and was martyred during Emperor Decius's persecutions in A.D. 250. The legend goes that the decapitated saint picked up his head, walked across the river, climbed up the hillside, and didn't lie down to die until he reached this spot. He and other Christians were buried here, and a shrine was raised on the site as early as the 4th century.

The current building began to take shape in 1013, under the auspices of the powerful Arte di Calimala guild, whose symbol, a bronze eagle clutching a bale of wool, perches atop the **facade** ⍟⍟. The Romanesque facade is a particularly gorgeous bit of white Carrara and green Prato marble inlay. Above the central window is a 13th-century mosaic of *Christ Between the Madonna and St. Miniato* (a theme repeated in a slightly later mosaic filling the apse inside).

The **interior** has a few Renaissance additions, but they blend in well with the overall medieval aspect—an airy, stony space with a raised choir at one end, painted wooden trusses on the ceiling, and tombs interspersed with inlaid marble symbols of the zodiac paving the floor. The frescoes on the walls are mostly 15th century, except the enormous *St. Christopher* on the right wall near the door, which may date back to before the 1300s. At the nave's end is the **Cappella del Crocifisso,** a tabernacle (1448) designed by Michelozzo to house the miraculous *Crucifix* that nodded its head to St. Giovanni Gualberto (now in Santa Trínita). Still in the tabernacle is the Crucifix's painted backdrop, cabinet doors painted by Agnolo Gaddi (1394–96), and the enameled terra-cotta coffered roof by Luca della Robbia.

Catching Calcio Fever

To Italians, calcio (soccer) is something akin to a second religion. You don't know what a "fan" is until you've attended a soccer match in a country like Italy, and an afternoon at the football stadium can offer you as much insight (if not more) into Italian culture as a day in the Uffizi. Catch the local team, the Fiorentina, Sundays September to May at the Stadio Comunale, Via Manfredi Fanti 4 (*© 055/579-743*). Tickets go on sale at the stadium box office 3 hours before each game.

Below the choir is an 11th-century **crypt** with small frescoes by Taddo Gaddi. Off to the right of the raised choir is the **sacristy,** which Spinello Aretino covered in 1387 with cartoonish yet elegant frescoes depicting the *Life of St. Benedict* ✸. Off the left aisle of the nave is 15th-century **Cappella del Cardinale del Portogallo** ✸✸, a brilliant collaborative effort by Renaissance artists built to honor young Portuguese humanist Cardinal Jacopo di Lusitania, who was sent to study in Perugia but died an untimely death at 25 in Florence. Luca della Robbia provided the glazed terra-cotta dome, a cubic landscape set with tondi of the four *Virtues* surrounding the *Holy Spirit* to symbolize the young scholar's devotion to the church and to humanist philosophy. It stands as one of della Robbia's masterpieces of color and classical ideals. Antonio and Piero del Pollaiolo painted the altarpiece (this is a copy; the original's in the Uffizi) as well as some of the frescoes, the rest of which were finished off by Alesso Baldovinetti, including the *Annunciation.*

The unfinished **bell tower** seen from the outside was designed by Baccio d'Agnolo.

Via del Monte alle Croci/Viale Galileo Galilei (behind Piazzale Michelangiolo). *©* 055/234-2731. Free admission. Easter to early Oct daily 8am–noon and 2–7pm; winter daily 8am–noon and 2:30–6pm. Bus: 12, 13.

Museo Stibbert Half Scotsman, half Italian, Frederick Stibbert was nothing if not eccentric. A sometime artist, intrepid traveler, voracious accumulator, and even hero in Garibaldi's army, he inherited a vast fortune and this villa from his Italian mother. He connected the house to a nearby villa to create an eclectic museum housing his extraordinary collections, including baroque canvases, fine porcelain, Flemish tapestries, Tuscan crucifixes, and Etruscan artifacts. The museum was partially rearranged in past decades to try and make some sense out of 57 rooms stuffed with over 50,000 items. More recently, however, the city has come to appreciate this rare example of a private 19th-century museum and is busily setting it all back the way Stibbert originally intended.

Stibbert's greatest interest and most fascinating assemblage is of **armor** ✸—Etruscan, Lombard, Asian, Roman, 17th-century Florentine, and 15th-century Turkish. The museum has the largest display of Japanese arms and armor in Europe. The high point of the house is a remarkable grand hall filled with an entire cavalcade of mannequins in 16th-century armor (mostly European, but with half a dozen samurai foot soldiers thrown in for good measure). Stibbert even managed to get some seriously historic Florentine armor, that in which Medici warrior Giovanni delle Bande Nere was buried. And, it must be said, the museum is also the resting place of the world's greatest collection of spurs.

Via Stibbert 26. ✆ **055/475-520**. Admission 8,000L (4.15€, $4). Easter to early Oct Fri–Wed 10am–1pm and 3–6pm; winter Mon–Wed and Fri 10am–2pm, Sat–Sun 10am–6pm. Bus: 4.

6

Shopping

The cream of the crop of Florentine shopping lines both sides of the elegant **Via de' Tornabuoni,** with an extension along **Via della Vigna Nuova** and other surrounding streets. Here you'll find big names like Gucci, Armani, Ferragamo, and Mila Schön ensconced in old palaces or modern minimalist boutiques.

On the other end of the shopping spectrum is the haggling and general fun of the colorful and noisy **San Lorenzo street market.** Antiques gather dust by the truckload along **Via Maggio** and other Oltrarno streets. Another main corridor of stores somewhat less glitzy than those on the Via de' Tornabuoni begins at **Via Cerretani** and runs down **Via Roma** through the Piazza della Repubblica area; it keeps going down **Via Por Santa Maria,** across the **Ponte Vecchio** with its gold jewelry, and up **Via Guicciardini** on the other side. Store-laden side tributaries off this main stretch include **Via della Terme, Borgo Santissimi Apostoli,** and **Borgo San Jacopo.**

General Florentine **shopping hours** are daily 9:30am to noon or 1pm and 3 or 3:30pm to 7:30pm, though many shops are increasingly staying open through that mid-afternoon *riposo* (especially the larger stores and those around tourist sights).

1 Shopping the Markets

Haggling is accepted, and even expected, at most outdoor markets (but don't try it in stores). The queen of Florentine markets is the **San Lorenzo street market,** filling Piazza San Lorenzo, Via del Canto de' Nelli, Via dell'Ariento, and other side streets. It's a wildly chaotic and colorful array of hundreds of stands hawking T-shirts, silk scarves, marbleized paper, Gucci knockoffs, and lots and lots of leather. Many of the stalls are merely outlets for full-fledged stores hidden behind them. Haggling is tradition here, and though you'll find plenty of leather lemons, there are also great deals on truly high-quality leather and other goods—you just have to commit to half a day of picking through it all and fending off sales pitches. From March to October, most stalls are open daily about 8am to

Getting Your VAT Refund

Most purchases have a built-in **value added tax (IVA)** of 12% to 19%. Non-EU (European Union) citizens are entitled to a refund of this tax if they spend more than 300,000L (155€, $150) at any one store, before tax. To claim your refund, request an invoice from the cashier at the store and take it to the customs office (*dogana*) at the airport to have it stamped *before* you leave. *Note:* If you're going to another EU country before flying home, have it stamped at the airport customs office of the last EU country you'll be in (if flying home via Britain, have your Italian invoices stamped in London).

Once back home, mail the stamped invoice back to the store within 90 days of the purchase, and they'll send you a refund check. Many shops are now part of the "Tax Free for Tourists" network. (Look for the sticker in the window.) Stores participating in this network issue a check along with your invoice at the time of purchase. After you have the invoice stamped at customs, you can redeem the check for cash directly at the tax-free booth in the airport—in Rome, it's past customs; in Milan's airports the booth is inside the duty-free shop—or mail it back in the envelope provided within 60 days.

8pm (it varies with how business is doing); from November to February, the market is closed Mondays and Sundays, except for the 2 weeks or so around Christmas, when it remains open daily.

Somewhere in the center of this capitalist whirlwind hides the indoor **Mercato Centrale food market** (between Via dell'Ariento and Piazza del Mercato Centrale). Downstairs you'll find meat, cheese, and dry goods. There's one stall devoted to tripe aficionados, a second piled high with *baccalà* (dried salt cod), and a good cheap eatery called **Nerbone** (see chapter 4, "Where to Dine," for more information). The upstairs is devoted to fruits and veggies—a cornucopia of fat eggplants, long yellow peppers, stacks of artichokes, and peperoncini bunched into brilliant red bursts. In all, you couldn't ask for better picnic pickings. The market is open Monday to Saturday 7am to 2pm and Saturday also 4 to 7:30pm.

As if two names weren't enough, the **Mercato Nuovo** (Straw Market) is also known as Mercato del Porcellino or Mercato del Cinghiale because of the bronze wild boar statue at one end, cast by Pietro Tacca in the 17th century after an antique original now in the Uffizi. Pet the well-polished porcellino's snout to ensure a return trip to Florence. The market specialized in straw goods in the late 19th century, but most of the straw stalls disappeared by the 1960s. These days, the loggia hawks mainly poor-quality leather purses, mediocre bijoux, souvenirs, and other tourist trinkets. Beware of pickpockets. In summer it's open daily around 9am to 8pm, but in winter it closes at 5pm and all day Sunday and Monday.

Besides these major daily markets, you may also want to stop by the food stalls at the **Mercato di San Ambrogio,** the Santa Croce district's daily produce market. Chefs from the local restaurants show up at 5am to pick over the vegetables and haggle prices, and the stalls shut down by 1:30pm. Nearby is the weekday **Piazza dei Ciompi flea market,** which converts to a semi-antiques and junk market on the last Sunday of every month. A junky crafts and near-antiques flea market fills the **Oltrarno's Piazza Santo Spirito** on the second Sunday of each month; the following Sunday, the square hosts an organic produce market.

2 Shopping A to Z

Here's **what to buy in Florence:** leather, high fashion, shoes, marbleized paper, hand-embroidered linens, lace, lingerie, Tuscan wines, gold jewelry, pietre dure (aka Florentine mosaic, inlaid semiprecious stones), and Renaissance leftovers and other antiques. Here's where to buy it:

ART & ANTIQUES

The antiques business is clustered where the artisans have always lived and worked: the Oltrarno. Dealers' shops line Via Maggio, but the entire district is packed with venerable chunks of the past. On "this side" of the river, Borgo Ognissanti has the highest concentration of aging furniture and art collectibles.

Gallori-Turchi   This gallery's large showrooms specialize in furnishings, paintings, and weaponry (swords, lances, and pistols) from the 16th to 18th centuries. They also offer majolica and ceramic pieces and scads of excellent desks and writing tables of handcarved and inlaid wood. Via Maggio 14r. © **055/282-279.**

Gianfranco Luzzetti   For the serious collector who wants his or her own piece of Florence's cultural heritage, this refined showroom offers artwork and furniture from the 1400s to 1600s. They have a gorgeous collection of 16th-century Deruta ceramics and majolica, canvases by the likes of Vignale and Bilivert, and on last visit even a glazed terra-cotta altarpiece from the hand of Andrea della Robbia. Bring sacks of money. Borgo San Jacopo 28A. ✆ **055/212-232.**

Guido Bartolozzi   Under family management since 1887, this old-fashioned store concentrates on the 16th to 19th centuries. They might be offering a 17th-century Gobelin tapestry, an inlaid stone tabletop, or wood intarsia dressers from the 1700s. Not only do they have beautiful furniture in excellent shape, but they often manage to lay their hands on matching pieces. The quality is impeccable: The owner has been president of Italy's antiques association and secretary of Florence's biannual antiques fair. Via Maggio 18r. ✆ **055/292-296.** There's another showroom at Via Maggio 11.

BOOKS

Even the smaller bookshops in Florence these days have at least a few shelves devoted to English-language books. **Feltrinelli International,** Via Cavour 12 (✆ **055/292-196**), is one of the few of any size.

BM Bookshop   BM Bookshop is a bit smaller than Paperback Exchange but more central and carries only new volumes. They also have a slightly more well-rounded selection—from novels and art books to cookbooks and travel guides. A special section is devoted to Italian- and Tuscany-oriented volumes. Borgo Ognissanti 4r. ✆ **055/ 294-575.**

G. Vitello   This shop sells coffee table–worthy books on art and all things Italian at up to half off the price you'd pay in a regular bookstore. Via dei Servi 94–96r. ✆ **055/292-445.** Other branches are at Via Verdi 40r (✆ **055/234-6894**) and Via Pietrapiana 1r (✆ **055/241-063**).

Libreria Il Viaggio   Here's a cozy niche specializing in travel guides, related literature, and maps, with a sizable selection in English. It's a good place to find specialty guides—hiking in the Chianti, touring Elba, wine estates that offer *agriturismo,* and the like. Borgo degli Albizi 41r. ✆ **055/240-489.**

Paperback Exchange   It's not the most central, but it is the best for books in English, specializing in titles relating in some way to Florence and Italy. Much of their stock is used, and you can't beat the prices anywhere in Italy—dog-eared volumes and all Penguin books go for only 4,000L to 6,000L (2.05€ to 3.10€, $2 to $3). You can also trade in that novel you've already finished for another. Via Fiesolana 31r. ✆ 055/247-8154.

DEPARTMENT STORES

Florence's central branch of the national chain **Coin,** Via Calzaiuoli 56r (✆ **055/280-531**), is a stylish multifloored display case for upper-middle-class fashions—a chic Macy's. **La Rinascente,** Piazza della Repubblica 2 (✆ **055/219-113**), is another of Italy's finer department stores. This six-floor store serves as an outlet for top designers (Versace, Zegna, Ferré, and so on) as well as for fine china and other housewares, cosmetics, perfumes, and jewelry. It also has areas set up to sell traditional Tuscan goods (terra cotta, alabaster, olive oils, and wrought iron).

But the **Standa** chain, Via dei Banchi, between the Duomo and Piazza Santa Maria Novella (✆ **055/239-8963**), is where real Italians go to shop. It's the place that runs back-to-school specials and carries bulk dish detergent, frying pans, cake mix, and everyday clothes—a sort of upscale Kmart. (Since the parent corporation of Coin recently bought Standa, it's busily converting about half the Standas in Italy to Coins, so don't be surprised if the name changes.)

DESIGN, HOUSEWARES & CERAMICS

Emporium   The watches, pens, place settings, and bookends here tend to be memorable and unique design items. Some of them are beautiful, some are "why didn't I think of that?" useful, and some are just silly, but it's always fun to browse. Via Guicciardini 122r. ✆ **055/212-646.**

La Botteghina   This tiny shop is about the best and most reasonably priced city outlet for true artisan ceramics I've found in all Italy. Daniele Viegi del Fiume deals in gorgeous handpainted ceramics from the best traditional artisans working in nearby Montelupo, the famed Umbrian ceramics centers of Deruta and Gubbio, and Castelli, high in the Abruzzi mountains. If you can't make it to the workshops in the hill towns themselves, La Botteghina is the next best thing. If you like the sample of pieces by **Romano Rampini** you see here and want to invest in a full table setting, Rampini has its own classy showroom at Borgo Ognissanti 32–34 (✆ **055/219-720;** www.chiantinet.it/rampiniceramics). Via Guelfa 5r. ✆ **055/287-367.**

Richard Ginori   Head here for big-name production-line china and tablewares. Colorful rims and whimsical designs fill this warehouselike salesroom of the firm that has sold Florence's finest china since 1735. Other houseware bigwigs are represented as well—Alessi coffeepots, Nason and Meretti Murano glass, and Chrisofle flatware. Via Rondinelli 17r. ☏ 055/210-041.

Viceversa (Finds Here you'll find one of the largest selections of the latest Robert Graves–designed teakettle or any other whimsical Alessi kitchen product. The friendly staff will also point out the Pavoni espresso machines, Carl Merkins' totemic bar set, the Princess motorized gadgets, and shelf after shelf of the best of Italian kitchen and houseware designs. Via Ricasoli 53r (☏ **055/239-8281.**

FASHION & CLOTHING

Although Italian fashion reached its pinnacle in the 1950s and 1960s, the country has remained at the forefront of both high (Armani, Gucci, Pucci, Ferragamo, just to name a few) and popular (as evidenced by the spectacular success of Benetton in the 1980s) fashion. Florence plays second fiddle to Milan in today's Italian fashion scene, but the city has its own cadre of highly respected names, plus, of course, outlet shops of all the hot designers. Also see "Leather, Accessories & Shoes" below.

FOR MEN & WOMEN

Cinzia Cinzia is a grabbag of hand-knit, usually bulky wool sweaters offered by an elderly couple who've been sending their creations around the world for more than 30 years. Borgo San Jacopo 22r. ☏ 055/298-078.

Emilio Pucci The address may be a hint that this isn't your average fashion shop: Palazzo Pucci. Marchese Emilio Pucci's ancestors have been a powerful banking and mercantile family since the Renaissance, and in 1950 the marchese suddenly turned designer and shocked the fashion world with his flowing silks in outlandish colors. His women's silk clothing remained the rage into the early 1970s and had a Renaissance of its own in the 1990s club scene. The design team is now headed by daughter Laudomia Pucci. If you don't wish to visit the showroom in the ancient family palace, drop by the shop around the corner at Via Ricasoli 36r (☏ **055/ 287-622**) or the boutique at Via della Vigna Nuova 97–99r (☏ **055/294-028**). Via de' Pucci 6. ☏ 055/283-061.

Enrico Coveri Enrico started off in the nearby textile town of Prato and has a similar penchant for bright colors as contemporary Emilio Pucci. The major difference is that Enrico Coveri's firm produces downscale fashion that fits the bods and wallets of normal folk—not just leggy models. Some of the men's suits are particularly fine, but the children's collection may be best left alone. Via della Vigna Nuova 25–29r. ℂ 055/238-1769. There's another tiny branch at Via Tornabuoni 81r.

Giorgio Armani Impossibly smart suits line the walls at Florence's outlet for Italy's top fashion guru, and the service and store are surprisingly not stratospherically chilly (the Official Armani Attitude at the moment is studied, casual indifference). The **Emporio Armani** branch at Piazza Strozzi 16r (ℂ **055/284-315**) is the outlet for the more affordable designs. The merchandise is slightly inferior in workmanship and quality and greatly inferior in price—you can actually dig out shirts for less than $1,000. Via della Vigna Nuova 51r. ℂ **055/219-041.**

Gucci But the biggest name to walk out of Florence onto the international catwalk has to be Gucci, and this is the world flagship store. It's here that this Florentine fashion empire was started by saddlemaker Guccio Gucci in 1904, now run by a gaggle of grandsons. You enter through a phalanx of their trademark purses and bags. Forget the cheesy knockoffs sold on street corners around the world; the stock here is elegant. Wander from brightly chromatic silk scarves and ties past the shoes to men and women's clothing. Via de' Tornabuoni 73r. ℂ **055/264-011.**

Luisa Via Roma Head here for a selection of all the top names in avant-garde fashion, including Jean Paul Gaultier, Dolce & Gabbana, and Issey Miyake. Men can hand over their wallets upstairs, and women can empty their purses on the ground floor. Service can be chilly. Via Roma 19–21r. ℂ **055/217-826.**

FOR WOMEN

Alex This shop is designed to keep up with the volatile fashion scene, carrying a select crop of what's hot at fair, not inexpensive, prices. Choice labels may include Sonia Rykiel, Alaïa, or Joseph Tricot. Via della Vigna Nuova 19r. ℂ **055/214-952.**

Loretta Caponi Loretta Caponi is world famous for her high-quality intimates and linens made the old-fashioned way. Under Belle Epoque ceilings are nightgowns of all types, bed and bath linens of the highest caliber, curtains, and feminine unmentionables. There's also a large section for the little ones in the back. Peek through the pebble-glassed doors to see the workshop, kept right here under Loretta's watchful eye. Piazza Antinori 4r. ℂ **055/213-668.**

STOCK HOUSES

To get your high fashion at bargain-basement prices, head to one of the branches of **Stock House Grandi Firme.** The store at Borgo degli Albizi 87r (© **05/234-0271**) carries mainly the past season's models, while the Via dei Castellani 26r branch (© **05/294-853**) carries spring/summer remaindered collections, and the Via Verdi 28r (© **05/247-8250**) and Via Nazionale 38r (© **05/215-482**) store outfits from the past winter. **Stock House Il Giglio,** Via Borgo Ognissanti 86 (no phone), and **Stock House Pattaya 2,** Via Cavour 51r (© **055/210-151**), also carry big name labels at 50% to 60% off.

GIFTS & CRAFTS

Alice Atelier Professor Agostino Dessi presides over the traditional Venetian Carnevale–style maskmaking at this gallery. All masks are made using papier-mâché, leather, and ceramics according to 17th-century techniques, handpainted with tempera, touched up with gold and silver leaf, and polished with French lacquer. Via Faenza 72r. © 055/287-370.

Pitti Mosaici Florentine traditional "mosaics" are actually works of inlaid stone called *pietre dure*. The creations of young Ilio de Filippis and his army of apprentices at Pitti Mosaici reflect traditional techniques and artistry. Ilio's father was a *pietre dure* artist, and his grandfather was a sculptor. (The family workshop was founded in 1900.) Besides the pieces on display down the road toward the Arno at Via Guicciardini 80r and across the river at Lungarno Vespucci 36r, the firm will custom make works to your specifications. Piazza Pitti 16r and 23–24r. © **055/282-127.** www.pittimosaici.it.

JEWELRY

If you've got the financial solvency of a small country, the place to buy your baubles is the **Ponte Vecchio,** famous for its gold- and silversmiths since the 16th century. The craftsmanship at the stalls is usually of a very high quality, and so they seem to compete instead over who can charge the highest prices.

Angela Caputi The audacious bijoux here aren't for the timid. Much of Angela's costume jewelry—from earrings and necklaces to brooches and now even a small clothing line—is at least oversized and bold and often pushes the flamboyance envelope. Even though she has become an international grande dame of costume jewels, in the end she keeps designing merely for the fun of it, and her low prices reflect it. Borgo San Jacopo 82r. © 055/212-972.

Offbeat Shopping

Antonio Frilli, Via dei Fossi 26r (✆ 055/210-212). The show-rooms here are packed with full-scale reproductions and high-quality miniatures of Italy's most famous sculptures, from the imported Greek classical to Canova's neoclassical—all in the original materials: marble, bronze, and alabaster. For a few hundred thousand dollars, you can have a life-size gilded bronze replica of Ghiberti's *Gates of Paradise*. The more modest can settle for a pair of Michelangelo *Dawn* and *Dusk* bookends.

Bartolozzi and Maioli, Via Maggio 13r (✆ 055/239-8633). Master reproduction woodcarver Fiorenzo Bartolozzi over-sees a wonderful jumble of a store/workshop. Full baroque altars frame flocks of Renaissance candleholders, and pudgy, oversize cherubs flit around a Golgotha of gauntly Gothic crucified Christs. Upstairs are furnishings, including table bases so intricate and striking you'll need to buy a glass tabletop just so you can stare at the legs all day.

Farmacia Santa Maria Novella, Via della Scala 16 (✆ 055/216-276). Documents date this pharmacy to 1542, but it was officially established only in 1612—that still makes it one of the oldest pharmacies in the world. Dripping with stuccoes

Bijoux Cascio   This is a good place to come if you don't want your faux jewels to look fake. The shop faithfully apes the popular top patterns and produces some tasteful pieces of its own design as well. Via Por Santa Maria 1r. ✆ 055/238-2851.

Mario Buccellati   This Milan-based boutique is a more moder-ately priced outlet than the stalls along the Ponte. Since 1919 they've been making thick, heavy jewelry of high quality. In the back room is the silver; for the fine flatware collection, ask. Via de' Tornabuoni 71r. ✆ 055/239-6579.

LEATHER, ACCESSORIES & SHOES

It has always been a buyers' market for leather in Florence, but these days it's tough to sort out the jackets mass-produced for tourists from the high-quality artisan work. The most fun you'll have leather and frescoes from a mid-18th-century makeover, its large rooms are lined with glass-and-wood display cases almost as old. This is one of the few Florentine spots where life actually still operates the way it did in the Renaissance. It's worth coming in if only for the ambience and the great smell, even if you don't buy any of the home-recipe cremes, poultices, or beauty products. The Farmacia is no longer run by the Dominican friars but rather by the fourth generation descended from the nephew of the last monk to keep shop here.

Gabriele Mossa, Borgo degli Albizi 73r (© **055/247-6637**). This is Gabriele's studio and his shop, where he makes and sells his original bronzes, paintings, and his own take on commedia dell'arte Carnival masks.

San Jacopo Show, Borgo San Jacopo 66r (© **055/239-6912**). Mannequins, mannequins, mannequins, in every imaginable style, crowd this long, narrow shop. With hyper-sharpened features or rounded facelessness, in flesh tones, electric blue, or mirrored silver, the shop's sole products variously lounge in Jacuzzis, sit on each other's shoulders, walk their mannequin dogs, or simply do what they do best—pose in the window.

shopping is without a doubt at the outdoor stalls of the **San Lorenzo** market, even if the market is rife with mediocre goods (see above). Never accept the first price they throw at you; sometimes you can bargain them down to almost half the original asking price. The shops below should guarantee you at least quality merchandise, but not the bargaining joys of the market. (See also "Fashion & Clothing," above.)

It's also fun to watch the artisans at work at the **Scuola del Cuoio** (Leather School) **of Santa Croce.** You enter through Santa Croce church (right transept), Piazza Santa Croce 16, or on Via San Giuseppe 5r on Sunday morning (© **055/244-533;** www.leather-school.it). The very-fine-quality soft-leather merchandise isn't cheap. You can watch the embossers stamping gold-leaf designs on the products and get them to emblazon your new wallet with your initials or a Florentine lily.

Anna   This is a fine store for handcrafted leather coats and clothing set in the remains of a 14th-century tower. You can also pick up discounted Versace purses and funky colorful Missioni sweaters. For the best of the leather, head down the stairs in the back, where you'll find fur-collared coats, suede jackets, and supple pigskin vests. They'll do alterations and even full tailoring in 24 hours. Piazza Pitti 38–41r. ✆ 055/283-787.

Beltrami   Although they display a bit of everything here, Beltrami's forte is still beautiful well-built footwear, bags, briefcases, and luggage. Beltrami is based in Florence, so prices are as low here as you're going to find. Via de' Tornabuoni 48r. ✆ 055/287-779.

Ferragamo   In the imposing 13th-century Palazzo Spini-Feroni lording over Piazza Santa Trínita are the flagship store, museum, and home of Ferragamo. Salvatore Ferragamo was the man who shod Hollywood in its most glamorous age and raised footwear to an art form. His original creations are de rigueur in clothing/decorative arts sections of museums around the world. View some of Ferragamo's funkier shoes in the second-floor museum (call ahead at ✆ 055/336-0456) or slip on a pair yourself in the showrooms downstairs. Via de' Tornabuoni 16r. ✆ 055/33-601 or 055-292-123.

John F.   John F. is a purveyor of high-quality leather goods as well as Missioni sweaters, Krizia purses, and Bettina bags. The stock is fashionable and made of buttery soft leather. Lungarno Corsini 2. ✆ 055/239-8985. www.johnf.it.

Madova Gloves   Gloves are all they do in this tiny shop, and they do them well. The grandchildren of the workshop's founders do a brisk business in brightly colored, supple leather gloves lined with cashmere and silk. Via Guicciardini 1r. ✆ 055/239-6526. www.madova.com.

Peppe Peluso   To keep yourself in genuine Florence shoes without breaking the bank, pop by this shop. You won't find shoes of high quality here, but you will find lots of them, and as dirt cheap as they come—as low as 59,000L (30€, $30). If you don't mind the relative flimsiness, you can get plenty of high-fashion knockoffs to match almost any outfit. Via del Corso 1r. ✆ 055/268-283.

MUSIC

Italians invented the violin and the piano, and Tuscans were the ones who first came up with modern musical notation and something called opera, so you can get some quite fine classical and operatic recordings. Italy's music heroes both past and present are well represented, from Donizetti to Puccini and Caruso to Pavarotti.

Alberti This is the biggest homegrown outlet in town (which isn't saying much) for general music and Italian pop, though the majority of the stock is the ever-popular American and British rock. Borgo San Lorenzo 45–49r. ✆ 055/294-271. There's another branch around the corner at Via de' Pucci 10–20r (✆ 055/284-346).

Data Records Although restrictions are ever tightening, Italy still remains one of the best places in western Europe to get bootlegs. Quality, obviously, can vary drastically (most places will let you listen before you buy). Some of the more "reputable" pirate labels include Pluto, Great Dane, Bugsy, On Stage, Teddy Bear, Beech Marten, and Red Line. Data Records is a hip place with a sassy funk attitude, knowledgeable staff, plenty of cutting-edge music (Italian and international), and scads of good bootlegs. They also run a more mainstream outlet, **Super Records** (✆ 055/234-9526), in the pedestrian passage leading from Santa Maria Novella train station, with some of the best prices in town on first-run presses from major labels. Both are closed in August. Via dei Neri 15r. ✆ 055/287-592.

Disco Emporium For more than 30 years, this tiny shop has offered a large and well-selected collection of classical, opera, and instrumental music from Gregorian chant to Philip Glass. Via dello Studio 11r. ✆ 055/295-101.

PAPER & JOURNALS

Giulio Giannini and Figlio This shop offers an expensive but quality selection of leather-bound notebooks, fine stationery, and the shop's specialty, objects garbed in decorative papers. This was one of the first stores to paste marbleized sheets onto desktop items, but its real trademark are objects sheathed in genuine 17th- to 19th-century manuscript and choir-book sheets. Piazza Pitti 36–37r. ✆ 055/212-621.

Il Papiro Il Papiro is now a modest Tuscan chain of jewel box–size shops specializing in marbled and patterned paper, as plain gift-wrap sheets or as a covering for everything from pens and journals to letter openers or full desk sets. There are several branches, including the head office at Via Cavour 55r (no phone) and shops at Piazza del Duomo 24r (no phone), Via dei Tavolini 13r (✆ 055/213-823), Lungarno Acciaiuoli 42r (✆ 055/215-262), and Piazza Rucellai 8r (✆ 055/211-652).

Pineider   Since 1774, much of the international and Italian elite have had their business cards, stationery, and formal invitations engraved at the original branch of Pineider. The successful marriage of superior craftsmanship with refined classical elegance has made the personalized paper products of Pineider popular with everyone from Napoléon to Elizabeth Taylor. Piazza della Signoria 13r. 𝄐 055/284-655. There's another branch at Via Tornabuoni 76r (𝄐 055/211-605).

Scriptorium   Come here for hand-sewn notebooks, journals, and photo albums made of thick paper—all bound in soft leather covers. With classical music or Gregorian chant playing in the background, you can also shop for calligraphy and signet wax sealing tools. It's one of the few fine stationery stores in Florence with very little marbleized paper. Via dei Servi 5r. 𝄐 055/211-804. There's a new branch in the Oltrarno at Piazza de' Pitti 6 (𝄐 055/238-2272).

PRINTS
Little Bottega delle Stampe   Come here for prints, historic maps, and engravings from the 1500s through the Liberty-style and Art Deco prints of the 1930s. You can dig out some Dürers here, as well as original Piranesis and plates from Diderot's 1700 Encyclopedia. There are Florence views from the 16th to 19th centuries, plus a fine collection of 18th-century French engravings. Borgo San Jacopo 56r. 𝄐 055/295-396.

TOYS
La Città del Sole   Since 1977, Florence's owner-operated branch of this national chain has sold old-fashioned wooden brain teasers, construction kits, hand puppets, 3-D puzzles, science kits, and books. Borgo Ognissanti 37r. 𝄐 055/219-345.

WINE & LIQUORS
Besides these two strictly wine shops, you can pick up fine bottles at **Il Volpe e L'Uva** and **La Fiaschetteria,** both listed in chapter 7, "Florence After Dark."

Enoteca Alessi   The front room sells boxed chocolates and other sweets, but in the back and in the large cellars, you can find everything from prime vintages to a simple-quality table wine. This large store, 2 blocks from the Duomo, also offers tastings. Via dell'Oche 27–29r. 𝄐 055/239-6987.

Enoteca Gambi Romano   This is another central outlet for olive oil, vin santo, grappa, and (upstairs) lots of wine. There are well-priced Tuscan labels and a good small stock of the best of the rest of Italy. Borgo SS. Apostoli 21–23r. 𝄐 055/292-646.

7

Florence After Dark

Florence doesn't have the musical cachet or grand opera houses of Milan, Venice, or Rome, but there are two symphony orchestras and a fine music school in Fiesole. The city's public theaters are certainly respectable, and most major touring companies stop in town on their way through Italy.

1 The Performing Arts

Many concerts and recitals staged in major halls and private spaces across town are sponsored by the **Amici della Musica** (✆ **055/609-012;** www.amicimusica.fi.it), so contact them to see what "hidden" concert might be on while you're in town. You can get tickets to all cultural and musical events at the city's main clearinghouse, **Box Office,** Via Alamanni 39 (✆ **055/210-0804;** www.boxoffice.it).

CHURCH CONCERTS Many Florentine churches fill the autumn with organ, choir, and chamber orchestra concerts, mainly of classical music. The tiny **Santa Maria de' Ricci** on Via del Corso seems always to have music wafting out of it; slipping inside to occupy a pew is occasionally free, and sometimes there's a charge of 5,000L to 20,000L (2.60€ to 10€, $2.50 to $10). Around the corner at Santa Margherita 7, the **Chiesa di Dante** (✆ **055/289-367**) puts on quality concerts of music for, and often played by, youths and children (tickets required). **The Florentine Chamber Orchestra,** Via E. Poggi 6 (✆ **055/783-374**), also runs an autumn season in the Orsanmichele; tickets are available at Box Office (see above) or at the door an hour before the 9pm shows.

CONCERT HALLS & OPERA The **Teatro Comunale,** Corso Italia 16 (✆ **055/211-158**), is the city's main music hall. It opens its season in September with concertos and recitals. Opera season runs December to mid-January, followed by symphonies and orchestral concerts through April. Mediocre plays are staged throughout the year.

The Teatro Verdi, Via Ghibellina 99–101 (✆ **055/212-320** or 055/263-877), is Florence's opera and ballet house, with the nice habit of staging Sunday-afternoon shows during the January-to-April season. **The Orchestra della Toscana** (✆ **055/281-993;** www.dada.it/ort) plays classical concerts here December to May. Like the Teatro Comunale, they do a bit of theater, but not of the caliber of La Pergola (see below).

THEATER   The biggest national and international touring companies stop in Florence's major playhouse, the **Teatro della Pergola,** Via della Pergola 12 (✆ **055/226-4335;** www.pergola.firenze.it). La Pergola is the city's chief purveyor of classical and classic plays from the Greeks and Shakespeare through Pirandello, Samuel Beckett, and Italian modern playwrights. Performances are professional and of high quality, if not always terribly innovative (and, of course, all in Italian).

2 The Club & Music Scenes

Italian clubs are rather cliquey—people usually go in groups to hang out and dance only with one another. There's plenty of flesh showing, but no meat market. Singles hoping to find random dance partners will often be disappointed.

LIVE MUSIC

Chiodo Fisso   Andrea Ardia opened this laid-back tavern in 1979 to give his fellow singer and songwriters a place to play. It's the only club in town to hear live acoustic guitar sets. Drinks, including their specialty Chianti-based sangria, start at 8,000L (4.15€, $4). They open at 8 or 9pm with light meals; the performer takes the tiny stage around 10:30 or 11pm. Monday is devoted to American-style folk a la Joan Baez, Tuesday to Thursday various musicians perform and Friday and Saturday Andrea himself breaks out the guitar. Via Dante Alighieri 16r. ✆ 055/238-1290. Cover is 5,000L (2.60€, $2.50) on first visit for an annual pass.

Dolce Zucchero   "Sweet Sugar" is one of the better recent efforts to spice up Florence's nightlife and is popular with all ages. Under high ceilings are a long bar and a small dance floor with a stage for the nightly live musicians, usually a fairly talented cover act cranking out American and Italian dance songs for the packed crowd. Via dei Pandolfini 38r. ✆ 055/247-7894. Cover 10,000L (5€, $5) including 1st drink.

Cafe Culture

Florence no longer has a glitterati or intellectuals' cafe scene, and when it did—from the late-19th-century Italian *Risorgimento* era through the *dolce vita* of the 1950s—it was basically copying the idea from Paris. Although they're often overpriced tourist spots today, Florence's high-toned cafes are fine if you want designer pastries and hot cappuccinos served to you while you sit on a piazza and people-watch.

At the refined, wood-paneled, stucco-ceilinged, and very expensive 1733 cafe **Gilli**, Piazza della Repubblica 39r/Via Roma 1r (© **055/213-896**), tourists gather to sit with the ghosts of Italy's *Risorgimento*, when the cafe became an important meeting place of the heroes and thinkers of the unification movement from the 1850 to the 1870s. The red-jacketed waiters at **Giubbe Rosse**, Piazza della Repubblica 13–14r (© **055/212-280**), must have been popular during the 19th-century glory days of Garibaldi's red-shirt soldiers. This was once a meeting place of the Florentine futurists, but aside from organized literary encounters on Wednesdays, today it too is mainly a tourists' cafe with ridiculous prices.

Once full of history and now mainly full of tourists, **Rivoire**, Piazza della Signoria/Via Vacchereccia 4r (© **055/214-412**), has a chunk of prime real estate on Piazza della Signoria. Smartly dressed waiters serve smartly priced sandwiches to cappuccino-sipping patrons. **Giacosa**, Via de' Tornabuoni 83r (© **055/239-6226**), was a 19th-century hangout for literati and intellectual clutches as elegant as any of the others, but today it's really more of a high-class *bar*, with no outside tables. It makes a good shopping break, though, with panini, pastries, cold salads, and hot pasta dishes.

DANCE CLUBS & NIGHTCLUBS

Full Up Year after year this remains one of the trendiest clubs in town and also one of the more elegant. People dress up to come here, whether they plan to sip drinks on the velvet sofas around the piano bar or hit the smallish disco floor to groove to pop, dance, and hip-hop. September to June, it's open Monday to Saturday 11pm to 4am. Via della Vigna Vecchia 23–25r. ✆ **055/293-006.** Cover 10,000L (5€, $5), 25,000L (13€, $13) on weekends, including 1st drink.

Meccanò   You'll have to wait a long time in line and fork over upwards of 20,000L to 30,000L (10€ to 16€, $10 to $15) to get into Florence's biggest, baddest disco. There are four separate dance floors, as well as a piano bar and six other bars. Laser lights shows and caged dancers are a-plenty, while the music could be anything from disco and funk to techno, house, and pop, with the occasional live act. Upstairs in the mysterious *club privée* is a vaguely hoedown atmosphere (it looks like a barn), with people shaking it on long pic-nic tables—nothing kinky, just dancing. There seems to be no set criteria for getting the *privée* stamp on your hand—being female helps. You purchase drinks, 10,000L (5€, $5) and up, with a drink card, which you must take to the cashier and pay before they give you the pass you need to exit the club. It's open 11pm to 4am every day except Monday and Wednesday. The Cascine Park is pretty seedy after dark, so be careful as you leave and head straight for the Viale. Viale degli Olmi 1, at the entrance to the Cascine Park, Piazza Vittorio Veneto (✆ **055/331-371.**

Space Electronic   Located right in the centro storico, this is a big-city dance club in a small-city setting. It never quite seems to get full, but it's usually fun anyway. Upstairs, the dance floor is done up as a funky space port with an excellent sound system and an army of DJs—including one who controls the lasers of the highly sophis-ticated light show. The place has become something of a younger hangout in the past few years (sometimes it looks like the local high school showed up on a field trip), but customers into their 30s still show up in fair numbers. If nothing else, watching karaoke at the downstairs bar is more amusing than in the States, if only to hear American pop hits belted out with Italian accents. Via Palazzuolo 37 (✆ **055/293-082**).

3 Pubs, Bars & Wine Bars

PUBS & BARS   There's an unsurprising degree of similarity among Florence's half-dozen Irish-style pubs: 7,000L to 8,000L (3.60€ to 4.15€, $3.50 to $4) for a pint of Guinness or cider; dark, woody interiors usually with several back rooms and plenty of smoke; and a crowd (stuffed to the gills on weekends) of students and 20- and 30-something Americans and Brits along with their

Italian counterparts. The better ones are the Florence branch of the successful Italian chain **Fiddler's Elbow,** Piazza Santa Maria Novella 7r (© 055/215-056); **The Old Stove,** Via Pellicceria 4r (© 055/ 284-640), just down from Piazza della Repubblica; and, under the same management, **The Lion's Fountain,** Borgo Albizi 34r (© 055/234-4412), on the tiny but lively Piazza San Pier Maggiore near Santa Croce. You'll find plenty of others around town—they pop up like mushrooms these days, but often disappear just as quickly.

Red Garter, Via de' Benci 33r (© 055/234-4904), is a speakeasy attracting a 20s-to-30s crowd of Italians and some Americans, Australians, and English. The hooch will run you 8,000L (4.15€, $4) and up. There's a small bilevel theater room in the back with live music some nights—the last time I was here it was a one-man band playing American and Italian rock hits with some blues mixed in.

WINE BARS   The most traditional wine bars are called *fiaschetterie,* after the word for a flask of chianti. They tend to be hole-in-the-wall joints serving sandwiches or simple food along with glasses filled to the brim—usually with a house wine, though finer vintages are often available. The best are listed in chapter 4, "Where to Dine," including **I Fratellini,** Via dei Cimatori 38r (© 055/239-6096); **Antico Noè,** off Piazza S. Pier Maggiore (© 055/234-0838); and **La Mescita,** Via degli Alfani 70r (© 055/239- 6400). There's also a traditional wine shop in the Oltrarno called simply **La Fiaschetteria,** Via de' Serragli 47r (© 055/287-420), that, like many, doubles as a small locals' wine bar with 1,000L (.50€, 50¢) glasses.

A more high-toned spot is the **Cantinetta Antinori,** Piazza Antinori 3 (© 055/292-234), also listed in chapter 4. It's housed in the palace headquarters of the Antinori wine empire at the top of Florence's main fashion drag, Via Tornabuoni. For a trendier wine bar focusing on handpicked labels offered with plates of cheese and other snacks, head to the Oltrarno and a real oenophile's hangout, **Il Volpe e L'Uva,** Piazza de' Rossi, behind Piazza Santa Felícita off Via Guicciardini (© 055/239-8132). The Avuris, who run the Hotel Torre Guelfa (see chapter 3, "Where to Stay"), have recently opened a great little wine bar right across from the Pitti Palace called **Pitti Gola e Cantina,** Piazza Pitti 16 (© 055/212-704), with glasses of wine from 7,000L to 12,000L (3.60€ to 6€, $3.50 to $6) to help unwind from a day of museums. They also have light dishes, meat and cheese platters, and cakes for 8,000L to 18,000L (4.15€ to 9€, $4 to $9).

4 The Gay & Lesbian Scene

The gay nightlife scene in Florence isn't much, and for lesbians it's pretty much just the Thursday to Saturday nights mixed gay-and-lesbian party at the **Flamingo Bar,** Via Pandolfini 26r (© **055/ 243-356**), whereas the rest of the week it's men only. The main bar is downstairs, where an international gay crowd shows up in everything from jeans and tees to full leather. Upstairs are a lounge and a theater showing videos and the occasional show. September to June, the ground floor becomes a dance floor pumping out commercial pop and lots of disco. It's open Sunday to Thursday 10pm to 4am (to 6am Friday and Saturday). Florence's dark room is the **Crisco Bar,** Via Sant'Egidio 43r (© **055/248-0580**), open Wednesday to Monday 9pm to 3am (to 5am weekends).

The only real gay dance floor of note is at the **Tabasco Bar,** Piazza Santa Cecilia 3r (© **055/213-000**). Italy's first gay disco attracts crowds of men from all over the country. The music is techno, disco, and retro rock, but entertainment offerings also include cabaret, art shows, and the occasional transvestite comedy. In summer, foreigners arrive in droves. It's open Sunday to Thursday 10pm to 3 or 4am (to 6am Friday and Saturday). Tuesday, Friday, and Saturday it's all disco; Wednesday is leather night.

5 Films

The only all-English **movie theater** in town is the run-down **Cinema Astro** (no phone), directly across from Gelateria Vivoli on Piazza San Simone—which is really just a wide spot on Via Isole delle Stinche—near Santa Croce. Its tiny screen shows Hollywood hits twice nightly except Monday for 10,000L (5€, $5). For a much more elegant cinematic outing, the Art Nouveau **Odeon,** Piazza Strozzi (© **055/214-068**), screens current movies in the original language all day Monday for 12,000L (6€, $6). Overwhelmingly, the movie will be in English, but you might run into a French night. If you don't like what's playing at the Odeon, the **Goldoni,** Via dei Serragli (© **055/222-437**), shows movies in the original language on Wednesdays. In summer, you can watch movies in Italian under the stars at the **Forte di Belvedere** (© **055/293-169**) above the Boboli Gardens.

Index

See also Accommodations and Restaurant indexes below.

FROMMER'S® COMPLETE TRAVEL GUIDES

FROMMER'S® DOLLAR-A-DAY GUIDES

FROMMER'S® PORTABLE GUIDES

FROMMER'S® NATIONAL PARK GUIDES

FROMMER'S® MEMORABLE WALKS

Chicago	New York	San Francisco
London	Paris	

FROMMER'S® GREAT OUTDOOR GUIDES

Arizona & New Mexico	Northern California	Vermont & New Hampshire
New England	Southern New England	

SUZY GERSHMAN'S BORN TO SHOP GUIDES

Born to Shop: France	Born to Shop: Italy	Born to Shop: New York
Born to Shop: Hong Kong, Shanghai & Beijing	Born to Shop: London	Born to Shop: Paris

FROMMER'S® IRREVERENT GUIDES

Amsterdam	Los Angeles	San Francisco
Boston	Manhattan	Seattle & Portland
Chicago	New Orleans	Vancouver
Las Vegas	Paris	Walt Disney World
London	Rome	Washington, D.C.

FROMMER'S® BEST-LOVED DRIVING TOURS

Britain	Germany	New England
California	Ireland	Scotland
Florida	Italy	Spain
France		

HANGING OUT™ GUIDES

Hanging Out in England	Hanging Out in France	Hanging Out in Italy
Hanging Out in Europe	Hanging Out in Ireland	Hanging Out in Spain

THE UNOFFICIAL GUIDES®

Bed & Breakfasts and Country Inns in:	Florida with Kids	New Orleans
California	Golf Vacations in the Eastern U.S.	New York City
New England	The Great Smoky & Blue Ridge Mountains	Paris
Northwest		San Francisco
Rockies	Hawaii	Skiing in the West
Southeast	Inside Disney	Southeast with Kids
Beyond Disney	Las Vegas	Walt Disney World
Branson, Missouri	London	Walt Disney World for Grown-ups
California with Kids	Mid-Atlantic with Kids	Walt Disney World for Kids
Chicago	Mini Las Vegas	Washington, D.C.
Cruises	Mini-Mickey	World's Best Diving Vacations
Disneyland	New England & New York with Kids	

SPECIAL-INTEREST TITLES

Frommer's Adventure Guide to Australia & New Zealand
Frommer's Adventure Guide to Central America
Frommer's Adventure Guide to India & Pakistan
Frommer's Adventure Guide to South America
Frommer's Adventure Guide to Southeast Asia
Frommer's Adventure Guide to Southern Africa
Frommer's Britain's Best Bed & Breakfasts and Country Inns
Frommer's France's Best Bed & Breakfasts and Country Inns
Frommer's Italy's Best Bed & Breakfasts and Country Inns
Frommer's Caribbean Hideaways

Frommer's Exploring America by RV
Frommer's Gay & Lesbian Europe
Frommer's The Moon
Frommer's New York City with Kids
Frommer's Road Atlas Britain
Frommer's Road Atlas Europe
Frommer's Washington, D.C., with Kids
Frommer's What the Airlines Never Tell You
Israel Past & Present
The New York Times' Guide to Unforgettable Weekends
Places Rated Almanac
Retirement Places Rated